An Enemy of the State

The Life of Erwin Knoll

Bill Lueders

Common Courage Press

MONROE, MAINE

First edition, first printing

Common Courage Press
Box 702
Monroe, Maine 04951
Phone: (207) 525-0900
Fax: (207) 525-3068

Typeset by Strong Silent Type, Madison, Wisconsin
Cover photo by Brent Nicastro
Back cover photo by Zane Williams
Cover design by Matt Wuerker

Library of Congress Cataloging-In-Publication Data

Lueders, Bill.
An enemy of the state : the life of Erwin Knoll / by Bill Lueders.
p. cm.
Includes bibliographical references and index.
ISBN 1-56751-098-1. -- ISBN 1-56751-099-X
1. Knoll, Erwin. 2. Journalists--United States--Biography. 3. War in the press--United States. I. Title.
PN4874.K62L84 1996
070'.92--dc20 96–14004
CIP

Contents

The most dangerous man, to any government, is the man who is able to think things out for himself, without regard to the prevailing superstitions and taboos. Almost inevitably he comes to the conclusion that the government he lives under is dishonest, insane, and intolerable, and so, if he is a romantic, he tries to change it. And even if he is not a romantic personally, he is very apt to spread discontent among those who are.

H.L. Mencken

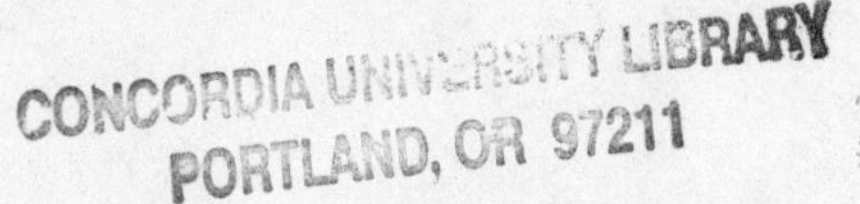

Acknowledgments

Thanks to Doris Knoll for providing me with a lifetime of records and recollections; to David and Jonathan Knoll, for their stories; to Alice Allen and Erwin's extended family, especially Eric Nash, Rita Penn and Alan Lemberger; to the folks at *The Progressive,* especially Matt Rothschild and Teri Terry; to Marc Eisen and *Isthmus,* for giving me the time; to the people who offered wise counsel, especially Judy Davidoff, Dean Robbins, and Sam Day; and to the many librarians and archivists who helped me get information. Thanks also to Phyllis Rose and Linda B. Clifford for proofreading; to Eric Parker, Heather Despres-Burack and Mark Pitsch for putting me up in New Jersey, New York and Washington, D.C.; to Chris Deisinger for putting up with a book-writing roommate; to Sheldon Rampton and Matt Wuerker for their layout and cover design; to literary agent Tom Wallace for his guidance and support; to Greg Bates and the other folks at Common Courage Press for having the uncommon courage to publish books they care about; and to Deirdre Green, my best friend.

For my son, Jesse

Introduction

Erwin Knoll called one morning, summoning me to Madison for an interview at *The Progressive.* A few days earlier, I had sent Knoll a letter and some of my published writing in response to a mention in his monthly "Memo From the Editor" about the availability of editorial internships. I drove the seventy miles from Milwaukee on Oct. 25, 1983, the day President Reagan declared war on the Vietnam Syndrome by invading the tiny island of Grenada.

I expected, based on my impressions of *The Progressive*, to be meeting with august older men. To my surprise, Matt Rothschild and Keenen Peck, the two associate editors who together with Knoll formed the interview team, were about my age, twenty-four. Knoll led the questioning, and things went well: I was promised an internship in the summer of 1984. After the interview, Knoll pulled me aside to jab his finger at my letter's most effusive line: "When I cracked open the October issue and came across your 'Memo' regarding openings for editorial interns, my heart broke into a sudden gallop. I have scarcely been able to think of anything else since."

"If you wrote that for *The Progressive*," he told me, leaning forward to whisper, "I'd tell you that you were breathing a bit too heavy."

Knoll laughed pleasantly, the tuft of hair on his chin becoming the dot on an exclamation point. To this day, I don't know whether I got the interview based on the strength of my published writing, or the depth of Knoll's desire to deliver that line.

Erwin Knoll was, by this time, already well-known. During much of 1979, he appeared on front pages and television screens across the nation, defending *The Progressive*'s right to publish a closely guarded "secret" of hydrogen bomb design. In the early 1980s, he gave weekly commentaries on National Public Radio. His popularity—and his success at reaching large numbers of people—would continue to grow until Knoll became the closest thing the political Left had to a national spokesperson. In the end, when he died in his sleep on November 2, 1994, at age sixty-three, he was appearing regularly on public television's "MacNeil/Lehrer NewsHour," hosting a nationally syndicated weekly radio show, delivering daily two-minute radio commentaries, and researching a book he planned to write about capital punishment—as well as being editor of *The Progressive*, the nation's oldest monthly political magazine.

Knoll, I learned in bits and pieces, was born in Austria but fled the Nazis as a child. His family reunited in New York City, where he went to school and began to learn English. He had worked for *The Washington Post* as a reporter and news service chief, and for Newhouse newspaper chain, covering Lyndon Johnson. He was married to Doris and had two sons. He told stories about himself all the time, at the slightest provocation.

In fact, Erwin Knoll lived his whole life at the edge of history. Wherever he happened to be, was, at the time, one of the best vantage points from which to witness some of the 20th Century's most profound events: the Holocaust, McCarthyism, the Korean and Vietnam Wars, the Administration of Lyndon Johnson, the rise and fall of Richard Nixon, the fading of the American Left, the insane proliferation of nuclear arms, and the ascendance of the political Right. Knoll's response to each of these events was to become more radical.

Knoll was, in the end, a monumental figure on the American Left, skillfully pitching radical ideas to millions of people. He consistently staked out fresh, witty, principled positions, and defended them with great passion and verve. During his final "MacNeil/Lehrer" appearance on October 28, 1994, Knoll remarked that the theory advanced in the right-wing tract, *The Bell Curve*, was easily disproved: "Spend an evening watching Congress on C-Span, and you can't possibly accept the notion that America's elite is endowed with high IQ."

My internship, by chance, coincided with the halfway point of Knoll's twenty-one-year career at *The Progressive*. The magazine's paid circulation was then higher than ever—43,000 copies a month. A staff of sixteen people (plus interns) tended to every task: editorial, circulation, bookkeeping, advertising, production. Because *The*

Progressive paid so poorly, the staff was quite young: Knoll, who that summer turned fifty-three, was old enough to be just about everybody's father—and that's how many staff members thought of him, as a father figure. He could be cantankerous. He could deliver devastating rebuttals and cast withering looks. But he treated people around him with respect, even as he quarreled with them.

The Progressive, then as now, is located in Madison's oldest neighborhood at 409 East Main Street, four blocks from the state Capitol. A small sign identifies the magazine; T-shirts hang in the front windows; across the street is St. Patrick's Catholic Church. The office's tiny work areas are littered with newspapers and books and cluttered with wall hangings and postings. There's a large, messy basement, with thousands of old issues stacked against walls and decades of history packed into boxes piled upon boxes in heaps on the floor, amid bales of T-shirts and stacks of posters.

In May 1984, when I began my internship, the magazine was working on its July issue—a special package of articles commemorating *The Progressive*'s 75th anniversary. Knoll gave me the nod to write a piece about the magazine's founder, Robert Marion "Fighting Bob" La Follette, the legendary Wisconsin governor, senator, and leader of the Progressive movement. The parallels between the two men are inescapable.

Like La Follette, Knoll was a dynamic public speaker, although the public's appetite for speech was much greater in La Follette's time. Both had their moments of greatest fame coincide with the times when they were most reviled. For La Follette, this was his opposition to the United States' entry into World War; for Knoll, it was the H-bomb story. Both came to be respected not despite but *because* of the unpopular positions they took during these times. And both died at the zenith of their careers: La Follette after he garnered 16.5 percent of the vote in the 1924 presidential elections, Knoll after he rose again to national prominence as the U.S. media's most prominent critic of the Persian Gulf War.

Knoll never left any doubt about where he and *The Progressive* stood. His call for humane values never wavered, no matter what justifications for inhumanity were in vogue at the time. He could be irascible and pugnacious, but he believed so strongly in others' right to disagree with him that it was hard to fault him for even his most extreme positions. Knoll spoke often and eloquently on the right to free speech—which he believed applied to all speech, even that intended to cause hurt and stir up hatred. He upheld *The Progressive*'s tradition of opposing war and militarism, and thrust it defiantly into the national limelight over the issue of nuclear secrecy. He weaned it of faith in the electoral process. He made it a more radical magazine.

That July 4, as always, the Knolls had a party. Knoll grilled burgers and brats and vainly cried "David, No!" as his twenty-four-year-old son blew off firecrackers. Rothschild and Peck were present, as was Erwin's father, Carl Knoll, who had recently moved to the Madison area. Tacked to trees were copies of the Declaration of Independence and the Bill of Rights—decidedly radical documents that Knoll, an immigrant to America, revered.

Erwin Knoll believed it was better—tactically as well as morally—to be uncompromising on matters of principle. Being an absolutist had its benefits. He never found himself in a quandary over whether a certain sort of expression ought to be allowed or a certain act of savagery condemned. But Knoll's eagerness to take things to absolutes and his refusal to compromise on matters of principle also had a price: It relegated him to the margins of political discourse, and it often put him at odds with the Left.

One day that summer of 1984, an activist from the Israeli peace group Yesh Gvul came to *The Progressive*, seeking affirmation. He soon found that his failure to renounce violence in all its forms—including the violence of the oppressed against their oppressors—made him, in Knoll's eyes, anything but a kindred spirit. Knoll disparaged his visitor's professed commitment to peace, and assailed his failure of courage. In the end, the fact that the two men agreed in their critique of the Israeli government seemed almost inconsequential.

Knoll also parted ways with many on the Left over the issue of electoral politics. In 1984, *The Progressive* blasted Democrats Walter Mondale and Geraldine Ferraro as being "afraid to enunciate anything more than a sweetened version of Reaganism." Less predictable was the magazine's rejection of Jesse Jackson, in an editorial stating that Jackson's highly publicized reference to New York City as "Hymietown" should "rule out support" from the Left. This infuriated many longtime subscribers, who registered their dissent. ("Write me a letter," Knoll shouted into the telephone one afternoon. "I don't have time to listen to your bullshit.") Knoll used his August "Memo," which ran under the headline "Jesse Jackson's Claque," to rub salt in the wounds of people whom the editorial offended. Privately, he called Jackson supporters "ignorant."

I questioned the intensity of Knoll's dislike for Jackson, who I thought deserved credit for articulating a radical agenda and giving impetus to a new political movement, the Rainbow Party. "Indeed," I wrote in a memo to Knoll, "the argument could be made that Jackson has done as much to radicalize the American public in one campaign as has *The Progressive* in 75 years."

Knoll called me into his "office," a cramped, messy space in the back of the magazine. The walls were covered with posters and plaques, most prominently one touting Knoll's inclusion on Nixon's Official Enemies List. He said the first time he saw Jackson—while covering a civil rights march in the late 1960s—he was awed. He called Doris to say that Jesse Jackson, this man he had just seen, was destined for greatness. But time and again since then, Knoll said, Jackson had proven himself more beholden to his own interests than to the cause of building a progressive movement. Soon after, Jackson went to the Democratic National Convention and got nothing but a broken Rainbow in exchange for embracing Mondale and the Democrats on a death march to the polls.

Contrary to the core, Knoll disputed that presidential elections are a meaningful forum for discussing serious issues, since so few serious issues—such as the steady decline in the average U.S. worker's standard of living—are ever discussed. Elections, he felt, were a distraction from the real work of politics. In time, he came to reject the process so thoroughly that he refused to even cast a vote for president. One of his favorite quotations—indispensable during presidential elections—was from *The Progressive*'s roving editor, Milton Mayer: "We are not disillusioned, because we were never illusioned."

In November 1994, six days after Erwin Knoll died, the Republican Party captured the U.S. Senate and House of Representatives, catapulting Newt Gingrich and Jesse Helms to new heights of power, and driving Bill Clinton even farther to the right. What would Knoll have thought about this event? He would have disputed that the differences between the two major parties were consequential, compared to the yawning gap between his views and theirs. He would have said that the Democrats got what they deserved, and that if people wanted to build a progressive movement they had better be prepared to leave the Democratic Party behind.

So too, in 1996, Knoll would doubtless find little to champion or admire. He would call on progressives to renounce Clinton in his hour of need, to repay him properly for his betrayal of progressive causes. And then, he'd say, after the elections are over, we can turn our attention to building a movement.

My internship ended on September 15, 1984, the day of *The Progressive*'s 75th birthday party. Five hundred people came out to Fighting Bob La Follette's former homestead in Maple Bluff. Studs Terkel led a chorus of speakers in singing the magazine's praises: "It ought to have a million readers." But Knoll, taking the microphone, distanced himself from this celebratory tone. He urged his audience not to applaud *The Progressive* but to do the work that needed to be done to build a movement for progressive change.

Knoll's life, it's true, lacked a sense of completion. Fortunately, though, he had been so clear and so consistent for so long there was really no question how he would want people to respond to the sense of incompletion that his passing brought. Erwin Knoll would have wanted them to become more radical, to escalate the intensity of their commitment to progressive change. (Which reminds me of the story about the woman who accosted Knoll after a speech, shaking her umbrella and shouting, "I hold you and your magazine responsible for my son's refusal to register for the draft." To which Knoll responded, "I hope you are as proud of him as I am.") It was a lesson his own life had taught him—importantly, by way of regrets. He was sorry he allowed himself to be inducted into the U.S. Army and even sorrier he did not defy the federal judge who barred *The Progressive* from publishing the H-bomb story. He was a man who sometimes gave in to what seemed safest, only to regret it, and sometimes would not budge, which he never regretted. This was the agent of his lifelong radicalism.

One of Knoll's favorite quotations, which his family included in the program for his memorial service, was from Jean-Paul Sartre:

"Naturally, in the course of my life, I have made lots of mistakes, large and small, for one reason or another, but at the heart of it all, every time I made a mistake it was because I was not radical enough."

CHAPTER ONE

Vienna

Erwin Knoll was one of the lucky ones; he got out of Vienna, and Europe, with his life. Many members of his family were not so fortunate. Some were beaten to death, some starved, others gassed. Knoll would later call the Holocaust "the formative experience of my life and the frame of reference from which I draw my politics." This may seem odd, since Knoll's politics, in his later life, were built on two bedrock principles: an absolute commitment to nonviolence (he even opposed the use of violence to stop Hitler) and an absolute commitment to freedom of speech (he went to the mat to defend the right of bigots to preach hate). Knoll was a few months past seven years old on *Kristallnacht*, the Night of Broken Glass.

Beginning that night of November 9, 1938, the Nazis orchestrated a two-day anti-Semitic rampage throughout Germany and Austria. The windows of Jewish-owned businesses were smashed; Jewish homes were looted and trashed. Some 4,600 Viennese Jews were sent to Dachau, the German concentration camp; thousands more were arrested, mistreated and detained. More than 1,000 Jewish places of worship—virtually every synagogue, temple, and prayer house in the land—were set on fire. In Vienna, the city of his birth, young Erwin watched the synagogue down the street from his home burn to the ground. "The fire department turned out and sprayed water from their hoses on the adjacent buildings, so the adjacent buildings wouldn't also catch fire," he recalled. "I saw that."

Erwin and his sister Alice, then three years old, lived with their parents, Carl and Ida (Nüchim and Jüdes), in the largely Jewish section of Vienna known as the Leopoldstadt. The former ghetto was bounded by the Danube Canal and the Danube proper; thus its residents acquired the joking nickname, "Islanders." Carl's three brothers and three younger sisters had by 1912 all migrated to Vienna from Stanislawow, Galicia, part of the Austro-Hungarian Empire (later part of Poland, then part of Russia and now part of Ukraine). Carl, then thirteen and off in Lwow to earn a livelihood, was the last sibling to arrive. Ida Schachter, Erwin's mother, had come to Vienna from another small Polish town; she and Carl married in 1930. Carl's parents, David Knoll and Mindel Diringer, also made their way to Vienna, after their grain-selling business failed. It was a warm and close-knit family; members got together often at each others' homes.

Carl Knoll and his brother Simon lived with their families across the hall from each other in an apartment building at *Hammer-Purgstallgasse 3*. Erwin and his cousin Rita, who was two years younger, used to ride their tricycles in the hallway between the two apartments. Erwin, recalls Rita, was a bit of a bully. "He used to beat me up," she says of their childhood encounters. "I knew Erwin before he was a pacifist."

Others remember young Erwin as unusually bright and well-behaved. "An unbelievable child," says Eric Nash (Erich Nasch), then a Czechoslovakian medical student at the University of Vienna. Nash was dating Erna Knoll, Carl's youngest sister, when Erwin was born on July 17, 1931. As a young boy, Erwin was "adopted" by his aunt and uncle-to-be. The couple would take Erwin to restaurants or on walks, and pretend he was their child. "He liked this game because he was crazy about Erna," says Nash. "She was an unusually beautiful girl and she showered him with love and he liked that."

Carl and Simon were also in business together, at a shop in the Leopoldstadt called Knoll & Co. Electromotoren. Much of their business came from installing electric motors into modified manual sewing machines. At the time, many Viennese women earned money by sewing at home. Carl's idea was to offer the machines for a free monthly trial, followed by low weekly payments (two shillings). Of the first 1,000 machines installed, only about a half-dozen were returned. Most users found they could sew faster and make more money. Carl, a pacifist and socialist of intellectual bent—relatives remember him as the family philosopher, well-read and almost professorial—ran the business end of things. Simon, an apprenticed mechanic, installed the motors and taught women how to use them. While Carl would never learn to drive a car, Simon became the first member of the Knoll family to own one. It was confiscated—as was Simon and Carl's business—when Nazis took control of Austria in the spring of 1938. Anna "Anny" Knoll, Simon's wife and Rita's mother, later saw the car being driven by one of the family's neighbors. A small doll that Rita had given her father still hung from its rear-view mirror; Anny asked the driver if she could have it back. The embarrassed man complied. "The people," recalled Simon charitably, "were not so bad."

But how they loved Adolf Hitler. The German fuehrer's own anti-Semitism was nurtured during his five-year stay in Vienna three decades before. ("Vienna," he later wrote, "gave me the harshest but also the most thorough education of my life. In that city I acquired a point of view, and a political approach which . . . has never left me.") Days after German troops on March 12 poured south into Austria, Hitler was afforded a hero's welcome as great as that of any conqueror in history; a half-million Austrians poured cheering into the heart of Vienna to greet him. "Our last march, the reoccupation of the Rhineland, is completely eclipsed by this event—especially as far as the joy of the people is concerned," declared Hermann Goering, Hitler's second-in-command. "The Fuehrer is deeply moved." In this high spirit, Hitler on April 10 held a plebescite in Germany and Austria on whether the two countries should be combined. Austrians overwhelmingly approved the *Anschluss* (annexation); the 99.75 percent "Yes" vote was fraudulent, but even the fairest election would have produced a lopsided win.

"Plainly, what had happened was the fastest and fullest mass conversion in history," wrote George E. Berkeley in his book, *Vienna and Its Jews*. "Virtually overnight, millions of Austrians who had previously supported their country's independence had executed a 180-degree turn."

Austrians, as Berkeley and others have noted, were wildly fond of Hitler's unvarnished hatred of Jews. Indeed, Hitler had to tone down his anti-Semitic rhetoric in Germany because it wasn't sufficiently rousing the public; in Austria, the public could not get enough.

"The Germans make good Nazis but lousy anti-Semites,"

observed the writer Alfred Polgar. "The Austrians make lousy Nazis, but what first-class anti-Semites they are!" It was true. Austrians shared little of their German counterparts' enthusiasm for discipline and hard work. Militarily, their ranks were disordered, and rife with corruption—so much so that Hitler sent some Austrian Nazis to Dachau. Conversely, the Germans responded less to Hitler's anti-Semitism than they did to his nationalism. Adolf Eichmann, the Nazi in charge of ridding Austria of its Jews, worked with Jewish officials to set up a processing center in the confiscated Rothschild Palais to streamline Jewish emigration; Austrian anti-Semites regularly sabotaged the operation.

As the Nazis came marching in, Austrians unleashed a virulent and sadistic anti-Semitism, the worst in the Reich. Mobs took to the streets, attacking Jews. They paraded through the Leopoldstadt, chanting "*Jude verrecke*" ("Croak, Jews!") Throughout the country, Jews were subjected to grotesque humiliations. Some, ordered to wear their best clothes, were forced to scrub the streets and sidewalks, using toothbrushes and water mixed with acid. In the streets of Vienna, a young girl was made to bend up and down in front of her parents' store wearing a sign that said, "Please do not buy from me—I am a Jewish sow." Jews were commanded to spit in each others' faces and to dance on desecrated Torah scrolls. While reports from Germany tell of Nazi thugs forcing horrified citizens to partake in the abuse of Jews, in Austria the citizenry responded to the same opportunities with glee. "We could scarcely hold back the crowds from mishandling the Jews," stated one Gestapo report. "There were frequent cries such as 'Beat them to death, the dogs.' [Sympathy for the Jews] was almost nonexistent, and the very few who voiced it were set upon by the mob."

The Austrian public also responded enthusiastically, after the *Anschluss*, to the declaration of economic war against Jews in their midst. Marveled *Das Schwarze Korps*, the official Nazi Party journal, "The Viennese have managed to do overnight what we have failed to achieve in the slow-moving, ponderous north up to this day. In Austria, a boycott of the Jews does not need organizing—the people themselves have initiated it." Some Austrians would with great satisfaction walk into Jewish-owned stores, help themselves to whatever they wanted, and leave without paying. Others reveled in the job opportunities brought about by the economic displacement of Jews. Austrians even turned on Jews they knew. One Jewish man's longtime barber suddenly cut off a piece of his ear; when the Jewish man complained to his doctor, he was told, "You should be glad the barber did not cut off the whole ear."

Austrian Jews protested this outbreak of mass hatred, but were outnumbered and overwhelmed. Moreover, the Jews of Austria—ninety percent of whom lived in Vienna—were deeply divided between Zionists, who sought the creation of a Jewish state in Palestine, and those historian Marsha Rozenblit calls "integrationists," who felt it was better for Jews to assimilate into Austrian society. Zionists called the integrationists "Jewish anti-Semites," while the integrationists charged that the Zionists, in calling for a separate Jewish national identity, were playing into Hitler's hands. Carl Knoll and his brothers leaned to Zionism.

As a young boy, Erwin Knoll saw the signs that went up on public benches, *"Fur Juden Verboten"* ("Jews Forbidden"). One day a kindly older couple in Erwin's apartment building—the wife gave him candy, the husband taught him to whistle through his teeth—hung up a new piece of needlework. "Heil Hitler," it said. Erwin's teacher, an Austrian nationalist, disappeared suddenly. "The new teacher," Knoll recalled, "wore a button that had a swastika with a laurel wreath around it." The wreath meant that the wearer had been a Nazi even before the *Anschluss*, when the party was illegal. "To this teacher," said Knoll, "adherence to Hitler was not a matter of convenience or of keeping his job, but a deep-set ideological conviction." Teachers were at the forefront of Austrian anti-Semitism. The Teachers Association journal decried "the totally demoralizing and corrupting Jewish influence which of necessity springs from the moral and intellectual characteristics of the race."

One night, Erwin heard a commotion outside his apartment, and looked out the window to see a standoff across the street between a gathering crowd and a non-Jewish janitor known to give refuge to Jews and others in trouble. (The Leopoldstadt, while containing one of the largest concentrations of Jewish people in Europe, was sixty percent Gentile.) Some people who were being beaten had ducked into the janitor's dwelling for protection; the crowd was demanding that they be surrendered for further abuse. Knoll later did not remember how the matter was resolved, but he never forgot the spectacle of a "howling mob across the street from our house." Likewise, he never forgot the day his mother sent him down the street to buy oranges at the *Karmelitermarkt*, a cluster of outdoor vendors. The woman at the fruit stand knew Erwin, for she had sold to him before. On this day she shook her head: "We have no oranges for Jews." Erwin burst into tears and ran home.

Vienna was then, as now, among the world's most elegant cities—its architecture stunning, its culture thriving, its pastries second-to-none. Austrian inventors lay claim to producing the world's first internal-combustion engine, typewriter, and sewing machine. Culturally, Vienna gave the world the waltz, and was home to such composers as Beethoven, Brahms, Mozart, Schubert, and Strauss, at various times in their lives. In 1931, when Erwin Knoll was born, the city had seventeen daily newspapers and three stoplights.

Although Vienna's 200,000 Jews never accounted for more than ten percent of its population, they contributed disproportionately to its success. Jews made up more than half of the city's physicians at a time when Vienna was a world-renowned medical center. Jewish philosophers Martin Buber and Ludwig Wittgenstein put Vienna on the cutting edge of 20th Century thought. In 1936, Austrian Jews won a Nobel Prize and an Olympic Gold Medal, adding to impressive records in both areas of endeavor. The city's most famous resident was a Jew, and an outspoken one: Sigmund Freud.

For hundreds of years, Vienna had served as capital of the Holy Roman Empire, a vast group of nations. Napoleon, in 1806, put an end to all that. In 1859 the remaining Austro-Hungarian Empire, twice defeated in the field, was forced to relinquish much of its Italian territory. In 1866, just as the skies above Austria glowed with a rare, spectacular display of northern lights, the nation was devastated by northern neighbor Prussia in a war that lasted a mere seven weeks. Austria was further afflicted by fiscal collapse in 1877, an event for which the nation's Jewish minority was widely blamed.

Battles over language, national identity, and religion reduced Austrian political life to chaos. In 1890, militant Catholics staged a failed attempt to take over the government. Raging discord spread to the Austrian Parliament, where factions pounded on drums, crashed cymbals and blared wind instruments to drown out the speeches of their rivals. In 1897, Austrian monarch Franz Joseph, who by that time had ruled the country—fairly and wisely, in the estimation of most—for half a century, was so disgusted he dissolved Parliament for a decade.

After World War I, Austria's fortunes fell further; the victorious Allies treated the nation like a spoil of war, giving away large sections to Czechoslovakia, Yugoslavia and Italy. What remained of Austria was called "a mutilated stump bleeding from every pore."

Many Austrians responded in destructive ways. Vienna led the world in suicides; self-indulgence was rampant; favoritism and obsequiousness became crucial to success. Freud himself was belatedly promoted to full professor at the University of Vienna only after a patient donated a valuable artwork to a new public gallery in his name. The Austrians were notorious complainers: "Vienna," one writer observed, "is a city for people who have chosen the wrong profession."

Anti-Semitism had been, for as long as anyone could remember, a staple of Austrian society and politics. Twice before—in 1421 and 1670—the country purged itself of Jewry. In the late 1600s, when capital was needed, Jews were allowed back, but subjected to a dizzying array of special taxes and restrictions. They were barred from most of the learned professions, except medicine, and for a time required to wear the Star of David. In 1849, Austria became the last major western country to extend full citizenship to Jews. The Catholic Church, long a mainspring of European anti-Semitism, registered its firm dissent.

Austrian Jews were resented for their economic success, although a great many were desperately poor. Longstanding lies about Jews—that they killed Christ, participated in ritual murders, or plotted endlessly against non-Jews—were in resurgence. A group called the Reform Union, created in 1882, sold watch-chain effigies of a Jew being hanged. Soon thereafter, the Catholic Church helped launch the baldly anti-Semitic Christian Social (*Christlich Soziale*) Party. By 1895 the Christian Socials were in the majority on the Vienna City Council—making Vienna, says Berkeley, "the first major city in [Europe] to fall under control of a political party openly and officially committed to hating the Jews."

Concurrently, a wave of government-sanctioned pogroms

in Russia and a Church-sponsored boycott of Jewish businesses in Galicia prompted many east-European Jews to head for Vienna. Between 1860 and 1900, Vienna's Jewish population rose from 6,000 to 147,000.

The problem was, many Vienna-born Jews had assimilated so fully they didn't much care for the new arrivals, who spoke Yiddish and maintained old traditions. Some prominent Austrian Jews, including the writer Karl Kraus, called on their fellow Jews to eschew the beliefs, rituals, and customs of Judaism. During this period, thousands of Austrian Jews converted to Christianity. This eagerness to fit in also applied to the few Jewish members of Parliament. When it was proposed that a session be rescheduled so as to not conflict with Yom Kippur, Jewish members objected. A joke made the rounds in Vienna: Anti-Semitism had become so popular the Jews had taken it up themselves.

Carl Knoll, the third child of David and Mindel Knoll, was born in 1899. David Knoll, an orthodox Jew, had started off in business at age ten, buying vegetables from farmers on his way home from school and selling them to dealers at a profit. Later, he set up a small grocery store and grain outlet.

But it was getting harder than ever for Jews to make a living in Galicia. Carl's two oldest brothers—Jacob and Joseph—fled to Vienna in the years just prior to World War I. David Knoll soon followed, but floundered in his early attempts to make a new start. He wanted to return to Stanislawow, but this was not possible: His wife Mindel had liquidated the family business there, and was on her way to Vienna, children in tow.

The Knolls were part of an influx of Jewish refugees—called *Ostjuden*—who swelled Vienna and became the focal point of anti-Semitic anger. Leaflets distributed at churches and coffee houses marked these new arrivals as "the refuse of humanity" against whom God's Commandment "Thou Shall Not Kill" purportedly did not apply. The Social Democrats—the party to which Carl, his brothers, and most other Austrian Jews belonged—offered little resistance, often supporting and even instigating anti-*Ostjuden* legislation. "It would be nicer to be hospitable," the party's newspaper opined, "but naked self-preservation compels us to be otherwise."

World War I, sparked in June 1914 by the assassination in Sarajevo of Austrian Archduke Franz Ferdinand, further inflamed passions against the Jews, who were depicted as traitors and war profiteers. This although thousands of Jews—including Jacob and Joseph Knoll—served in the Austrian Army.

The Jews' greatest protector, Emperor Franz Joseph, died in 1916 at age eighty-six, after a sixty-eight-year reign. The Christian Socials soon edged out the Social Democrats to take control of Parliament. New laws were passed to restrict the rights of Jews; the Christian Socials proposed a new Austrian national anthem, replacing the words "God protect and God preserve our emperor from harm" with "God protect, God preserve our land from the Jews." The streets of Vienna, and especially the Leopoldstadt, hosted sporadic riots in which mobs of anti-Semites pounced on and beat up people who looked Jewish (mistakes were made), sometimes stopping trolleys to snare victims. In 1919, the Social Democratic governor of Lower Austria, which included Vienna, called for the *Ostjuden*'s mass expulsion. The idea fizzled; the sentiment remained.

Throughout the 1920s, random acts of violence against Jews became an Austrian fact of life. Jewish suicides rose sharply (one prompted the sign, "Neighbors, Please Copy"), and the Jewish birthrate steadily declined, from 2,733 births to Viennese Jews in 1923 to a mere 757 in 1933, the year Alice Knoll was born. Jews were effectively squeezed out of civil service (government) jobs, and made to bear the brunt of a hurt economy. Anny Appel, later Simon's wife, remembers standing in line with her mother at 4 a.m. to get bread and milk. Meanwhile, the hardship brought on by the Great Depression and the success of Hitler's National Socialist (Nazi) Party in Germany buoyed Austria's own Nazis. In January 1933, when Hitler became chancellor of Germany, the party's Vienna branch had 40,000 members, up from 600 three years before.

Eric Nash, suitor of Erwin's beloved Aunt Erna, had been vexed by anti-Semitism all his life. At the end of World War I, when he was seven, Eric and his family fled to Vienna from Czechoslovakia to escape a massive pogrom. He entered the third grade in Vienna, where classmates sized him up and demanded, *"Bist du Jud´?"* ("Are you a Jew?") Now, in 1933, he was a medical student at the University of Vienna, where many professors openly aligned with the Nazi cause. Nash was involved in a bizarre battle with other medical students during an anatomy lesson. It began with a Nazi student whispering "Dirty Jew" and ended in an all-out brawl in which two groups of students, at a loss for weapons, attacked each other with the parts—an arm here, a leg there—of corpses being dissected by the class.

In 1934 the Social Democrats, the political party to which Nash belonged, was outlawed following a brief but bloody civil war. Nash, a party stalwart, used an illegal printer to produce thousands of leaflets. Once, he was arrested while handing leaflets out. "Thank God they didn't come to my home, because I had this printer in my bathroom," says Nash, who told his mother it was photographic equipment.

Because he had never been able to obtain Austrian citizenship, Nash remained a Czech, subject to military conscription. A two-year rotating internship in Vienna forestalled the inevitable, but in October 1936 Nash was ordered to defend the homeland he had been forced to flee. He served as a doctor, treating soldiers. Erna stayed with her family in Vienna, visiting every few months.

Toward the end of 1937, Austrian Nazis renewed a campaign of terror bombings, which did nothing to improve their sagging standing with the Austrian public. Anti-Semitism was still the party's main card—Nazi thugs would sing into the Vienna night the words of "*Horst Wessel*": "Just you wait you matzoh-devouring people. Soon will come the night of the long knives"—but the ruling Christian Socials could steal this thunder simply by ratcheting up their own anti-Semitic rhetoric. For whatever reason, many Austrians had serious qualms about aligning with Hitler and the Nazis.

As 1938 began, the skies over Austria hosted a rare display of northern lights—just as had happened in 1866, when Austria was crushed by her neighbor to the north. The Austrian public rallied behind Chancellor Kurt von Schuschnigg's call for Austrian independence. Hitler, infuriated, brought Schuschnigg to his knees and troops to his door. Immediately, the Austrians were sieg-heiling Hitler with the rest of them—but with a bit more feeling.

Shortly after the *Anschluss*, Bert Knoll, Erwin's cousin (the son of Carl's brother Joseph), was expelled from high school for being Jewish. He began to work at his uncles' business, installing electric motors into sewing machines. But then the Nazis confiscated the business, and began liquidating its stock of electric motors. Since the motors belonged to the Knolls, they felt justified in taking a piece of the action. At night, they sneaked into the shop through a back door and carried out motors, to sell illegally on the black market.

Nazi authorities entered the Vienna home of Sophie Littman, Carl Knoll's cousin, and confiscated valuables. The family sent word to its most influential relative—David Diringer, an archeologist who worked for the Italian government. Diringer and his wife journeyed to Vienna, where he paid an unannounced visit to Gestapo headquarters, demanding the return of this property. "They gave back everything they took," recalls Sophie's son Walter, who was nine at the time.

But the days when Jews in Vienna might secure an occasional dose of justice were rapidly nearing an end. Most of them were now actively trying to flee the country. Bureaucratic red-tape and anti-Semitism confounded this process, but, at least until the start of World War II, getting out was not nearly as difficult as finding some place to go. In July 1938, U.S. President Franklin D. Roosevelt convened a 32-nation conference in Evian, France, to ponder an international response to the mass exodus of Jews from the Third Reich. Only three nations—Denmark, Holland, and Santo Domingo—professed a willingness to take in additional Jewish refugees. "They weep crocodile tears over the Jews," chided the *Voelkischer Beobachter*, a leading Nazi newspaper, "but nobody is willing to make any sacrifices for these 'unfortunates,' since everyone knows what the Jew means within a national community. Those countries who themselves refuse to take any Jews merely justify the German Reich's defensive measures against the Jews, measures which are in any case not yet sufficiently far-reaching."

At a meeting in Munich on September 29, 1938, Hitler secured the acquiescence of the governments of Britain, France, and Russia to "reoccupy" the *Sudetenland*, the southern portion of Czechoslovakia. (Six months later, Hitler broke his part of the bargain by invading and plundering the rest of Czechoslovakia. Laws were quickly passed to strip the nation's Jews of their money and dignity.) The signing of this Munich pact, a proud moment for the Reich, occasioned a new outbreak of anti-Semitic violence in Austria. According to Berkeley, "So many people with broken arms and legs, smashed-up faces, and other injuries were brought to the [local Jewish] hospital that they were put first in the corridors and then, when those filled up, on the lawn."

On *Kristallnacht*, even these horrors were surpassed. In Vienna, more than 4,000 Jewish businesses were looted; 2,000 Jewish families lost their homes. Jewish women in detention facilities were forced to entertain their captors by dancing naked with high-kicking legs and having sex with female prostitutes.

Norbert Seiden, Erwin's cousin and playmate, remembers that on November 10, 1938, his father, Ignaz, walked to the Jewish day school that Norbert had been attending and watched it burn. On that day, Ignaz Seiden was forced to hand over the keys to his housewares business to a Nazi officer.

At the Littman residence, *Kristallnacht* began with a knock at the door in the early morning. Local Nazi thugs entered the home to "search for weapons." Finding none, they nonetheless arrested Leo Littman, the husband of Carl Knoll's cousin Sophie. Later, the door burst open again, and the Nazis began helping themselves to whatever they wanted, including the new pillowcases that Sophie had just made. These they loaded on a bedsheet; Sophie persisted in taking items back. Finally, as young Walter watched, her insouciance earned her a sharp punch in the back of the neck. The door was open and a neighbor looked on in horror. Walter and his mother were banished that night to a small part of the apartment; the next day they had to get out for good.

Joseph Knoll, Erwin's uncle (his father Carl's older brother), was also arrested on November 10 by Austrian Nazis. The owner of a business that sold bags for shipping, Joseph was sent to the same makeshift detention facility as Leo Littman. It was a horseback riding school. There, Leo Littman watched the Nazis beat Joseph Knoll savagely. For three days Joseph, bruised and bleeding, was denied food or medical attention. He was taken in a coma to a public hospital, where family members found him. Joseph Knoll died of his injuries without ever regaining consciousness. It is not known whether he is among the ninety-one people the Nazis officially counted as killed on *Kristallnacht*.

Leo Littman was released from the detention facility after four days, but the ordeal left him badly shaken. He began having nightmares, as his son Walter recalls: "He'd wake up staring at the colored brown windows across the street. He thought they were stormtroopers."

On November 12, the Nazis imposed a fine—equal to $400 million in today's currency—on Austria's Jewish population, to pay for the damage caused during *Kristallnacht*. And insurance payments to Jews for losses incurred were confiscated by the state.

The message of *Kristallnacht* to the 175,000 Jews who still remained in Austria was loud and clear: Get out. Many did, through whatever means available. Others remained in Vienna—because they had no place else to go or because they believed, erroneously, that Hitler's downfall was soon at hand. Erwin Knoll's family, for the most part, decided it was time to go. By September 1939, when Hitler sparked World War II by invading Poland, three-fourths of Austria's Jews had fled.

With Joseph Knoll dead, taking care of wife Regina and son Bert, then fifteen, became the family's most immediate concern. In early 1939, Carl Knoll, Erwin's father, tried escaping with Bert. The pair traveled across Germany to the Belgian border, but it was closed to emigration just as they arrived; next, they took a train to Austria's southwestern corner and paid a guide to take them on the half-day trek into Switzerland. But after crossing the border into Basel, Carl Knoll and his nephew were apprehended by Swiss authorities, who turned them over to the Gestapo. The Gestapo sent them back home.

Carl Knoll's next escape attempt was with his son Erwin. Alice Knoll says her mother, Ida, insisted on it: "The family was a matriarchy. Women made the decisions. We kept people alive." What happened, says Alice, is that "my mother decided to send my father and brother away." Why? "They used to accost the soldiers in the streets and get into arguments with them. They would tell the soldiers what civil rights they had. You did not tell Nazi soldiers what your civil rights were and expect to live."

Even if he kept his mouth shut, Carl Knoll was in great danger. He was a Jew, and a formerly successful businessman. He was among the hated *Ostjuden*, a refugee from Galicia. He belonged to the outlawed Social Democrat Party. And he had a history of radicalism, including a brief prison term for anti-war activities during World War I.

Erwin Knoll remembered standing, for days on end, with his mother at the Rothschild Palais, waiting for a passport. In April 1939, he got one. It had a swastika on the cover and in five places inside. A large red "J" was stamped on the first page. His name was entered Erwin Israel Knoll, in accordance with a Nazi directive giving the middle name "Israel" to every Jewish male and "Sarah" to every female.

Carl's attempt to flee Austria with Erwin, like his earlier escape attempt with Bert (who in July 1939 safely joined his mother in England), did not go off without a hitch. Erwin, on the day of their first planned escape, had thoughtfully returned his books to his teacher, explaining he would not need them anymore since he and his father were leaving that night for Switzerland. Unfortunately, the teacher he said this to was the one who wore the swastika with the laurel wreath. The plan was delayed and it was impressed upon seven-year-old Erwin that this was not a good time to be absolutely truthful. Soon thereafter, in what Erwin remembered was great haste, they tried again. As before, Carl and his charge took a train ride and paid for safe passage across the border into Switzerland. This time it worked.

A third of a century would pass before Erwin Knoll would return to the land of his birth. In January 1973, he and his wife Doris visited Vienna for a week. They were awed by the architecture and the music, and Erwin, especially, loved the pastries. They visited his old apartment at *Hammer-Purgstallgasse 3*. It was just as he remembered it, although a sign announced that the building had been restored after being damaged in the war. He noticed that Jews—once so vital to Vienna's standing as a mecca of music, medicine and ideas—were almost nowhere to be seen. This did not seem to trouble the Austrians he met, otherwise fine and charming people.

On January 20, the day Richard Nixon was being sworn in for his second term as president of the United States, Erwin Knoll went back to the *Karmelitermarkt*, from which he had been turned away in tears as a child. He found the fruit stand in the same place it had been. This time, he was allowed to buy two oranges. Later, Doris noticed the label on the peel. They were Jaffa oranges, imported from Israel.

CHAPTER TWO

Refugee

Throughout its history, the Knoll family has displayed a profound ambivalence toward war. In fact, the family traces its very name to an act of draft-dodging.

Toward the end of the 18th Century, four brothers named Landau are said to have fled military service by making the 400-mile horse-and-buggy trek from the city of Przemysl to a town named Nadworna, also in Galicia. (This family legend is suspect, since military service was not compulsory at that time; perhaps the brothers left to take advantage of *Schutzjuden*, a historically documented institution wherein Jews were given protection by Gentiles, in exchange for some consideration.) The brothers, traders all, chose the new name Knoll. It had two meanings—little hill, and of high-bound station—but was probably picked because it was short and had a distinctive ring.

The family fragmented, its members moving to neighboring towns and as far as Romania. But whenever Jews named Knoll met, they knew they were cousins and could trace the relationship. Among Erwin Knoll's papers is a *New York Post* article about Felix G. Rohatyn, the legendary powerbroker of New York City; it relates that Rohatyn was born in Vienna, the son of Edith Knoll. Scrawled in the margin, "It's a small world."

Although the name Knoll was of Anglo-Saxon, not Jewish, origin, family members were marked nonetheless. Charles Knoll, a descendant of one of the original Knoll brothers, in 1925 moved from Stanislawow to France, where he married a French woman, ran a successful business, and served with distinction in the French Foreign

Legion. He was captured in 1940 after a vigorous standoff with German forces. Blond-haired and blue-eyed, Knoll gave the Gestapo a letter, from a French priest, falsely attesting to his status as a good Christian. The Gestapo let Knoll go. A couple of months later they picked him up again; their records showed that all Knolls from Galicia had descended from four Jewish brothers who changed their name in 1794 and hence all were Jewish. Charles was sent to a concentration camp for a year; his business was confiscated.

Other family members also achieved military distinction—of a sort. In World War I, Carl's oldest brother Jacob was in the Austrian army. One day, he and a small group of German-speaking Austrian infantrymen were suddenly surrounded by a much larger contingent of Russian soldiers. The two sides stared at each other down the barrels of their guns. "Does one of you speak Polish?" a Russian soldier asked. "I speak Polish," replied Jacob. The Russian continued: "Tell your men that, as they can see, we are much stronger. A fight would make no sense for you. Tell them not to be nervous. Drop your weapons and you will be taken prisoners of war. No harm will come to you." Jacob translated these words to German, and his frightened comrades surrendered. It's not the kind of thing they give war medals for, but, as Carl Knoll noted in a family history he wrote in 1964, "In one group as well as in the other, a man who spoke a language unknown to his comrades saved their lives."

Unfortunately for Jacob Knoll, the Russian soldier's pledge—"No harm will come to you"—proved overly optimistic. Jacob and the others were dispatched to Siberia, where they found themselves among a group of 7,000 POWs fighting off an outbreak of typhus. The Russians did nothing to help the prisoners, and more than two-thirds died. Jacob, one of the survivors, again proved his peculiar heroism: At the urging of a Russian priest, he began recording information on the dead, so that after the war their families could be told.

Some Knolls, following family tradition, did everything they could to avoid military service—especially since they were being ordered to serve a nation that had marginalized them as citizens. Carl's cousin Muni Diringer, sent to the Italian front soon after he turned seventeen (the age of mandatory conscription), deserted. As Fred Diringer, Muni's son, tells it, "He took one look at the soldiers around him and said, 'We're not going to win this thing and I'm not going to get killed with these guys.'" Muni, who stayed in Prague until the war ended, was right on both counts.

Carl Knoll turned seventeen in November 1916, and for the next two years passed himself off as his brother Simon, who was not old enough to be drafted and had the papers to prove it. Simon had less need for papers; he was apprenticing as a mechanic and his blue work clothes afforded some protection.

In 1939, the brothers were fleeing war again, and this time it was a war against the Jews. Simon's papers came through first, and he left for England on the last day of April, leaving behind his wife Anny and daughter Rita. Jacob Knoll fled illegally to Yugoslavia, leaving his wife Bronia and two children, Heinrich and Gertrude, in the Vienna apartment they shared with his mother Mindel Knoll. (David Knoll, the father, died in 1935 of diabetes and pulmonary tuberculosis.) Ida and Alice Knoll also stayed in Vienna, as Carl and Erwin made their way across the border into Switzerland.

Carl Knoll was interned, along with hundreds of other Jews, in a refugee camp at Gossau. His son Erwin, who that summer turned eight, was sent to live with a Lutheran minister and his family in a nearby town named Flawil. The two got to see each other occasionally and exchanged letters. One from Erwin to Carl dated August 9, 1939, reads in part (as translated from German), "Dear Dad! I've since Tuesday not had any school. Why haven't you written to me this week? Are you picking me up tomorrow? . . . When will I be getting the shoes back that I gave you to repair? How are you? I'm good. In Flawil, you see a lot of soldiers nowadays. I close with many greetings and kisses. Love, Erwin. P.S. Thanks for the letter I've now received.

The minister and his family—a wife and five children—were good to Erwin, as he later recalled: "It was just terrific. They took me in and let me live with them for a year. These were people who had no radio in a tiny village that had no automobiles. When a car came through it was a big event, and kids came running to see it. Having moved to this from the very cosmopolitan city of Vienna, it was quite a dramatic change."

Every Sunday, from 2 to 5 p.m.—after the morning church service and before dinner—the minister and his family would gather in their living room to play chamber music. Each member played an instrument. Erwin was greatly impressed: "These were the most civilized people I ever lived among."

Young Erwin also met a Swiss man who, while he had just one leg, was an accomplished skier. Erwin would cling onto his back for thrilling rides through the mountains.

One day Erwin's most valuable possession, his bicycle, was badly damaged in a mishap. He dreamt he covered the bike with gravel, went away, and returned to find it in perfect condition. The images were so vivid that, upon waking, he rushed to his bike, which was just as badly damaged as before. Erwin later told this story to his son David, who had had a similar dream about recovering his own prized but stolen bike.

As Erwin lived apart from his mother, his attachment to her—never as strong as to his father—grew fainter. But in a letter back home to Vienna, Erwin wrote of his loneliness and his sadness of being separated. "His letter was all very dramatic about how much he missed his family," recalls Rita. But what most impressed those who saw Erwin's letter was that it was streaked with tears. Just to see it made their hearts ache.

Erwin later told his wife Doris about this letter. He told her how, when he had finished writing it, he had dipped his hand in a glass of water and sprinkled "tears" all over it.

At the end of July 1939, Rita and Anny Knoll took a train through France and then a boat to England. Anny had found work as a domestic, a common occupation among Jewish women allowed into England. The family had to leave almost all its valuables behind; Anny sewed a gold chain and some rings into the elastic of Rita's underwear, where they remained safe from harm. Because Simon was from Austria, and hence from Greater Germany, he spent the start of World War II in internment camps, similar to those set up by the United States to imprison Japanese-Americans. Most of the time he was at the Isle of Man, where he became camp cook, using a garbage can to prepare huge quantities of food.

Anny, then thirty-three, was told she could not bring her daughter with her to work. She objected, saying "Rita is the only thing Hitler let me keep and I'm not going to part with her." Anny took Rita with her to several jobs. For a while they lived in Andoversford, where Rita attended school; the house they lived in lacked electricity and hot water and, remembers Anny, to use the outhouse "you had to make like this [waving arms] so the rats and mice would go away." After about a year, Simon was released to reunite with his family; they moved to Cheltenham, in Gloucestershire County, where he found work as a taxi-cab driver and as a mechanic for the taxi fleet.

The rest of the family also scattered, in search of refuge. Muni Diringer and his family were the first to come to the United States, in 1937. The Seidens—Carl's sister Pepi, her husband Ignaz, son Norbert and daughter Trudie—in 1939 left for Shanghai, which had opened its borders to Jews. The Lembergers—Carl's sister Lisa and husband Kurt, fled first to England in 1939 before arriving in New York in 1940, then on to Belleville, New Jersey. The Littmans—Carl's cousin Sophie, her husband Leo and son Walter—escaped to Sweden in May 1939, after depositing the requisite sum in a Swedish bank. In early 1941, they made their way to the United States—by going to Finland, then Russia, then Japan, then across the Pacific to Seattle. They settled in New York, where Leo sold fabrics, eventually owning a store on Elridge Street.

In Czechoslovakia, Erwin's beloved Aunt Erna married Eric Nash on November 19, 1938, a week after *Kristallnacht*. In March 1939, Hitler's troops marched into Czechoslovakia and Nash, a doctor just starting his own practice, was pressed into service as medical director of a refugee camp near Brno. This position, Nash would later note, "was both dangerous and debilitating, since it meant working constantly under and against the Gestapo, which had charge of the camp." Bit by bit, the rights of Jews in Czechoslovakia were stripped away. The Nashes—Erna, Eric and his mother Irma—lost their apartment, and had to move in with Eric's sister Trude and her husband Henry; all five shared one small room. Later, the Nashes were ordered to move to Eibenschutz, where the refugee camp was located. Still, they had a small but comfortable apartment, and lived relatively well.

After her husband and son left, Ida Knoll continued to seek passage to the United States, and had obtained the necessary affidavits from her relatives, a family named Greenspan, in New York City. (All Jews immigrating to the United States had to have sponsors who promised to take care of them lest they become a burden to the Government; many thousands of Jews were thus excluded, some fatally.) In April 1940, Ida and Alice, then four years old, took a train to Italy and an ocean liner to New York, where they arrived just ahead of Carl and Erwin. As Alice Knoll saw the Statue of Liberty for the first time, her mother told her that, from now on, "You are an American child." From then on, she was.

The Knolls moved into a cold-water flat, paid for by the Greenspans, on Freeman Street in the Bronx. Carl Knoll, at age forty, found a job as a busboy. Ida Knoll, also forty, worked in a textile mill, sewing by hand. After a year the family moved to a nicer apartment in Brooklyn. Alice, who stayed with neighbors during the day, grew up learning English. Erwin began learning the language when he entered the fourth grade in a Bronx public school. Ida and Carl attended classes at night school. Both learned the language well, but Carl in particular had a hard time adjusting to life in the United States, as Alice recalls. "My mother said it nicely: 'Most of the family never quite crossed the ocean.'"

Erwin, says Alice, "retained European values. I never did." (Erwin's son David takes the point further: "Erwin wanted to be a member of the 18th Century European intelligentsia. This was a man who didn't think they've created one note of civilized music this century. He thought, you get past Mozart, and it's all junk.") Whereas Alice would become, in her own estimation, "the apolitical sister who lives in the world as it is," her father Carl arrived in New York "still fighting the authorities" in Vienna. "I don't think he ever recovered," says Alice, "and I don't think my brother ever recovered from that period, either." She says Erwin, like his father, would "never stop fighting those men in the street, telling the soldiers what his civil rights were."

Even before the family came to New York, says Alice, her brother's defiant character was set. She points to a photograph taken in Switzerland. Erwin is sitting on a fence, on the far-left-hand side, with a group of seven adults. He's wearing a Swiss outfit, arms folded across his chest. "See," exclaims Alice, "he's protesting already." She points to another photo of Erwin with his father. Erwin's arms are again folded, and his face is scrunched up into a scowl, or perhaps it's a smirk. "He's imitating his father's expression," says Alice.

Carl Knoll, after losing several jobs, opened his own business, a print shop on Wall Street called Knoll Duplicating Service. He ran the presses; Ida ran the business; it was finally a job from which he would not get fired. The main problem when Carl worked for others, says Alice, "is that he kept on asserting his rights. I don't think the employers liked it anymore than the soldiers did." Carl Knoll once told his son a printer could make more money working for others than he could owning his own shop. "One day, you'll understand," he said. One day Erwin did.

Photo courtesy of Alice Allen

Erwin with father Carl: Imitating his expression?

Growing up in Brooklyn, where he attended PS167 elementary school and Erasmus Hall High School, Erwin felt isolated. His parents tapped into a large community of Jewish immigrants they found in New York, "but my world was the kids on the block and the kids in the school who were not part of that community of immigrants." Worse still, "I encountered in New York the kind of street-bully anti-Semitism from which I had fled." As he walked down the sidewalk, these other kids—"And they weren't Germans; they weren't Nazis"—accused him of killing Jesus Christ. He thought of himself not as a victim but as a refugee.

After the war in Europe ended in the spring of 1945, Erwin on several occasions accompanied his father to Jewish refugee-aid organizations in New York; the walls were covered with postings from Jews seeking to reestablish contact with displaced relatives. That September, a man who had known the Knolls in Vienna called excitedly to say that a New York Yiddish-language paper had made reference to Eric Nash, the Czech doctor who had married Erwin's Aunt Erna just before the war. The article said Dr. Nash had come to the Supreme Allied Headquarters in Paris as a representative of a Jewish group that was seeking to locate death-camp survivors. Carl Knoll sent a cablegram to Paris, and it was forwarded to Nash in Prague. Nash promptly wired back: "AM WELL BUT ALONE.

LETTER FOLLOWS."

The letter that arrived soon thereafter was typed, single-spaced, on both sides of four sheets of flimsy paper. It was entitled *"Ich habe es gesehen"* ("I have seen it"), dated September 28, 1945, and addressed to "*Meine Lieben*" ("My Dears"). Carl Knoll somberly read this missive to his family. Alice, ten at the time, has no recollection of this event; Erwin, then fourteen, never forgot it. "I can still see and hear my father reading it aloud to us," he wrote. "I believe no other document, no text, no piece of paper has ever had such a profound effect on me." His thirteen-year-old cousin, Norbert Seiden, whose family received the same letter in China, also remembers "as though it were yesterday."

After his father died in 1986, Erwin searched through his belongings for the letter. It was not there, and he was "bitterly disappointed at the loss of so important a family document." But at Carl's funeral in New York, Erwin asked Nash whether he still had a copy. "Of course," he replied. Erwin, over a period of many months, translated the letter into English. Nash—who after the war came to New York, opened a general practice, and became physician to Carl and other family members—looked over his nephew's version, and made various refinements. This is how the letter began:

"Ever since my liberation on May 2 in Southern Bavaria, I've made repeated attempts to write to you. I . . . will now try to relate what has transpired since we were last in touch by mail. The world collapsed and a new one has not yet been created. Words can't describe what we were forced to endure and how we were destroyed. But you have a right to know what happened."

The letter goes on to recount the fates, so far as Nash knew, of various family members. Jacob Knoll, who had fled illegally to Yugoslavia, was the next (after Joseph) to die. In a letter dated January 25, 1941, Jacob expressed concern for himself and his family in Vienna, hoping they would find safe passage to the United States. "I know I must learn to wait patiently," he wrote, "but who knows what we can expect with the threatening situation in Europe? I'm not certain of anything. Not even the Revolution." Hitler's troops invaded Yugoslavia in April 1941; Jacob, his family learned, burned to death in a barracks the Nazis had set on fire.

A child, it's been said, is an expression of God's opinion that the world should go on. In the case of Eric and Erna Nash, the child they conceived in mid-1941 was an expression of their optimism that the war would soon end. They were terribly wrong.

In January 1942, the German high command devised a "Final Solution" to the problem of European Jewry. Austrian engineers designed the world's first gas chamber, after the Nazis' custom-designed gas vans proved unreliable. It was tried out first in Austria, at Hartheim Castle near Linz, on some 30,000 physically or mentally impaired Austrians. Throughout the Reich, Jews were rounded up and put on transports—mass shipments of people packed into railroad cars.

For several months, there were no transports from Czechoslovakia; but then, in March 1942, Brno and its environs began to be evacuated. The Nashes didn't think they'd be affected, since the refugee camp still needed his medical services. On April 1, just days before Erna's due date, the couple was enrolled in a transport, but were told it was an error. The Germans said they had to show up as ordered, but would not be sent. Erna Nash packed for the whole family, including her expected newborn, as Eric sent a final shipment of supplies and money to family members still in Vienna. The family—Eric, Erna, Irma, Trude and Henry—arrived at the assembly point, a school.

"There we received a small foretaste of what awaited us," Nash wrote. "We were cooped up in a classroom with covered windows. Ventilation was permitted only at night so that no one on the outside could see what it was like on the inside—children, sick people, old people, all thrown together in filth and stench, with no food and little water."

As night fell, the detainees were "loaded under SS blows into railway wagons" and shipped to Theresienstadt, a so-called model ghetto recently established in Czechoslovakia. "What we found when we arrived there on April 4, 1942, was horrible," wrote Nash. "Thousands of us crammed into small barracks; men and women separated and unable to see each other, even at work; hardly anything to eat. The terror consisted of beatings and executions. But at least we knew the women were in the same city, a few doors away."

On April 9, 1942, Erna Nash gave birth to a son—the seventh of 256 children born at Theresienstadt. His name was Michael Joseph, after his mother's brother Joseph Knoll, the first family member to die. The delivery went well, but Erna nearly bled to death due to complications afterwards. "When I finally overcame tremendous difficulties and gained access to the women's barracks, it was all over," Nash related. "Erna, very pale but extremely happy, was lying on a white bed."

As a physician, Nash was able to arrange almost daily visits with his wife and child. Irma and Trude helped Erna greatly. But then, on April 28, Trude and husband Henry, a successful architect, left on a transport from Theresienstadt to the area near Lublin in Poland. Trude's last letter is dated August 16, 1942. Neither she nor Henry were heard from again.

Transports were pouring into as well as out of Theresienstadt, and that summer one of them brought Mindel Knoll, Erwin's grandmother, from Vienna. Joseph's wife Bronia and two children, eighteen-year-old Heinrich and ten-year-old Gertrude, were put on another transport to parts unknown; they were never heard from again. Fewer than 700 Jews remained in Austria, all in hiding, at war's end. In 1945, Nazis fleeing Vienna briefly occupied the Leopoldstadt, where the Knolls had lived. They found nine Jews—including an eighty-two-year-old woman—hiding, as they had been for months, in a cellar. They machine-gunned them to death.

Mindel Knoll moved in with the Nashes and began attending to her daughter Erna and new grandson, both of whom had measles—a serious illness, in Erna's case. Conditions in the ghetto had worsened, due to a policy of malign neglect. Dysentery and starvation ruled; some days as many as 200 people died. But life for the Nashes was not without joy. Eric managed to turn an old stable into a room for his family; there, Mischa learned to walk and talk. "He wanted for nothing," attested Nash of his son. "Both grandmothers competed in this love for him, constantly knitting, darning, washing for him. He was the focal point of our family." Theresienstadt had a rich cultural life: parks, theaters and concert halls. Eric and Erna had many friends; he had his profession; they both had Mischa. "We loved each other very much, perhaps more than in our earlier years in Vienna, for now we knew each other through and through," Nash wrote his family. "Yes, there was happiness in Theresienstadt!"

Hardship intervened, as Erna came down with tuberculosis and had to be parted from her child; eight months passed before she was completely well. Nash, in his letter, applauded her perseverance, and heaped praise on their son: "I must tell you I've seldom seen such a child. . . . Can you imagine," Nash wrote his relatives, "how much we yearned for the end of the war, how much we talked about it, how we planned proudly to introduce you all to him?"

Maintaining optimism was getting harder by the day. Eric's brother Willi had been picked up in 1941 on the streets of Brno because "he did not jump fast enough out of the path of a visiting SS officer," and put on a transport to a labor camp in Minsk. The two brothers remained in contact through smuggled letters. In his last letter, dated October 20, 1943, Willi warned that he might not write again: "I must go the way of my fate." He never mailed the letter; it was sent by a friend, who added a few scribbled lines: "Today, on October 21, my comrade Willi was taken away. Where to? The thing that is hard to take is how good and honest people suffer at the hands of the monsters [*Unmenshen*]." Eric Nash speculates that Willi was killed in an "action," then a common practice: Hundreds of Jews were rounded up and made to dig a mass grave; then they were machine-gunned backwards into it and covered with dirt, sometimes while still alive.

On eight occasions, the two grandmothers were enrolled in transports to the east; each time, Nash managed to get their names off the list. Then, in December 1943, there was nothing he could do: The two women were put on a train to Auschwitz, the last stop for 1.9 million Jews. Irma Nash, her son later learned, died at Auschwitz in January 1945 of exhaustion and hunger. Mindel Knoll also died at Auschwitz, most likely the same way. But the Nashes did not then know this: "We lived in sorrow, but in the constant hope that we would find our mothers again. Our child helped us a great deal in coping with all this."

In October 1944, the Nazis ordered the evacuation of Theresienstadt. Nash and his family were put on the "blue list" of people who were not supposed to be shipped out. But on October 19, they were. It was a grueling journey—in a railroad car without food, water or a toilet, packed with eighty people and their belongings—and it lasted three full days. Two-year-old Mischa, reported his father, had a good time on this, "his first and last railroad trip"; he never lost his sense of humor and delighted in entertaining other passengers. At last the train stopped, and the doors were opened. The sign on the station said "Auschwitz." The new arrivals—1,500 in all—were immediately set upon by Polish Jews in uniforms who roughly drove them out, tearing off their watches and confiscating their bags. They were led before the notorious Nazi doctor Josef Mengele, who sorted them into two lines: the strong to the right; the old, the sick, and all women with children to the left.

Eric Nash was directed to the right, but when he saw that children were being sent to the left he snuck over to that side. He was apprehended and sent back. Then his group was marched off to be subjected to horrors beyond anything Nash had seen at Theresienstadt. ("If Auschwitz was hell," reflected one survivor, "Theresienstadt was the anteroom.") The new arrivals were pushed into cold showers and forced to stand naked in the cold for hours, as guards beat them and whipped them and searched their every body opening for hidden valuables. Nash says a third of those around him did not survive this ordeal. "At this point," Nash says, "something in me turned to steel: I was firmly resolved that . . . I would see my wife and child again."

From his first night at Auschwitz, Nash heard the rumor—that all those directed to the left were put to death. "Into the starry night sky," he wrote his family, "visible from every corner of the huge camp, loomed the symbol of Auschwitz: the chimney. Huge, black, hideous, it burned day and night, and at night the flames leaped meters high into the black sky. The thought that my wife and child were burning there was too absurd to be believed." Others hastened to assure him that it wasn't true. People were being killed and burned, they said, but only those who were crippled, very old or very ill; women and children were just sent to another camp. Nash "allowed myself some hope."

On October 24, after just three days at Auschwitz, Nash was dispatched to Camp Kaufering in Bavaria. The camp, an annex of Dachau, was designed as a place to work people to death. Nash experienced "the heaviest labor, outdoors in all kinds of weather, almost nothing to eat, beatings, standing in formation, sleeping in lice-infested earth bunkers, freezing, dysentery, typhus, 'selections,' shootings. People died like flies. They died everywhere—while eating, while working, while sleeping, while the roll was called, in the latrine, on the march. Still, I knew that I had to survive, for I wanted to see my Mischa and Erni again."

Those who could no longer work were killed. So Nash "worked when I was feverish, when I had bloody stools, when I was freezing." It was at Camp Kaufering that Nash was shot in the head by a Nazi soldier who caught him stealing a beet from a field; it was a glancing shot, but it bled terribly and those who saw Nash dragged away assumed he was dead. Nash, in his letter to his family, neglected to mention this horror—it fell into the category of "I won't describe further what we had to endure"—and many family members never knew.

Nash was at Camp Kaufering for five months. On April 24, as advancing U.S. forces drew so near that artillery fire could be heard in the distance, the Germans ordered the camp evacuated. Thus began the Dachau Death March, as Nash describes: "Fifteen-thousand ghostlike skeletons were set in motion, marching night and day, virtually without provisions. The Germans who saw us pass wept bitterly; we didn't know why because we didn't know what we looked like. People who threw bread at us were shot by the SS. Our people who sank to the ground and could go no further were dispatched with a bullet to the head when we were in open country, or with a chloroform injection when we were in a city, so as to arouse no protest."

Eight days and 100 miles passed before American troops overtook and put an end to this grisly procession. Barely 3,000 of the original 15,000 marchers—Jews and prisoners of war—were still alive. Nash was one of them. He weighed 93 pounds, down from his normal 165. He recuperated, and made his way to Paris. There, he lost the rest of his hope. He met the former camp historian at Auschwitz who confirmed to him that all the mothers and children who came to Auschwitz in October 1944 were immediately sent to the gas chambers. They were for the most part spared beatings, and may have been blessed not to know what was happening to them; but afterwards, their corpses were plundered in search of gold teeth. Nash told his family of his torment: "I have these images constantly before me: How my wife and child were taken there, poisoned, their bodies desecrated and burned. I see it in every detail. I can find no peace."

In all, about a third of the members of Erwin Knoll's family were killed in the Holocaust. Erwin lost his grandmother Mindel, his Uncle Joseph, his Aunt Bronia, and cousins Heinrich and Gertrude. He lost his Aunt Erna—who had loved him so much she pretended he was her son—and Michael Joseph, the two-year-old cousin he never knew. More than a dozen other relatives, on both sides of his family, were put to death because they were Jews. Most of the rest, like Erwin, became refugees.

Different family members dealt with the enormity of their experience in different ways. Alice Knoll—later Alice Allen, a career civil servant with the New York City Housing Authority—saw it as something that had no relevance to her life. Efraim Elrom, a descendant on the Diringer side of the family who went to Israel, was, as chief of a Tel Aviv police agency, one of the first people to interrogate Adolf Eichmann, the Nazi leader who had purged Austria of its Jews, after his 1960 capture by Israeli agents in Argentina. Eichmann was convicted of war crimes and hanged. Carl Knoll became a more fervent Zionist, and an indefatigable defender of Israel; he would occasionally complain that the Israeli army—after some or another adventure that shocked the conscience of other Jews—wasn't being tough enough. Erwin, explains his son David, "didn't think it was excusable for Israelis to become as bad as their oppressors. We [Jews] had, until the state of Israel, remained relatively clean of shedding other peoples' blood. He thought it was a shame the culture lost that."

The issue of Israel, recalls David, was a source of "constant and loud and elevated discord between my father and grandfather." David, who thinks the Jews' only proud moment in the Holocaust was when they violently rebelled in the Warsaw ghetto, derides both positions. "My father," he says, "found some dignity in the relative passivity of Jews who were slaughtered in the Holocaust." On the other hand, "My grandfather was caught up in the Holocaust survivor psychology: He'd always hold up his bony finger and say, 'Never again.'"

Erwin Knoll, late in his life, took issue with this sentiment in a challenging way: "People talk about the Holocaust and they say, 'Never again.' And what they often mean by 'Never again' is that 'Never again must this be allowed to happen to the Jews.' But to me this means that never again must this be allowed to happen, period. And the tragedy is that at one place or another in the world, holocausts are going on all the time—whether the victims are the people of East Timor, or the people of Tibet. These are all holocausts. These are all savage crimes. And the fact that people are capable of committing such monstrous acts against each other is never terribly far from my consciousness."

Photo courtesy of Norbert Seiden

As a young man.

CHAPTER THREE

Educating Erwin

Entering public school in the Bronx knowing only a few words of English was for Erwin Knoll a powerful lesson in the importance of language. From the start it marked him—as a refugee, as a European, as a Jew. It brought ridicule from some grade-school classmates, but also inspired acts of kindness. Knoll later recalled that his fourth-grade teacher "took the trouble of communicating with me in Yiddish, which I could understand because I spoke German, and this made my life easier."

Already, Knoll knew that words were his key to the world around him. It was a message he had gotten from his father, Carl, who read voraciously, loved discussing politics, and, most importantly, used language to assert his rights. "He had a sense of mission from the get-go," says Erwin's sister Alice. "He wanted to express himself." Her statement is true so far as it goes, but it doesn't go far enough. Erwin Knoll wanted to express himself *correctly* and *well*.

Throughout Knoll's adult life, people would marvel at the way he used language—never carelessly or imprecisely. He would engage in spirited discussions about words and their use—arguing, say, that "both" is often not needed and "upon" almost never better than "on." From the dictionary, on which he relied, Knoll received guidance and affirmation. His approach to what Mencken called the American language was based on respect, the kind a person develops for something he covets. Perhaps that's because he learned it as a second language, in an environment where those who knew it better had a clear advantage. Perhaps it's because learning was so hard.

David Knoll, Erwin's son, later delighted in discovering some of his famed father's first literary efforts, the lined pages besieged with red ink. Once, after reading a paper David had written for a high-school class, Erwin remarked that it was in most ways terrible—except in the ways that counted toward grades. "You'll probably get an A," he said unhappily. "Oh, yeah?" replied David, producing a sampling of his father's own schoolwork, "Well, it's a lot better than this and you only got a B."

Erwin, on his way to becoming one of the nation's best education reporters, was pleased by his experience in the New York public schools; he later expressed his gratitude in a letter to the principal of Erasmus Hall High School. Equally vital to Knoll's education was his extensive use of the neighborhood library, where he read *Das Kapital* and other writings by Marx. He skipped grades in both elementary and high school, graduating from the latter in May 1948 at age sixteen.

By this time, Knoll knew what he wanted in life. He wanted to be a journalist. His idol was I.F. Stone, then writing for the newspapers *PM* and the *New York Star*. In September 1948, Knoll wrote a letter to the editor deriding the *Star* for its endorsement of Harry Truman. "Despite the *Star*'s poor choice and the ensuing contradictions, I shall continue reading it, for Albert Deutsch, Jennings Perry and I.F. Stone have fortunately not fallen into your blunder."

As Knoll completed his senior year in high school, he wrote a letter and sent a resume ("imagine how extensive it was when I was 16 years old") to "every single listing under the heading of 'Publications' in the Manhattan phone book." Knoll's mass mailing got him a job at *Editor & Publisher*, the trade publication of the newspaper industry. He began working as a copy boy in July 1948; his starting salary was $28 a week. He liked it so much he changed college plans for that fall, enrolling as a night student at New York University so he could keep his day job.

Around this time, the Knoll and Diringer families, scattered from Vienna to almost every corner of the globe, began reuniting in and around New York. In 1949, after ten years in England, Simon Knoll and his family were finally allowed to immigrate to the United States. They came to Belleville, New Jersey, where Simon's sister Lisa Lemberger had moved before the war. Alan Lemberger, then five years old, remembers waiting with great excitement for his long-lost relatives to arrive at his home, where they lived for six months before getting their own apartment in the same building. "All of a sudden, they came, and I hid in the closet. I wasn't prepared to deal with these people."

The Knoll family and its recent history were a lot to deal with. Rita's parents shielded her from the truth. After the war ended in 1945, her uncle Eric Nash visited her family in England. "They wouldn't let me listen," says Rita, who was twelve at the time. "They made me go to bed. The next morning it looked like they had been up all night talking. I asked what was going on. 'You don't want to know,' they said." Fifty years would pass before Rita would learn about Nash's letter, which her parents had received.

Simon Knoll was family-oriented, and especially fond of his brother Carl, as Rita recalls: "Every Sunday we'd get in the car, drive to New York and visit with the cousins." Rita and Erwin, who had known each other as playmates riding tricycles in the hallway between their two apartments in Vienna, became reacquainted at the Knoll's apartment at 913 Eastern Parkway in Brooklyn. Rita was impressed with Erwin, and proud of his being a writer: "I used to refer to him as my cousin who worked at *Editor & Publisher*." And Rita found Erwin's company easier to take: "At that point, he didn't beat me up anymore."

Alan Lemberger, who was born in New Jersey when Erwin was twelve, grew up in the shadow of his older cousin. "He turned out to be a role model for me," says Lemberger. "Many of his interests became my interests." Chief among Erwin Knoll's interests at that time—unknown to many who knew him in later life—was photography. He had one of the first 35-millimeter cameras, and would take color slides. These he'd show off in presentations at family get-togethers at the Knolls' tidy but sparsely furnished Brooklyn apartment.

In June 1950, a phalanx of family members—Alan and his parents, Erwin and Carl, Rita and Simon—piled into Kurt Lemberger's '48 Dodge and hit the road for Canada, where Bert Knoll was to be wed. The car overheated, and Kurt pulled over by a field of flowers. Erwin took six-year-old Alan's picture amid the flowers in the field. He also photographed the wedding. It was the first time Bert

Knoll had seen his cousin Erwin since 1939, when they each fled Vienna after Bert's father was killed.

There were many more such reunions. The Seidens, the family of Carl's sister Pepi, in 1951 arrived in Belleville, New Jersey, after ten years in China. They moved into the same apartment house as did the families of Lisa Lemberger and Simon Knoll. It was what Alan Lemberger calls an "extended transplanted family." Erwin became reacquainted with his cousin Norbert Seiden, six months his junior.

By day, Erwin worked at *Editor & Publisher*, successively as a copyboy, reporter, and feature writer. Beginning in July 1951, he began writing a weekly feature about syndicated columnists and comic-strip artists. He got to interview big names in the field, including archreactionary columnist Westbrook Pegler and cartoonist Walt Kelly, creator of "Pogo." "I always thought the comic-strip people were a lot smarter than the people who wrote political columns," said Knoll, "but it was a good beat. It was interesting and I learned a lot about the newspaper business." Each day at lunch, he bought a half-dozen different papers from the out-of-town newsstands in Times Square, to search out things he liked and things he hated.

By night, Knoll attended evening classes at New York University. While Knoll achieved some efficiencies by turning in writing he did for *Editor & Publisher* as journalism assignments, he found other ways to stretch himself to the limit. In time, he became involved with *The Evening News*, a twice-monthly paper, the Evening Organization, a student group, and Doris Ricksteen, a fellow evening student. He would go on to become editor of *The Evening News*, president of the Evening Organization, and husband of Doris, in that order. He also served as president of the Evening Forum Club, another student group, and vice-president of the Evening Organization Honor Society. It was a busy period, especially since, after the Korean War started in 1950, Knoll had to attend college full time to maintain his draft deferment. How did he do it? "I sort of gave up sleeping." He also took up smoking, a habit he continued into middle age.

NYU at the time had two campuses: Washington Square College in Greenwich Village, which Knoll attended, and University Heights in the Bronx, which he remembered as "sort of an elite campus for out-of-state students, where they had dormitories, they had fraternities, and all those trappings of American higher education that we didn't have at the downtown campus, thank God." The same disdain is reflected in Knoll's response, as editor of *The Evening News*, to a proposal to replace all five campus student newspapers with a single paper: "One newspaper would mean one editorial stand, and that stand, we fear, would be more closely tied to the University administration than any now taken by the various independent newspapers." Besides, he noted, evening students, being "for the most part older and more mature," had different interests: "We shudder at the prospect of wading through an all-University paper filled with accounts of fraternity antics, sports upsets, and school shenanigans of students who have more time on their hands."

Irwin Berkman, Knoll's predecessor as editor of *The Evening News*, says the Washington Square College campus consisted of "a couple of buildings—some old factories that had been converted. It was a very unacademic kind of place, physically." The newspaper had no office as such, but was given a desk or two in a large open area that by day housed NYU administrators. Most evening students lived in New York and worked during the day; many were Jewish radicals who watched in horror as Julius and Ethel Rosenberg, two New York Jews of leftist bent, were sentenced to death for allegedly leaking atomic secrets. Says Berkman, "We were all very liberal, very much part of the upwardly mobile working class culture of New York City." Into this mix were thrown World War II veterans taking advantage of the GI Bill; by 1948-49, Knoll's first year, they accounted for nearly half of NYU's 50,700 students and, recalls Berkman, exerted a subversive influence: "They would challenge the teachers, wouldn't take any crap from them."

Knoll, late in his life, recalled with fondness his days at NYU, "playing chess in Washington Square by candlelight with old Italian men who had no common language with me except for the chess board, and drinking beer with the flotsam of the Beat Generation at a bar called Cedar Street." The closely connected Evening Organization and *The Evening News*, says Berkman, drew students who were "more intellectually curious and more politically active," and Knoll fit the bill. "He was extremely bright, well-informed, with a readiness to be iconoclastic. He had an enormous variety of interests."

Knoll loved literature and music, especially Mozart and Schubert. "Erwin was a very cultivated man, very civilized," says Berkman, a psychiatrist who lives a stone's throw from Central Park. "I admired him." Once, Erwin and Doris took Berkman to Wolftrap, an open-air theatre near Washington, D.C., for a classical music recital. "It turned out to be advanced modern French music with a fat soprano," says Berkman. "Erwin said to Doris, 'I'm never going to another recital unless you show me the program first.'"

Erwin and Doris met on the last day of 1951 at a New Year's Eve Party held by her cousin, Carmelita Gillespie, a friend of Erwin's. Doris, a native of New York, studied nursing by day at New York Medical College and took classes by night at NYU. Doris was an excellent pianist, and for a while sang in a paid church choir; Erwin, says Berkman, had a "wonderful musical ear." The two hit it off. Doris was smart, good-looking, wickedly funny, opinionated, and unafraid to speak her mind. Erwin was in love. The two were friends with another couple who would also marry: Burt Wenk and Dina von Zweck. They would get together often at Cedar Street and a franchise restaurant called Chock Full o' Nuts. Doris, as part of her training, worked nights in an emergency room in Spanish Harlem. Erwin liked to hang out, waiting for her shift to end, watching what was going on.

From the start, Erwin and Doris built their relationship on rough terrain. Erwin's parents, especially his mother, disapproved of her son dating a girl who wasn't Jewish. Her family was Protestant, attending Lutheran and Episcopalian churches, "whichever was closer." This baffled him, since neither of his parents was religious. Erwin had to endure their disapproval; he still lived at home.

On other fronts, Erwin Knoll found his courage challenged. In 1950, Knoll took over from Berkman as editor of *The Evening News* just as a wave of McCarthyite hysteria—loyalty oaths, faculty purges, suppression of student dissent—was sweeping the nation's campuses. That October, nearby Brooklyn College revoked the charter of its student paper, *The Vanguard*, for running an editorial criticizing the Brooklyn College administration's suspension of a campus group that had opposed U.S. participation in the Korean War. William Taylor, the editor of the suddenly defunct paper, said the action "can only be construed as an attempt . . . to gain control of the newspaper and squelch the expression of any student opinion which does not agree with that of the administration."

Knoll, in his next issue, rallied to *The Vanguard*'s defense. "The action of Brooklyn College authorities in suspending . . . the Labor Youth League is itself a violation of student rights. The suspension of *The Vanguard*, the student newspaper, for opposing that motion, is totally indefensible. If college papers are denied the right to criticize administration policies, one of their major reasons for existence has been destroyed."

As it happened, the NYU administration would provide many opportunities for Knoll and *The Evening News* to perform this essential function of criticism. In 1950, Prof. Lyman R. Bradley, the former chairman of its German department, was jailed for contempt of Congress after he refused to testify before the House Un-American Activities Committee. NYU promptly suspended Bradley without pay, and barred him from speaking on campus. That September, Knoll sent Bradley a letter thanking him for his "courageous and self-sacrificing stand in behalf of civil liberties" and offering "any possible help in securing reinstatement to your position." Bradley thanked Knoll, but said he wanted to let the process play out. In June 1951, he was fired, without severance pay.

NYU also prevented novelist Howard Fast from speaking at Washington Square College on grounds that he had recently served a prison term. Knoll's editorial support drew a stirring letter from Fast. "I do not thank you merely for coming to my personal defense. The issue is far broader than that," he wrote. "The threat implicit in this banning is directed far more against every student of the University than against myself. When any voice is silenced, there should be a grave moment of reflection and doubt." Fast, noting that his beliefs were a matter of public record ("I have stated them in book after book"), concluded: "It is less that I have been judged than that you people have been judged. And the verdict was that you were not to hear anything that might contradict the increasing tempo of falsehood and hatred which is taking the American people to fascism and war. This is your world as well as mine, as well as Harry Truman's. It is up to you to see what manner of a world it should be."

Erwin Knoll took this charge seriously. For the 1951-52 school year, he stepped down as editor of *The Evening News* and became president of the Evening Organization, the student political group, and chairman of the Student Council. In February 1952, Knoll was appointed to serve on Washington Square College's Student Committee on Educational Policy, an advisory group. Knoll was, *The Evening News* reported, "the first evening student ever appointed to the committee." NYU's new chancellor, Dr. Henry Townley Heald, was taking what appeared to be strong stands in favor of academic freedom. "Generally speaking," he told a press conference, "students are sufficiently mature to make up their own minds about a speaker without having to be protected from those whose opinions differ from those you and I might hold." Heald also defended dissident teachers: "I deplore the irresponsible charges occasionally made against university faculty members because someone thinks they represent an unpopular point of view."

At that time, academic freedom needed vigilant protectors. The witchhunt for communists and their sympathizers was in full swing at NYU, led by Professor Sidney Hook, chairman of the Philosophy Department. Hook, formerly a prominent intellectual Marxist, was one of the founders of the ironically named Committee for Cultural Freedom, which called for purging the academy of professors of "communist" bent. In his frequent contributions to *The New York Times* and *The Washington Post*, Hook argued that since Communist Party members had explicit instructions to "inject Marxism-Leninism into the classroom," they should not be allowed to teach. Universities, he wrote, needed to be vigilant; professors had to police themselves: "Nobody enjoys the right to plot to overthrow the Government of the United States." Precisely because communism posed so great a threat to academic freedom, he argued, people in academia needed to give up some of their freedom: "The realities of the Cold War have pushed us reluctantly toward compromises."

Such rhetoric, of course, fueled public hysteria about "pinko" professors able to infiltrate and poison minds. Early in 1952, NYU education Professor Theodore Brameld was barred from giving a scheduled talk by the Board of Education in Red Bank, New Jersey. Board president Stanley Haviland Jr. said the action was prompted by "inferences that [Brameld] had associated himself voluntarily or involuntarily with persons, organizations and institutions regarded as anti-American." Voluntarily or involuntarily?

That fall of 1952, Knoll was reappointed as editor of *The Evening News*, with the staff's unanimous consent. It was the paper's 25th year of publication, and perhaps its most important.

On October 13, Chancellor Heald suspended English Professor Edwin Berry Burgum, a popular evening instructor, for refusing to answer questions put to him that day by the U.S. Senate's infamous McCarran Subcommittee. Burgum had cited his First and Fifth Amendment rights. Heald declared that Burgum had committed "a breach of his duty to the Government and to the University." The chancellor's erstwhile commitment to academic freedom, apparently, had been pushed toward compromise. "I regard membership in the Communist Party as disqualifying a teacher from employment in New York University," he now said.

The Evening Organization Student Council passed a sharply worded resolution attacking Heald: "We believe that for one citizen to take punitive action against another because that other exercised his right to appeal to the Constitution is to use coercion to enforce submission to personal opinion." Stronger still was Knoll's editorial in *The Evening Star*. Under the headline "NYU's Shame," it listed a litany of grounds for collective chagrin: "We are ashamed of the University administration for making NYU the first privately endowed school in the nation to knuckle under to the McCarran Subcommittee. . . . We are ashamed of Chancellor Henry T. Heald because he has betrayed the faith students and faculty put in him. . . . We are ashamed of our faculty because it has failed to protest. . . ." And so on.

Much of the next several issues of *The Evening News* was devoted to the Burgum affair. In its issue of November 10, the paper reprinted excerpts of a letter heralding Heald's action from red-baiter Hook—along with Burgum's reply. Hook's letter, sent to other NYU campus papers but not to *The Evening News*, asserts that since communists are pledged to "the triumph of a formidable international conspiracy against freedom (including academic freedom)" they should be barred from the classroom. Nor could academia, in his view, afford the luxury of judging professors based on how well they seemed to do their jobs: "It is easy to flatter students about their perceptiveness, but the truth is that the kind of indoctrination Communist teachers are advised to conduct can rarely be detected except by a knowledgeable and critically trained observer who is almost continually present." Burgum, in his published reply, said Hook's letter reminded him of McCarran and crew: "Vituperation is mingled with declaration of high principles. Flaws in logic are concealed by appeals to prejudice and hysteria. Guilt is established by association and non-sequitur."

Student response to NYU's purge of leftist faculty was for the most part subdued. Doris remembers friends telling Erwin he was "crazy" to be so critical of the university administration, saying it would get him kicked out of school. For her, the most galling thing was hearing about the reception afforded a delegation of NYU students who had gone to raise issues of academic freedom at the University of Wisconsin, McCarthy's home state. "They sat there swilling beer, laughing. They didn't give a damn."

Burgum's appeal of Heald's suspension—as well as a motion to dismiss him from NYU altogether—was heard by a committee of the NYU faculty Senate. Knoll, in an editorial, expressed optimism in the process, remarking hopefully that "in recent weeks educators have become aware of the implications of having semi-literate legislators pass on the merits of faculty members and have begun to protest the Congressionally sponsored witchhunts."

In March 1953, as Knoll headed for graduation with a degree in journalism and government, the faculty committee—after eleven three-hour sessions—pondered Burgum's fate. Meanwhile, Harold Goodman, editor of the *Heights Daily News*, a student paper serving NYU's uptown campus, was reprimanded by a joint student-faculty committee for his paper's opposition to a plan to tear down beautiful, old, ivy-covered buildings and displace whole departments to accommodate an ROTC armory on campus. At the time, NYU was receiving more than $2 million a year—one-third its total research budget—from the military.

"We can't see why a student editor should be reprimanded for being anti-armory," Knoll wrote in an editorial. "Student editors aren't always right. But they're right at least as often as Army Reserve officers." The next month, the administration of NYU issued a statement with 37 other universities reminding professors of their "duty" to cooperate with outside investigations even when those conducting them abuse their power. That's about the same position the faculty Senate committee took regarding Burgum: On April 30, it fired him from NYU, without severance pay. In 1959, after a prolonged probe, the American Association of University Professors censured NYU for its treatment of Bradley and Burgum. Two years later, this was rescinded, even though NYU remained steadfast in refusing to pay either professor a year's severance, as the AAUP stipulated.

Knoll had just one more issue as editor of *The Evening News*. It appeared on May 11, 1953. Its front page carried news not just of Burgum's dismissal, but also the resignation of William Olson, another popular professor who was summoned, uncooperative, before the McCarran Committee, and the suspension—from both the paper and the university—of *Heights Daily News* editor Goodman, for taking a slap at the ROTC armory that was deemed in poor taste. On Page 2, Knoll bade farewell to his alma mater in a column. But whereas departing editors, he noted, usually offered up "nostalgic remembrances and paeans of praise for the Dear Old School," Knoll was in an altogether different mood.

"I'm damn glad to be getting out of NYU," he wrote, chiding, "The NYU which will give me my degree next month is not the same NYU I entered in September, 1948. This is an NYU which fires professors for their political views, regardless of their teaching ability. This is an NYU which tears down liberal arts buildings to put up armories. This is an NYU which suspends student editors because they don't approve of tearing down liberal arts buildings to put up armories. In short, this is an NYU in which a sickening atmosphere of fear has replaced the spirit of free inquiry which is so essential to education."

Hook, in reply, wrote a letter denouncing Knoll and suggesting that he shouldn't be allowed to graduate. But it was too late. Knoll's student days were over—and so was his deferment from military service. The door to his future was open, and he felt a "draft."

From Erwin's slides, courtesy of Doris Knoll

Doris and Erwin, circa 1952.

CHAPTER FOUR

To Hell and Back

Carl Knoll once speculated that the Knoll family's checkered military history, its tales of draft-dodging, surrender, and desertion, owed to "a distaste for drill and cruelty toward men—even toward those who are occasionally identified as enemies." Whatever the reason, his son Erwin would continue the family tradition of passionate disdain for military service.

At the time, though, Erwin Knoll lacked the courage of his convictions. Later, he reflected that "allowing myself to be drafted was an act of moral cowardice on my part. Of all of the things I've done in my life, that is the one I regret most—not because I had a bad time in the Army. I didn't. But I knew then that I was opposed to war, and to the particular war in Korea that was going on at the time. I was opposed to militarism. I was opposed to wearing a uniform. I was opposed to carrying a gun. But because there was no support system out there, or none that I knew of, for somebody like me to refuse induction, I went in. And I'm really sorry about it. I regard it as something wrong that I did."

Instead of becoming a draft resister, Knoll contented himself with merely smarting off to members of his local draft board: "I told them I was prepared to fight for the territorial integrity of the borough of Brooklyn." They drafted him anyway.

In September 1953, Knoll was inducted into the United States Army at Fort Dix, New Jersey, and sent to Indiana for basic training. The Korean War was winding to a close, but there was always the chance Knoll might be sent there, as was his cousin Norbert Seiden. For this reason, Knoll was "very adamant" in insisting that he and Doris not marry until he was out of the Army: "I started changing my mind, oh, about four hours into my military service." The couple made plans to wed as soon as Erwin was stationed.

On November 1, Knoll got his hands on a typewriter for the first time since he entered the Army and pounded out a letter to his cousin Alan Lemberger, who was nine at the time and much in awe of Erwin. "As you've probably heard," Knoll wrote, "the Army decided to send me out to Indiana. I don't know why, except that it's very inconvenient to me and the Army seems to take extra special pleasure in doing things that are inconvenient to me." He remarked that the flat Indiana landscape "will be a very nice feature when it comes to going on long marches," whereas the cold climate "will not be so nice when it comes to sleeping on the ground." He wrote about how the Army had given him "a helmet, a rifle, a bayonet, half of a puptent, a canteen and mess kit, a couple of packs, and a pick-and-shovel exactly like the one I gave you before I left. You may remember that I never even liked cap pistols much, so you can imagine that I'm not very friendly with my rifle and bayonet. And that goes for my helmet, too.

"The rest of the stuff is just like being in the Boy Scouts, though. Except that when I was a Patrol Leader in the Boy Scouts, I was much smarter than most sergeants in the Army are. As a matter of fact, you can be sure that *you're* much smarter than most sergeants in the Army are. And that goes for lieutenants, too." The letter concludes by asking Alan to give Erwin's regards "to all the New Jersey contingent in the family," followed with the postscript: "I'll bet you an ice-cream cone you don't know what the word 'contingent' means. Don't be lazy—look it up in the dictionary. That's why I used the word in the first place."

After basic training, Knoll was sent to the Army Home Town News Center in Kansas City, Missouri. There he and about two dozen soldiers spent all day, every day, providing newspapers across the nation with press releases on the order of "Corp. Philip Green of Backwater, Louisiana, was this month awarded a Good Conduct Medal." On February 3, in a belated reply to young Alan's request for military paraphernalia, Erwin wrote another letter: "I'm enclosing a couple of brass U.S. insignia, and a regimental crest. This latter is the emblem of the 200th Infantry Regiment, which I was in until very recently. The words on it are in Latin, and mean 'Believe and Conquer.' The red gadget at the top is an Indian war club, I am told. Just why you want this stuff is beyond me. Most of the fellows who are wearing it will really celebrate the day they can take it off. There's an old Army jingle which goes: 'Soldiers who want to be a hero / Are practically zero; / But soldiers who want to be civilians / Brother, they run into the millions.' " Erwin's postscript—to his typed letter signed in pencil—was as follows: "It is considered poor manners to type a personal letter, and even poorer to sign it in pencil. Just so you'll know." "That left quite an impression on me," says Alan. "It's okay to break the rules under some circumstances."

Doris, at this time, was all set to come to Kansas City to marry Erwin. Then, days before the wedding, Erwin was abruptly transferred to Fort Sheridan, Illinois, about forty miles from Chicago. When he was sent out, he wrote Doris, "one of the sergeants at the news center pulled me aside and told me—in strictest confidence—that he had heard that CIC (Counter-Intelligence Corps) insists that I be reassigned to a non-classified job." This moved Erwin in two directions. One was to declare his intention to fight the charges: "I know damn well what my political views were and are, and I know that they offer no justification for regarding me as a menace to the republic. I have no illusions about 'clearing myself' or any such nonsense, but having been active in behalf of other witch-hunt victims, I'd hate to sit back passively while I get the guilt-by-association treatment." The other was to apologize to his bride-to-be: "With the change in my situation, I am once again assailed by the old doubts about dragging you into an obviously difficult situation—perhaps for a long time. At the same time I must confess—very selfishly—that I need you now more than ever. I feel very much on my own in a hostile environment—and would do most anything to have you with me."

Erwin Knoll and Doris Ricksteen, both twenty-two, were married on March 1, 1954, in the Cook County Courthouse. In the change of plans, the couple had arranged to meet in Chicago at the Statler Hotel. Being from the east coast, it was unthinkable to them that Chicago did not have a Statler Hotel. Doris ended up at the Hilton, and eventually located Erwin at the Palmer, by calling other hotels and asking them to page Erwin Knoll. All the while her mother was haranguing her about what a bad idea it was to marry a journalist.

There were five people at the wedding: the happy couple, Doris's mother, Erwin's best man Sheldon Schiff, a friend of his since high school who happened to live in Chicago, and Judge Elmer Tone, who performed the vaguely Jewish ceremony. Erwin did not tell his parents about it. For the next year and a half, the couple would lead a secret life—secret from Knoll's family. Doris remembers her mother always asking, "Has he told his parents yet?" and living in fear of becoming pregnant. At the time, Doris didn't object to this subterfuge; now she's irked by it: "Why didn't he have the guts to tell his parents? I told *my* parents."

Doris and Erwin rented an apartment above a bar in Highwood, a suburb of Chicago right next to the base, and Doris took a job as a nurse at Highland Park Hospital. Erwin would sneak off base to be with her most nights and weekends. It was the first time, aside from Erwin's basic training, that either of them had lived away from their parents. Remembers Doris, "We lived on pizza for a month." At first, Erwin didn't have any civilian clothes; Doris bought him a pair of blue jeans and a plaid shirt. After a while, the couple moved to another apartment on top of a farmhouse in Lake Bluff, Illinois. They rented from an older couple, who lived downstairs. The man, Doris recalls, was "a nasty old S.O.B." One day, his wife—a woman named Proxmire (a relative of Bill Proxmire, soon after elected by Wisconsin to the late Joe McCarthy's U.S. Senate seat)—up and left him. "Can you beat that?" the man told his tenants. "She left me and she didn't even do the canning."

At Fort Sheridan, Knoll worked on an Army newspaper called the *Tower*, named after the huge tower in the fort's headquarters. His editor was Bob Satran, a twenty-four-year-old graduate of Marquette University whose family had for years owned a weekly newspaper in Wisconsin—first in Denmark, a town near Green Bay, and more recently in Eagle River, in the part of Wisconsin known as "Up North." Satran had come to the Army through the National Guard in February 1953 and was, like all recruits, sent to the processing center at Fort Sheridan. He was flagged as having newspaper experience, and asked to try his hand at putting out the *Tower*. After a couple of issues, the brass invited him back as editor after retraining.

The only thing was, that retraining would entitle him to the rank of second lieutenant, which was higher than the position of editor called for. So Satran was given a choice: Either he could go to Korea as a second lieutenant in the Infantry, or he could come back to Fort Sheridan as a corporal and edit the eight-page weekly tabloid. Satran put out the paper alone for six or seven months before his pleas for help were answered in the form of a new arrival: an enlisted man named Erwin Knoll who had journalism experience.

The *Tower*, part of Fort Sheridan's office of Troop Information and Education (another division offered classes to help soldiers get their G.E.D.s), ran stories about soldiers who got medals, dignitaries who visited, events on base, and sports. Satran and Knoll split up duties, and eventually were aided by another staffer: Ray Lane, later the radio voice for the Detroit Tigers.

The technology was basic: Satran, sometimes accompanied by Knoll, would take dummy layouts to the printer, have the copy set in type, and help arrange the linotype slugs in metal chases. All stories were reviewed prior to publication by the base's executive officer; this cut down on the potential for muckraking, but did not prevent an occasional mishap. Once, an article by Satran about a new NIKE nuclear missile training center at Fort Sheridan, based on information a colonel had released, was later deemed classified. The colonel—not Satran—took the heat.

Like Knoll, Satran had little enthusiasm for military service. His family had just taken over the Eagle River paper, the *Vilas County News Review*, and needed him desperately. Satran and his wife, Lois, lived on the base in a small house trailer with Susie, their newborn baby girl. The two couples became fast friends. The Knolls took a fancy to Susie, and would buy her gifts. Doris, a nurse at Highland Park Hospital, helped Lois get treatment for severe asthma attacks. Says Lois, "They were extremely kind to us."

It was an unusual but enduring friendship. "They were devout Catholics," says Doris. "Wonderful people." Lois Satran brought the Knolls to her parents' dairy farm, about forty miles from base. One day Erwin blurted out, "I'm so hungry for a bagel," and Lois asked, "What the heck is a bagel?" The Knolls soon gave the Satrans a taste, long before Bagelmania spread to the Midwest. The Satrans—Bob served as co-editor of the *Vilas County News Review* for thirty-three years—were pleased when the Knolls later moved to Wisconsin.

Eventually, the Army admitted that Knoll's reassignment to Fort Sheridan was due to security concerns over past associations. Specifically at issue, said the Army in a letter, was that Knoll had at NYU belonged to a group called Young Progressive Citizens of America and that he and his father had registered to vote for the American Labor Party. Knoll was told he could respond to the charges in several ways: either alone or with council at a military proceeding, or by writing a letter. "Get a lawyer," urged Doris. Erwin didn't agree. "I'm a writer," he said. "I'd rather use my craft."

In December 1954, Pvt. Knoll sent a letter to the Commanding General of the Fifth Army "in rebuttal and explanation" of these allegations. He admitted attending meetings of the Young Progressive Citizens of America, but noted it was an officially sanctioned campus group and that these meetings were "utterly devoid of any disloyal or subversive nature." He had registered to vote for the American Labor Party in 1952, but that stroke of a pen "marks the full extent of my participation in the party's activities."

Knoll then countered the charges head-on. "Although I have held political opinions which may be described as liberal, I have never endorsed any totalitarian doctrine or participated in any activity endangering the security of the United States," Knoll wrote. "Since entering the service in September 1953, I have assiduously avoided public expression of personal political views and have participated in no form of political activity or controversy."

It was the last time Knoll would be able to say that, and it worked. The Army notified Pvt. Knoll: "Your case has been reconsidered by the Department of the Army, and all restrictions and flagging actions against you have been removed as of this date." True to Army form, this notification was issued September 3, 1955, a few days before Knoll's tour of duty came to an end.

The Knolls moved back to New York City, to an apartment at 273 Bennett Avenue near upper Broadway that was larger and nicer than the ones they had in Illinois. Says Doris, "It took us until summer to notice our bedroom window looked down on an all-night gas station across the street."

In returning to New York, Erwin could no longer put off telling his parents the truth: He and Doris were married. As he had feared, they didn't take the news well. Erwin's mother, Ida, promptly disowned him. She even sat shiva—a Jewish act of mourning—for her son. Erwin was thunderstruck. "Why should they be so upset?" he asked his Uncle Muni. Doris converted to Judaism—a mere gesture, since she considers all religion "a crock"—as Knoll's family turned up the heat. In February 1957, the Lembergers pointedly invited Erwin and Doris to their son Alan's bar mitzvah, telling Carl and Ida to stay home if they wished. Carl came to the event; Ida did not. At one point, Erwin explained to his assembled relatives why he married Doris: "She's got everything I don't have." Anny Knoll, sizing up her good-looking, well-spoken, pipe-smoking nephew, whispered, "There isn't much *he* doesn't have."

Erwin went back briefly to *Editor & Publisher*, this time with the title of news editor. He didn't intend on staying: "I really just wanted to get a salary while I went looking for a job." In May 1956 he found one at an education newspaper called *Better Schools*, which, he later reflected, "blessedly no longer exists."

Better Schools was the monthly organ of the National Citizens Council for Better Schools, a New York-based public interest group. The group's president, Henry Toy Jr., was also the paper's publisher. Editor Don Morris, who hired Knoll as associate editor, saw the paper's mission to provide positive direction for the nation's schools as being noble, even awe-inspiring. But Morris had undermined his own authority by letting publisher Toy make content decisions.

In late August, Morris moved back to his hometown of Brownsville, Texas. That did not mean, however, that he stepped down as editor of a New York-based publication. It just meant that editorial discussions now had to take place through the U.S. mail over a 1,950-mile gap. Erwin wrote a fair number of stories, and was involved in editorial decisions. But he also accumulated a depressingly thick stack of correspondence from Morris. In one letter, dated October 30, 1956, Morris takes Knoll to task for his escalating discontent with Toy. "You are younger and perhaps more impatient about these things than I am. (Please read this letter thoroughly at least twice.) I can remember when I was impatient—and sometimes I still am. I have been a newspaper executive of one sort or another since I was 20, and I went through some terrific battles in my early days with my superiors—*mostly winning the battles but sometimes losing the WAR*—because I was impatient, because I was ahead of my time, because I could not see that they had anything worth considering in their conservative approach."

Knoll wrote back to tell Morris that, even after reading the letter "a half-dozen times," his disagreements with the paper's management were not something he could get over. Toy didn't know anything about being an editor, and yet he was running the show. His judgments made the paper looser, less readable, felt Knoll: "I am in no position, of course, to question Henry's integrity. As you point out, his responsibilities encompass a far greater area than the newspaper *Better Schools*. But I cannot help but feel that much of the interference with the newspaper's contents is dictated not by a sincere interest in the product offered to the reader, but by expedient circumstances involving people who are in a position to help or hinder the Council's financing. The criterion, I fear, is not 'How will this help someone working for school improvement?' but 'How will it affect [Council officials with ties to] the major corporations who are going to be asked to assume the burden of financing the Council's operations. The reader comes last, if at all." Knoll then gave notice of his intent to resign if the paper's management approved a plan to return to free circulation, as opposed to continuing to cultivate paid subscribers: "I came to work for a newspaper, and have no desire to stay and work for a house organ instead."

Morris, in ponderous and lengthy reply, urged Knoll to reconsider: Even if Toy were to decide "we have no alternative but to return to free circulation," wouldn't it be better to stick it out? "Realize that we may lose some battles before we win this war," Morris wrote from Texas. "If we lose the war itself, that'll be time enough to determine whether we change battlefields, or enlist under new flags."

At the time, there were plenty of battlefields. As Knoll waded through piles of memos in New York, revolution broke out in Hungary and war erupted in the Middle East. He notified Morris that "if and when" he decided to leave *Better Schools* he would give "not weeks but months" of notice.

Don Morris, in a sense, pushed Knoll over the edge. In a letter to his editor dated December 20, 1957, Knoll referred to their ongoing discussions "about ethics, compromises and such. And on this point, I must confess I am a 'moderate.' I think there is room for both the rebel and for the patient diplomat in our world; I think both have important contributions to make. And if I had a clear-cut choice—fortunately most of us don't—I think that I would choose to be a rebel.

"I am reminded at this season of the year," Knoll continued, "of a patient moderate man who did his best—within the bounds of moderation—to save the life of another man who was about to be unjustly put to death. The moderate man failed, and washed his hands. The other one—a hotblooded radical if ever one there was, who wanted to remake the world in a day—was nailed to a cross. And who's to say he should have been more moderate?"

In the end, Morris won the battle to keep paid circulation, but, despite his persistent attempts at persuasion, lost the war to keep his star associate editor. Erwin told Doris he couldn't stand it any longer. "So quit," she told him. He did.

CHAPTER FIVE

The Washington Post

Erwin Knoll gave notice at *Better Schools* before he found another job. And, as promised, he gave "not weeks but months of notice," informing Don Morris in early February that he would be leaving on June 15. Knoll even identified a successor: Arnold Bloom, the editor of a 5,000-circulation weekly newspaper in Belleville, New Jersey, for which Knoll's younger cousin, Alan Lemberger, then wrote. Bloom, in pursuing the job tip, asked Morris why Knoll had quit. Morris, in a letter, replied:

"He sees our operation as somewhat in the nature of public relations and propaganda, rather than newspapering. He also feels, I think, that he should not have to take suggestions which amount to orders from any non-newspaper people in the New York office, but only from me, a more experienced newspaperman. I sympathize with him on this, but feel there are policy decisions that have to be made on a higher level than mine, and even are going to be made whether or not I like it. They haven't bothered me. They do bother Erwin. Perhaps this is a matter of temperament and individualism. As a matter of fact, when Erwin mentioned you to me, he said . . . you might already be inured to 'front office' interference, which is what this amounts to, and which, though I cannot rejoice in it, is part of the cross of nearly every editor."

Bloom got the job. Knoll, meanwhile, was doing his utmost to leave it behind. He arranged to extend an assignment in Chicago into what he called a vacation; in fact, Erwin and Doris took off on a cross-country job hunt. They drove to Missouri, where he interviewed at the *St. Louis Globe-Democrat*; to Louisville,

Kentucky, where he interviewed with *The Courier-Journal*; and to the District of Columbia, where he interviewed at *The Washington Post and Times-Herald.* (The *Post* bought out the *Times-Herald*, its last morning competitor, in 1954, and combined names; by 1961, it had gone back to being just *The Washington Post.*)

Two weeks earlier, Knoll had written Al Friendly, managing editor of *The Washington Post and Times-Herald*, saying he "would welcome an opportunity to discuss with you the possibility of joining the news staff of the Washington Post and Times-Herald." Knoll expressed frustration with his job at *Better Schools*: "I have decided after a year of it that public relations is not for me—no matter how worthy the cause. I want to handle hard news for a responsible newspaper." Friendly passed the letter to the personnel manager who, while stating "we have a full staff at present," sent Knoll application materials and arranged for him to meet in mid-March with the paper's city editor, Ben Gilbert. After calling Morris for a reference, Gilbert brought Knoll on board. The Knolls packed up their belongings and moved to Washington, where Erwin began his new job on June 3, 1957.

The Knolls would live in Washington—all over Washington—for the next sixteen years. Erwin and Doris first got an apartment on Harvard Street, in the Mount Pleasant area near the zoo. After about a year, they moved to an apartment at 4200 W Street. Their oldest son, David, was born in March 1959, followed in January 1961 by Jonathan. In the fall of 1962, the family moved to a newly built townhouse in a housing cooperative called River's Place, on N Street on Washington's southwest side. After several years, they moved again, virtually across the street, to a house on M Street in Carrollsburg Square. A few years later, they returned to northwest Washington, to a house on River Road near Friendship Heights. "We were gypsies," says Doris.

Erwin's Washington work history showed similar signs of restlessness. He performed a variety of roles, including beat reporter, news-service editor, White House correspondent, free-lancer and author. He never did one thing for long, and always pursued an array of interests on the side. During his first two years at the *Post*, Knoll took graduate classes in journalism at George Washington University and was the Washington correspondent for a monthly newspaper called *Southern School News*. In 1959, Knoll was elected chairman of *The Washington Post* Unit of the Washington Newspaper Guild, a position he held for two years. He was also on the Guild's executive board and, in 1960-61, served as vice-president of the national Education Writers Association.

The Washington Post that Knoll came to in 1957 was, at eighty years old, a mere shadow of its future self. Although the *Times-Herald* merger pushed daily circulation beyond 380,000, making it the best-read paper in Washington, the *Post* still trailed its afternoon rival, *The Washington Star*, in advertising, and to some extent in prestige. During the Eisenhower era, the *Star*'s conservative disposition was more in favor among official Washington, which allowed it to break more national stories. The *Post* had little presence outside of Washington and its news-gathering operation was puny compared to what it would become. The editorial staff numbered about 150, compared to nearly 700 today. The paper had no overseas bureaus; it would later have fourteen. One of the first steps in this direction was taken in 1957, when the *Post* traded desk space with *The Manchester Guardian* so that it could have a correspondent in England.

But if its resources were modest, the *Post*'s sense of purpose was not. "Hardly anyone at the *Post* was there but for idealism," says Leslie "Les" Whitten, whose tenure at the paper overlapped with Knoll's. "It was and is a crusading newspaper."

City editor Gilbert, it turns out, had a special crusade in mind for Erwin Knoll: "I sized him up as someone who could cover education for the *Post*." This was an area of special interest to Gilbert, who was deeply committed to, as he puts it, "an end of racial apartheid in the District of Columbia." After the Supreme Court's 1954 ruling in *Brown v. Board of Education,* which the *Post* editorially applauded, President Eisenhower said he wanted Washington to be a "model" city for desegregation. Gilbert assigned this beat to Knoll, then age twenty-five.

Gilbert, the longest-tenured city editor in the *Post*'s history, was a good editor and a firebrand, with a driving sense of mission. But his people skills left much to be desired. As Chalmers M. Roberts puts it in his 1977 book, *The Washington Post: The First 100 Years*, Gilbert was "humorless, abrasive, and without patience for error or incompetence." Knoll, who developed a reputation for skill and accuracy, got along well with him. Others, like Whitten, detested Gilbert: "He was unpleasant to everybody." Once, Gilbert chewed out a woman reporter for misidentifying a bird in a photo caption; a fellow reporter, witnessing this, was so sickened he threw up. Morton Mintz, another *Post* reporter at the time, calls Gilbert "infuriating" and traces his "I know best" attitude to his early flirtation with communism. (Gilbert was, for a brief spell in 1936, a member of the Communist Youth League.)

Mintz was something of a firebrand himself. He came to the *Post* from St. Louis in late 1958 and soon established himself as one of the nation's best investigative reporters, especially in the mostly unexplored terrain of consumer protection. But Mintz was bothered by the *Post*'s reputation and practice of "injecting ideology" into its news decisions. In 1961, Mintz was assigned to pore over newly released Census data showing a substantial population decline in the District of Columbia beginning in 1955. He asked a district school official about it and elicited what he felt was an incautiously candid response. "It's *Brown v. Education,*" she said, referring to the Supreme Court decision mandating school desegregation: Whites were fleeing so their kids wouldn't have to go to school with blacks. Mintz was explaining this find to assistant city editor Seymour "Sy" Fishbein when suddenly he felt Gilbert's hot breath on his neck. Mintz turned as Gilbert angrily accused the school official of trying to "set policy for *The Washington Post.*"

"I was just astounded," says Mintz, who dropped the story idea on the spot, feeling it was pointless to try getting it into print "after that kind of emotional outburst from the boss." From Gilbert's point of view, says Mintz, "to print such a story would be to fan the flames of racial divisiveness and hatred, to see *Brown v. Education* as bad, not good. In his eyes, *Brown v. Education* was good. In mine, it was too." But Mintz hated having to suppress a story because it did not square with Gilbert's agenda: "Those of us who thought of ourselves as reporters first really hated this kind of crap." Gilbert doesn't remember the incident, but defends the position he took, saying much of this white flight from the district owed more to suburbanization than to school integration. Fishbein, Gilbert's former assistant, adds that reactionaries in Congress were then salivating for evidence that desegregation was a disaster, and "there *were* people in the school system doing their best to make desegregation look bad."

Knoll himself was frustrated by what he felt were the *Post*'s attempts to "manipulate or conceal" statistics that each year showed a higher proportion of black students in district schools. "I sometimes found it difficult to recognize my own stories under the headlines and rewritten leads that had been imposed on them," he later wrote. "These stories became an embarrassment to me—and a source of much wry commentary on the staff and in the community at large. I recall at least one occasion when our 'peak enrollment' story was posted on the newsroom bulletin board alongside *The Washington Star*'s story. The *Star*'s story had it right."

Some reporters couldn't stand it and quit. "You couldn't believe the turnover," says Whitten. "It was an unhappy paper." But Gilbert bore the scorn of his subordinates proudly; his tyranny was a tool for getting people to produce their best. Whitten tells of one evening when, right on deadline, a riot erupted at the Lorton prison in Virginia. Whitten reeled in the story from phones pressed against each ear—one connected to a police reporter, the other to a reporter on the scene—as "Ben with his fangs" stood over him, plucking copy from his typewriter two sentences at a time. "At that moment," relates Whitten, "I knew I was a newspaper man. I knew I was a pro." Later, Whitten became quite fond of Gilbert—"once I was out of his jaws and once he wasn't drinking my blood anymore." The metaphor is not idle: When Gilbert rearranged Whitten's schedule to make him work one day each weekend and have Mondays off, Whitten spent his Mondays writing a novel, *Progeny of the Adder*, about a vampire modeled in part after Gilbert. It was published in 1965, after Whitten left the paper to work for the Hearst newspaper chain.

Knoll became friends with Whitten, Mintz, and Laurence Stern, a reporter who would become a major player at the *Post*. All four toiled under Gilbert, were active in the Newspaper Guild, and shared a sense of mission about their work. "Erwin," says Whitten, "was the smartest of the four of us, and we were all smart." The Knolls, remembers Whitten, were wonderful parents. "Erwin and Doris would *listen* to those kids; they were very considerate of everything they said." Meanwhile, Mom and Dad were seen, at least by Whitten, as "perfect together. Doris kept Erwin from getting too full of himself. It was just incandescent, the way they were together."

Although Doris was considered the funnier of the two, Erwin was also known for his quick wit. Mintz tells the story about sitting next to Knoll at the office one day as Max Friedman, *The Manchester Guardian* correspondent who had a desk at the *Post*, walked past. Friedman had just returned from Egypt, where he had written a series of columns under a Cairo dateline. At the time, the Egyptian government was virulently anti-Jewish, and, says Mintz, "If anybody was unmistakably Jewish-looking, it was Max Friedman." So as Friedman walked down the aisle, Mintz said to Knoll: "Jesus Christ, Erwin. How the hell did Max Friedman get into Egypt?" Knoll, without a moment's hesitation, replied: "Reminds me of a story. A girl who was four feet tall and five feet wide got a job on the chorus line with the Rockettes at Radio City. Her friends got up the courage to ask her how she'd done it. The girl answered, 'I lied.'" Mintz nearly split a side.

Knoll worked at the *Post* during a period of great energy and expansion; the newsroom was packed with talent. In 1957, the same year it hired Knoll, the *Post* picked up a writer named Thomas K. Wolfe Jr., who later, as Tom Wolfe, would help redefine American journalism. Wolfe was a brilliant writer—his series from Cuba is still seen as a masterpiece—but ill-suited for the no-nonsense strictures of the *Post*. "He wouldn't do what they wanted him to do," says Whitten. Wolfe would puff up stories with salacious details and blow deadlines; the paper's management kept busting him down, until, by the time he finally left in 1963, recalls Whitten, "Tom was writing Bloodmobile briefs." Another writer brought on board during this time was Peter Benchley, who later wrote *Jaws*.

Whitten, formerly a reporter for Radio Free Europe and the International News Service, recalls the process of getting a job at the *Post*. Friendly and Gilbert each asked him to name the last three books he read. Whitten's list: a biography of Clement Attlee, an English translation of one volume of Proust's *Remembrance of Things Past*, and a collection of Haiku poetry. Whitten knew right away he'd hit the ball out of the park: "They were looking for an intellectual." Whitten, after making "some serious mistakes" early on, was put on the night police beat. The *Post*'s handpicked intellectual covered shootings and fires.

At that time, all writing at the *Post* was done on typewriters, on paper separated by carbons. The *Post*, recalled Knoll, issued carbon paper by the sheet "when you could prove that the last one was all used up." When reporters were finished, they'd shout, "Boy!—the term changed to "Copy!" after the paper hired copy girls—and their stories were whisked away. It was a chaotic environment, filled with noise, sweat, and smoke. Knoll loved it.

"He was a great reporter—intelligent, quick, a lean writer," says assistant city editor Fishbein (later with *National Geographic*). "He had command of his beat. He knew it better than I knew it. Of all the problems we had at the *Post*, he was not one of them." Wally McNamee, then a *Post* photographer (later with *Newsweek*), remembers Knoll as a tough reporter: "He seemed like a bulldog . . . like if he ever got hold of you he wasn't going to let go easily." Al Horne, then on the *Post* city desk (later the foreign desk), still marvels at Knoll's method of writing stories: "He would pace around the perimeter of the newsroom, walking all over, almost like an expectant father. He would not sit down to his typewriter until he had the story in his head. Then he'd sit down and write clean copy—almost never a strikeover or change. It was extraordinary." Others remember Knoll swaying back and forth at his desk, smoking nervously, pinching his cigarette in an odd way, like a piece of chalk, between his thumb and first two fingers.

Between July 1957 and April 1961, Knoll wrote more than 750 education pieces for *The Washington Post*, an average of four per week. He wrote about schools at the elementary, middle, high school, and college levels—not just in Washington but also New York, Virginia, and Maryland. His topics included school finances, class size, curriculum, homework, lunches, loyalty oaths, dress codes, delinquency, vandalism, smoking, and desegregation. And he wrote dozens of stories about Carl F. Hansen, the superintendent of schools for the District of Columbia, a powerful and charismatic educator.

"Hansen couldn't break wind without Erwin writing a three-paragraph mutt box about it," says Whitten, noting that Knoll's coverage of the superintendent was at times critical. "He called it the way he saw it; he just saw it the way [Hansen] did most of the time."

Knoll's 1958 series, "The Truth About Desegregation in Washington's Schools," was reprinted as a booklet and honored by both the Washington Newspaper Guild and the national Education Writers Association. The series concluded that desegregation was, with some wrinkles, working; Hansen called Washington's experience "a miracle of social adjustment."

In 1961, Knoll wrote another acclaimed series entitled, "Old Teaching in a New World." The sharply worded critique of outmoded educational approaches began: "In countless classrooms across the United States, children are being educated for a world that never will be, if it ever was." It went on to discuss how schools were teaching the same array of foreign languages, ignoring "tongues spoken by hundreds of millions of people." And how history and geography classes "pay only scant attention to scores of new nations and even deal with the Old World in cheery and comforting superficialities, while elsewhere in the 'social studies' such major developments as desegregation are present in the classroom but absent from the curriculum."

While Knoll's writing was straightforward and seemingly fair to all sides, his intense coverage and choice of cutting-edge topics reflected a bedrock belief that scrutiny from the press could improve the nation's schools. "It was a much more goal-directed kind of reporting," says Whitten. "He wanted to bring about certain things in the Washington school system."

As it turns out, Knoll would do more than just write about Hansen and desegregation; he would enlist his two children in the cause. In 1962 he and Doris moved to Southwest Washington so their two sons could attend Amidon, the superintendent's showcase school. The area had been one of the nation's first major "urban renewal" projects; older housing that had belonged to blacks was razed to make way for modern housing most blacks could not afford. Amidon was intended to draw new families—mostly middle-class and white—into the area. It did. But other schools just blocks away remained almost all black, a sure sign of troubled times to come.

At his new residence, Knoll began receiving an early edition of the *Post*—as he put it, "One of those smudged, typo-filled papers that had come off the press the night before." He asked the paper's circulation director, Harry Gladstein, why he was getting an edition intended for outlying areas even though he now lived closer to the *Post*'s plant. Gladstein, by Knoll's account, smacked his forehead and exclaimed, "Oh my God. I bet we still have that on the books as a nigger route." A few days later, the Knolls began receiving the paper's later city edition.

Knoll liked his job at the *Post*—to a point. "I was frustrated mainly by the politics of the paper," he later reflected. "Liberal politics are much harder to work under than conservative politics, because liberals are more determined to manipulate the news. Liberals think that it matters what people read. Conservatives are smarter. They know it doesn't make a difference." Knoll was also uneasy about the paper's close identification with official power, and the compromises this entailed. In 1950, for instance, the *Post* declined to publish a letter sent by President Harry S. Truman to its music critic, Paul Hume, in response to Hume's unfavorable review of daughter Margaret Truman's singing. The President called Hume "a frustrated old man who wishes he could have been successful"; declared that "a gutter snipe is a gentleman along side you," and threatened him outright: "Some day I hope to meet you. When that happens you'll need a new nose, a lot of beef steak for black eyes, and perhaps a supporter below!"

Erwin Knoll's *Washington Post* moment of truth—a moment he recounted dozens of times in later life—occurred in May 1960, when the Soviet Union shot down a U-2 spy plane piloted by Francis Gary Powers. The Eisenhower Administration was caught in a series of lies about Powers and his mission, and the incident led to the cancellation of a planned summit between the two Cold War adversaries. It was, Knoll noted, "a huge setback to U.S.-Soviet relations at a time when Eisenhower and Khrushchev were relaxing tensions. In fact, there was some speculation that it was deliberate." On May 6, as the *Post* headlined "RED AIRMEN GUN DOWN U.S. PLANE; CHILL HITS EAST-WEST SUMMIT SCENE," Knoll shared an elevator ride with Bob Estabrook, then the *Post*'s editorial page editor. Since Knoll normally did not have contact with folks like Estabrook—"there was a big wall between junior reporters like me and the executives at the paper"—he figured he'd better have something to say. "I said, 'That was a hell of a story today about that spy plane.' And he said, 'Yes, we've known about those flights for several years, but we were asked not to say anything.'

"That just staggered me," Knoll recalled of the incident. "Here I was working for a newspaper, goddamnit, and they were asked not to say anything about a major piece of news and they *complied* with that request? It just blew me away. It planted in me the first doubts about this line of work I had chosen for myself."

But Knoll's deepest divisions with management occurred over his role as union stalwart. Knoll had joined the American Newspaper Guild back in 1949, paying his dues as a student journalist at *The Evening News*. At the *Post*, he immediately became a member of the Washington Newspaper Guild and soon demonstrated his union affinities. On July 2, 1958, Knoll arrived at work to find the *Post* plant picketed by members of the International Union of Operating Engineers. That day, before his Guild unit had met to decide what stance it was going to take, Knoll dashed off a memo to Gilbert requesting a leave of absence, without pay, until the picket line was redrawn. Although Knoll feared his decision would "(1) cost me money and (2) jeopardize my position with the *Post*," he felt he had no other choice: "I have always believed that workers striking for higher wages or improved working conditions are entitled to the support of other workers." He was granted a leave.

A tireless recruiter for the union cause, Knoll headed the Guild's Washington Post unit from 1959 to 1961. It was a key time: In 1955, the *Post* had negotiated an unprecedented (and unrepeated) five-year pact with Guild members, which allowed it to keep labor costs low during a period of great prosperity. The pact expired on November 30, 1960, and Knoll led the union's negotiating team in nineteen separate bargaining sessions with company officials. In mid-November, the two sides were still so far apart that Knoll asked the membership to authorize a strike. Fishbein, a union member, asked that the vote be delayed pending further negotiations; Knoll declared that if the membership approved this delay, he would resign immediately. The motion perished, and the strike authorization was approved.

A strike office was rented and picket signs prepared. There was talk of a sympathy walkout by Guild members at the city's other daily papers, *The Washington Star* and *Scripps-Howard News*, and even the creation of a strike paper "if," as *The Guild Reporter* put it, "management deprives the reading public of all three of its daily papers." It was a powerful, credible, and most of all united threat. And a few minutes past midnight strike deadline, management gave in, offering higher raises, a reduced work week (down to 37.5 hours), severance pay hikes, and full pay for jury duty. The two-year contract was approved by a membership vote of 134 to 85.

On the management end, *The Washington Post* was at this time under the control, such as it was, of Phil Graham, the husband of Katharine Graham, whose financier father had bought the paper for $825,000 at an auction in 1933. Graham had taken over as publisher in 1946, and for the next decade led the paper, ably and with character. But around the time Knoll came on board, Graham's alternating currents of euphoria and gloom intensified to mania and depression. He had a nervous breakdown in October 1957, and for the next several years spent less time working at the *Post* than he did resting at the family farm in Virginia, or recuperating at a private psychiatric hospital in Maryland. But he remained charmingly manic, with an edge like a guillotine. Once, when the Knolls were attending a party at the Graham's house, someone pointed out to Phil that son Donny, then about twelve, had gotten hold of a pack of cigarettes and was augmenting his allowance by selling them to guests. "Wait till Donny takes over the *Post*!" his father joked. "He sure called it," says Doris. Donald Graham took over the paper in 1976.

Phil Graham's decline at the *Post* coincided with Erwin Knoll's ascent. In May 1961, Knoll was named Washington editor of the newly created *Los Angeles Times-Washington Post* News Service. The push came from the *Los Angeles Times*, which had just gotten a powerful reminder of its need to stay strong when *The New York Times* launched an ultimately unsuccessful attempt to start a west-coast edition. For both papers, it was a way to bolster their reputations by finding a broader market for their stories. For the *Post*, it was part of a larger effort to expand the paper's national and international coverage at a time of tremendous profitability. (In 1961, the *Post* ranked seventh in the nation in advertising revenue and its circulation topped the 400,000 mark.) On May 11, Graham typed Knoll a note: "Mr. Wiggins sent me the letter from Superintendent Hansen about your work. I was delighted to see the high regard you leave behind as you move onward. Congratulations." In pen, Graham put an asterisk by the word "onward" and wrote below, "*And I hope 'upward.' "

The news service had a barebones staff in each city; Knoll ran the Washington office, which in time consisted of one assistant, John "Jack" Carmody, and two teletype writers. These included a twenty-seven-year-old new hire named William Raspberry, who would go on to win a Pulitzer Prize as one of the paper's columnists. Doris remembers how impressed her husband was after interviewing Raspberry: "We've got to get him on the paper." Knoll later recalled that the *Post* hierarchy "was slow to respond" to his efforts to give Raspberry a regular newsroom job; it was only after Raspberry was about to leave for a Government job that "I was able to persuade the *Post* that it was about to lose an invaluable human being."

Knoll's news service perch, says Carmody, was a small table that jutted out into an aisle. The job consisted of editing and disseminating stories—a lot of work and not much glory. Knoll pushed himself to the limit; at one point, Phil Graham ordered him to undergo a complete physical, at Graham's expense. The news service itself became a huge success; by 1995 it was electronically offering about 80 stories a day (from the two papers as well as *Newsday*) to 550 subscriber papers.

Mintz took over as unit chairman, although Knoll remained a member of the bargaining team that negotiated the unit's 1962 contract. Carmody, hired in November of that year, recalls that Knoll made him march through the snow to vote on the final product, which gave *Post* writers and editors the highest top minimum wages ($175 a week) in the newspaper industry. It was nearly Christmas, and as the vote took place cars filled with families waited outside in the snow, engines running. The contract was approved, but Carmody says "Erwin and I agreed the previous management of the Newspaper Guild had not been too shrewd to negotiate a contract that came due Christmas Eve." One negotiator, of course, had been Knoll.

In early 1963, Phil Graham had left his wife and followed a *Newsweek* secretary to Paris, telling friends he intended to divorce and remarry. John F. Kennedy—who, holding his thumb and forefinger close together proclaimed, "The line is so damn narrow between rationality and irrationality in Phil"—outlived his friend long enough to attend his funeral. On August 3, on a weekend leave from his psychiatric hospital, Phil Graham killed himself with a .28-gauge sportsman's shotgun at the family farm, while wife (and successor) Katharine was in her room upstairs.

Another tragedy was playing out in Knoll's parents' home in Queens. Ida Knoll, Erwin's mother, had succumbed to depression, and illness. She stopped eating, and began wasting away. The Knolls, living in Washington, had no idea. That fall they visited Erwin's parents in New York and got the shock of their lives. Jonathan was just a baby and David was four. "I thought David was going to scream when he saw her," says Doris. "If we had known, we could have prepared him."

Carl Knoll, Erwin's father, insisted that Ida was getting all the medical attention she needed. Erwin left it at that, says Doris, who protested: "If that were my mother, I would not be satisfied with what's being done." Ida Knoll, once vivacious and appealing, withered away to about eighty pounds before she died in November 1963, a week before JFK. Doris got the news about this latter event from a fellow shopper who gleefully exclaimed, "They shot that snot in the White House." Erwin was at the U.S. Capitol, and wrote a story that day about how freshman Senator Edward Kennedy happened to be presiding over the U.S. Senate when word came that "your brother, the President, has been shot."

But Erwin Knoll, by that time, no longer worked for *The Washington Post*. In February 1963, after nearly two years of running the news service—his title was Assistant World Editor—Knoll felt that more was due him. Recalls Ben Bradlee, who came to the *Post* not long after Knoll's departure, "My recollection is that he left under some kind of cloud; he got in trouble with the *Post* hierarchy. I suspect it had to do with the Guild." Carmody says "Erwin hit up Al Friendly for a raise" and Friendly said no. Knoll was infuriated. The *Post*, he felt, was retaliating against him for his union activism. He thought he shouldn't have to take it, that a journalist of his proven ability didn't need *The Washington Post*. He told Doris he couldn't stand it any longer. "So quit," she told him. He did, in March 1963. As before, he did not have another job lined up. "I got calls from friends at the *Post*, 'If you need any groceries . . . ,'" says Doris. "People were appalled that he just quit."

The Washington Post would go on to more changes, glory, and collusions with power. A few years after Katharine Graham installed Bradlee to take over newsroom operations, the old guard—including Friendly and Gilbert—were gone. Some *Post* alumni credit themselves for Gilbert's eventual day of reckoning, believing Bradlee responded to their complaints about working conditions. At a party thrown by Stern, past and present *Post* workers waited in line to voice their grievances to Bradlee. When his turn came, Whitten says he "pissed on Gilbert with every last ounce of bladder pressure." But Bradlee, now the paper's vice-president at large, has only praise for Gilbert, and rejects the suggestion that he acted to improve morale. While Gilbert says he would "not quarrel with anyone who said I was too tough," Bradlee, in his cavernous white office, dismisses the workers' complaints: "Poor babies," he says.

It was what Mintz learned during his thirty-year career at the *Post* —that the paper was like a plantation: "They might treat you well, but you are never to forget your place. What they have is a structure in which what you have is what they give to you—not because you have, through your union, negotiated as equal parties." In the mid-1970s, a full-fledge plant strike turned ugly (one union official carried a sign that said, "Phil Shot the Wrong Graham") and left the Guild seriously wounded. But it was no longer Erwin Knoll's problem; he was off the plantation, for good.

CHAPTER SIX

From Newhouse to White House

Knoll was right: It was easier for an honest journalist to work under conservative politics than at a liberal organ like *The Washington Post*. His next job—as a writer for the Washington bureau of the Newhouse newspaper chain—represented a quantum leap forward in reportorial freedom.

"Nobody gave a damn," Knoll later said in praise of his bosses at Newhouse, which at the time owned twenty-two newspapers throughout the United States. "They didn't care about the editorial product at all. They wanted to make as much money as they could off their newspapers. They were mostly awful papers, but what I wrote got out on the wire and nobody messed with it. I got to do good stories and I was able to repackage them as magazine pieces here and there. It was a pretty good time."

Soon after being hired in early 1963, Knoll became fast friends with Jules Witcover, then beginning his second decade at Newhouse as a writer for papers in Syracuse, New York, and Huntsville, Alabama. There had been rumblings in Congress about the growing threat of newspaper monopolies, and, as Knoll remembered, "someone suggested to the head of Newhouse that he could head this off at the pass by opening a Washington bureau and saying, 'See, none of our papers could afford this on their own. Media consolidation makes for better newspapers.'" What had been a small regional office consisting of Witcover and four others burgeoned into a newly minted bureau with some two dozen reporters. They filed stories for the chain's papers, which included the *Staten Island Advance, Portland Oregonian, Long Island Press, Newark Star-Ledger, Harrisburg Patriot*, and *New Orleans Times-Picayune*.

There was, as the *Post*'s Ben Bradlee puts it, one problem: "Nobody read Newhouse. Nobody reads Newhouse. It cast no shadow, the Newhouse bureau in Washington." In 1967, *Time* magazine ran a story about the advent of news-service bureaus in Washington, including one-paragraph write-ups on a half-dozen of them. Newhouse was not mentioned. That year, Newhouse acquired its biggest paper, The *Plain Dealer* of Cleveland, which had a circulation of 377,000, almost as high as that of the *Post*. But there were no great papers in the group, and most were mediocre. "It was a frustrating place to work because the papers we worked for were so terrible," says Judy Randal, formerly the bureau's science and medicine reporter.

The Newhouse papers tended to be intensely local in focus. Some resented the suggestion that they needed outside help, and resisted using stories from the national wire. Witcover tells of filing, in the early morning hours of June 6, 1968, a first-person deadline account of Robert F. Kennedy's assassination, which Witcover had just witnessed at the Ambassador Hotel in Los Angeles while on assignment for Newhouse. This story was available only to the chain's twenty-two papers. Says Witcover, "Only three or four papers used it."

At Newhouse, Knoll was put on the education beat; Witcover covered the Pentagon. The two shared an office at the news service, located first at 711 14th Street and later at 1750 Pennsylvania Avenue. Says Witcover, "Erwin was head and shoulders above everyone else at the bureau in terms of his reportorial drive and talent." Indeed, in moving from *The Washington Post* to Newhouse, Knoll had gone from the big leagues to the minors, where he had no trouble batting .400. "He was, quite simply, the quickest writer, and he could produce the cleanest copy, of any reporter I ever knew," recalls Newhouse alumni Donald Bacon, later with *U.S. News & World Report*.

Reporters for the bureau—initially the Advance News Service, later the Newhouse National News Service—were expected to crank out four or five articles per week for the national wire. These were news-analysis pieces—short essays with original reporting on topics of the moment. They had to be tight, well-written, and clearly different from what was elsewhere available. Some veteran reporters could not make the transition, and quit. But Knoll was a pro.

"Erwin could hammer out a model Newhouse-type story in about 15 minutes," says Bacon. "I used to marvel at him. He would saunter into the office around 9:30, read two or three newspapers, make a phone call or two, go to lunch, come back, read, and converse with a parade of other staffers who would invariably drop by his office for a visit. At three o'clock, he'd type out a short description of his story for the day and give it to the news editor for the daily budget. Then he'd return to his reading and bull sessions until about 5:30. As other reporters, who'd been sweating for hours over their own articles, were trying to wrap up their day's work, Erwin would slip paper into his typewriter and start banging away. Fifteen minutes later, on his way out the door, he'd drop two-and-a-half pages of informative, precisely written copy into the news editor's in-basket."

Because he had so much extra time on his hands, Knoll began collaborating with Witcover on stories about President Lyndon Johnson's "War on Poverty." The TV show "Batman" was all the rage at the time, and around Newhouse Knoll and Witcover became known as "the Dynamic Duo." They relished the role, holding court in their tiny shared office. It became such a destination point for younger reporters procrastinating over their afternoon writing that Knoll and Witcover rigged up a sign that could be switched to say either "The Doctors Are In" or "The Doctors Are Not In."

Knoll, especially, was a rebel in the ranks. "Newhouse was very stodgy and mediocre," says Witcover, "and Erwin was always bucking up against the system." Dean Reed, then the paper's news editor, remembers it much the same way; "Erwin was always just short of fomenting rebellion. He was always delivering a criticism with a wink and a smile."

Throughout this period, Knoll kept his eye open for other opportunities. In 1964 he wrote to Ben Bradlee, then chief of the Washington bureau of *Newsweek*, which the Washington Post Company owned, about the possibility of being hired there. Bradlee on June 17 wrote Knoll to say he "would have liked to hire you," but for the powers-that-be at the *Post*: "You seem to have burned an uncommon number of bridges with the Washington Post Company." Knoll subsequently met with his former bosses at the *Post*, including Ben Gilbert and Al Friendly. It was Friendly who lowered the boom. "He said he resented the circumstances of my resignation from the *Post* early last year, regarding them as signs of 'immaturity' and 'irresponsibility' on my part," Knoll wrote Bradlee. "He made it clear that he regarded this as an obstacle to my joining *Newsweek*, and would continue so to regard it." But Philip Foisie, the *Post*'s legendary foreign editor, had nothing but good things to say about Knoll. He wrote, in a job reference to *The New York Times*, "I consider Mr. Knoll to be the most craftsmanlike and dedicated newspaperman I have ever met anywhere."

At Newhouse, Reed was just as pleased: "Erwin was one of the few top-notch education reporters in the country. Every time he bothered to enter something for an award, he'd win handily." (In 1964 and 1965, Knoll won national honors from the Education Writers Association.) Although Knoll was brazenly opinionated, Reed found "nothing ideological" in his reporting. Knoll was interested in covering the "mechanics of Government," not just what people in Government had to say.

But Knoll's biggest story at Newhouse—perhaps the biggest of his career—had nothing to do with education. It was about the girls next door.

Shortly after they moved into their River Park townhouse, at 314 N Street in Southwest Washington, Erwin and Doris began to notice the young women who lived at 308. "They were two gorgeous, knock-out women who worked on Capitol Hill," says Doris. They held lavish parties—black-tie, candle-lit affairs, usually catered—and seemed to have more money than their secretarial jobs would indicate. Theodor "Ted" Schuchat, a free-lance journalist and political ghostwriter—he wrote speeches for every U.S. President from Truman to Reagan—who lived at 298, was also suspicious. One day he said to Erwin and Doris, "You know, those girls: They toil not, neither do they spin, yet they live well."

River Park was organized as a co-op that tenants would eventually control. But, under the rules, the co-op managers ran things until 90 percent of the units were occupied. This threshold was reached, and a co-op organizational meeting was held on October 19, 1963. At this meeting, the organizers for the first time passed out a list of co-op members. Knoll and Schuchat first checked their own properties to make sure their names were spelled correctly and then ran their fingers to 308. The name of the owner, as entered, was R.G. Baker. Knoll and Schuchat got up and left the meeting.

R.G. Baker, the reporters realized, was Bobby Baker, the infamous secretary to the Senate Majority who had been forced to resign two weeks earlier, on October 7, 1963, amid charges that he used his position for personal gain. He had managed, on a salary that never topped $19,600, to acquire a net worth of more than $2 million. Baker was known as the "101st Senator" because of the power he wielded and as "Johnson's Boy" because of his many years of loyal service to Lyndon Johnson, who was Senate Majority Leader until he became vice-president under JFK. Baker had a reputation as a hustler. As a fourteen-year-old Senate page, he would arrange cab rides for senators, getting a quarter kickback from the drivers per ride. As Chief Senate Page at age sixteen, he would make other pages give back part of their salaries as political contributions. Later, he passed on money from certain givers to the people they wanted to influence. "Sophisticated givers," says Schuchat, "understood that some of the money would stick to the fingers of the messenger." Most of the wheeling and dealing for which Baker got in trouble occurred after Johnson left the Senate in 1961, a fact the President took pains to point out: "When he worked for me, he was too busy to take a piss, much less steal." The story had died down after Baker stepped down. But now, Knoll and Schuchat were in a position to blow it wide open.

They went from the meeting to the parking lot, and jotted down the license-plate number of the car in the space assigned to 308. The plates were from Tennessee, so Knoll had a reporter friend in Nashville trace the registration. The car was registered to Nancy Carole Tyler, and the address was a room number at the Capitol. Knoll reached for his directory. The room had belonged to Bobby Baker. Further research showed that Tyler was Baker's secretary—both during the time he was secretary of the Senate Majority and afterwards, at his law firm. Her roommate, Mary Alice Martin, formerly worked for Senator George Smathers.

It was a sensational discovery. Baker was violating the co-op's rule requiring owner occupancy, in circumstances strongly suggesting that he, a married man, was violating other rules as well. He had claimed on the application that Tyler, a former Tennessee beauty queen, was his cousin. Unfortunately for Baker, he was violating all these rules smack dab between two nosy reporters. Knoll and Schuchat had seen the heavy activity at the townhouse, although at the time, says Schuchat, "Erwin and I wouldn't have known Bobby Baker if we fell on him."

The next morning, Sunday, October 20, the two men met over coffee at Knoll's place, going over what they had. They could mention the parties and candle-lit dinners. Too bad they couldn't get a peek into the fenced-in backyard. Doris gestured to the door. "We have kids," she said, picking up a ball and tossing it into the women's yard. "Now we have to go get it, right?" Erwin got close enough to see the thick lavender carpet.

Knoll and Schuchat went to the Newhouse office that afternoon and wrote the story under a joint byline. They described the townhouse as "plush, heavy curtained," and Tyler as "a striking brunette in her early 20s who occasionally wears a blond wig." The next day, as the piece appeared in Newhouse papers, the phones at the bureau rang off the hook. Baker, who looked as though he might *be* off the hook, was the subject of renewed attention. The townhouse discovery, wrote *The New York Times*, "opened to investigation another aspect of Baker's outside activities while serving in the influential Senate post."

The River Park Co-op ordered Baker to sell, for violating the occupancy rule. A few days later, JFK was assassinated, and LBJ became president. Republicans in Congress, eager to make the new President look bad, seized on the Baker affair. Knoll and Schuchat each wrote more stories about the case, as questions were raised about Baker's ties to a shady private mortgage insurer and his ownership of the Carousel, an upscale motel in Ocean City, Maryland. The story was also pursued by Knoll's friends Larry Stern of *The Washington Post* and Les Whitten, then with Hearst newspapers (later a collaborator with columnist Jack Anderson). "No one owned that story," says Schuchat. "It was too big."

In February 1964, Baker and Tyler were compelled to appear before the Senate Rules Committee. Each pled the Fifth. The committee, after an eighteen-month investigation, concluded that Baker had committed "gross improprieties" and a federal grand jury indicted him on nine counts. Baker was convicted of tax evasion, conspiracy to defraud the Government and theft and eventually served seventeen months in prison. Still, he fared better than Tyler, who died in May 1965 when the private sightseeing plane she was on crashed into the Atlantic Ocean 1,000 feet from the Carousel Motel. "When that happened," says Schuchat, "Erwin and I just looked at each other and said, 'You couldn't make this stuff up.'"

During the Baker scandal, the Knolls were visited by their old friends from college, Burt and Dina Wenk. The two couples struck upon the idea of making a game—literally—out of Washington corruption. They called it "Influence." Erwin enlisted his friend Stern as co-inventor. Burt, a graphic artist, designed the gameboard.

"Influence" players rolled dice and moved markers in a circle around the board, collecting "Control Cards" and "Influence Cards" along the way. Picking "Joint Pork Barrel Committee" meant coughing up $30,000 for a pet project; "Counter-Insurgency Agency" was a windfall: "You did a great job of scouting the invasion beachhead—but the landing force discovered that Puerto Rico is already ours. Collect your $5,000 mustering-out pay." The "Whitewash" card conferred instant immunity from investigation. Most prized of all, the "Q" card entitled the bearer to control the Quid-Pro-Quid Club—a play on the real-life Washington Quorum Club, of which Baker was a charter member. The biggest player went first and arguments were settled in favor of whoever yelled the loudest. The instructions read, "For the young, it provides an antidote to the stale moralizing and sentimentality of standard civil textbooks—a life portrait of a hustling democracy in action."

The game was commercially produced by Washington Educational Enterprise Productions and distributed to stores in the summer of 1964. Despite ads in *The New York Times* and *The Washington Post* and favorable write-ups, "Influence" did not catch on. In the end, Knoll, Stern, and Wenk lost thousands of dollars.

Knoll's reporting on the Baker story bolstered his reputation. Doris Knoll remembers a party where Ben Bradlee of the *Post* asked Erwin if he was interested in coming back. "He'd be divorced," she answered. Bradlee doesn't remember this exchange but says Stern always talked highly of Knoll and that "There was no good reporter I didn't toy with trying to get on *The Washington Post*." Knoll knew so many people and was so well-known in Washington that it was impossible to walk down the street without running into two or three people he knew. Witcover, unnerved by his friend's popularity, ordered two dozen inch-and-a-half, black-on-yellow buttons that read, "Who Is Erwin Knoll?" Then Witcover threw a party, and secretly gave them to guests. "At an appropriate moment during the party," he says, "everybody put one on." Afterwards, Witcover collected the buttons so that he could continue the gag for years on end. When Knoll landed an interview with a member of Johnson's cabinet, the official greeted him wearing one of these buttons. When he went in for an operation on his knee, the anesthesiologist's button inquired, "Who Is Erwin Knoll?" When Erwin and Doris took a vacation in Nova Scotia, a man wearing one of the buttons showed up at their hotel. When Erwin traveled with President Johnson to Pago Pago in the South Pacific, he was greeted by a button-wearing native as he got off the plane. Says Witcover, "I tried to get one of the astronauts on the moon to wear a button. I talked to people at NASA. But they wouldn't do that."

Meanwhile, Knoll's free-lance career was taking off. In 1964, Knoll and Stern co-wrote articles on the Baker affair for the *Columbia Journalism Review, Esquire,* and *The Reporter*, a twice-monthly political magazine. In *Esquire*, their piece led off a package called "A Sampler of American Scandal." After reflecting that "the heart of the scandal is within Congress itself," Knoll and Stern issued an astute forewarning: "The problem of Congressional morality is bound to become more acute as Government becomes an increasingly dominant partner in the American economy." In January 1965, Knoll contributed a lead article on school desegregation to the premier issue of *American Education*, a slick magazine published by the U.S. Department of Health, Education and Welfare. He also wrote regularly for *Southern School News*, a monthly education newspaper that in 1965 became *Southern Education Report*, a monthly education magazine, published in Nashville, Tennessee. An article by Knoll and Witcover critiquing Johnson's War on Poverty appeared in *The Reporter* for June 3, 1965, and was promptly entered into the *Congressional Record* by U.S. Rep. Peter H.B. Frelinghuysen, Republican of New Jersey.

But the most promising new free-lance outlet in Knoll's Rolodex was a magazine in Madison, Wisconsin, called *The Progressive*. The relationship began in 1961, when a piece he had written for *The Reporter* about a divinity student expelled from Vanderbilt University for taking part in Nashville's lunch-counter sit-ins was rejected as "too political." Someone suggested that Knoll send it to *The Progressive*, which accepted it and paid him "the princely sum of $25"—one-tenth *The Reporter*'s going rate.

Thus began Knoll's relationship with Morris H. Rubin, who had been editor of *The Progressive* since 1940, when he turned twenty-eight. The magazine then had less than 5,000 subscribers and was on the brink of collapse. Rubin, in his memoirs, placed his salary at $250 a month "when there was money to meet the payroll, which was not nearly so often as we would have liked." His wife Mary Sheridan worked by his side, for the first two years without pay. Still, they simply ran out of money. In November 1947, the then-weekly magazine announced, in bold letters on Page 1, "The End of *The Progressive*." But it was not to be. The magazine was flooded with letters, telegrams and, most importantly, financial contributions—$40,000 in all. *The Progressive* was revived as a monthly in January 1948.

This was a difficult task, made more so by the bouts of depression that began afflicting Rubin soon after he became editor. "There were days at the office," he recalled, "when I was so sunk I could do nothing, literally nothing, but stare at the wall, watch the crawling clock for noon so I could go home . . . and bury myself under the sheets." Eventually, Rubin found some relief under the care of Dr. Joseph Kepecs, a Madison psychoanalyst.

Rubin and Sheridan were an able team, and by the mid-1950s the circulation of *The Progressive* topped the 30,000 mark. The pair's proudest moment was the magazine's special issue of April 1954, which went after Tailgunner Joe McCarthy. "It was the story," Rubin later reflected, "of a man who had lied and cheated and plundered and believed in nothing." The 96-page issue sold 180,000 copies, six times the norm. In the mid-1960s, the magazine ran impressive packages on military spending and the environment. Rubin's 1961 article based on his travels in Central and South America won that year's coveted George Polk Memorial Award for foreign-affairs reporting. The magazine's fortunes were also reflected in its array of contributors, including, in the 1960s, Martin Luther King Jr., James Baldwin, Senator George McGovern, and President John F. Kennedy. They joined such earlier contributors to *The Progressive* as Carl Sandburg, Jack London, William Jennings Bryan, Theodore Roosevelt, Harry Truman, Kay Boyle, Eric Sevareid, and Helen Keller.

It was a respectable magazine, and Knoll signed on for the long haul in 1964, when he and Stern debuted a monthly news column, "The Word From Washington." For the next ten years, Knoll and Stern would write the column jointly, using the pseudonym "Potomacus." The column consisted of small news items that they wrote interchangeably; no one could discern any difference in their styles. The two men, says Doris, spoke the same way, one picking up where the other left off, neither making sense to anyone else: "It was like primary speech." (Ben Bradlee never knew that Stern was co-Potomacus; otherwise, he says, "We would have told him to quit it.") Knoll also wrote articles for the magazine about the war on poverty, Johnson's Great Society, and runaway military spending.

In January 1966, Knoll was a member of the journalists' panel on "Meet the Press" when the guest was John W. Gardner, Johnson's secretary of Health, Education and Welfare. Knoll's star was rising, and when the position of White House correspondent at Newhouse became open around this time, he let his interest in it be known. Philip Hochstein, the senior editor at Newhouse, didn't like the idea one bit, as news editor Reed remembers. "He said Erwin Knoll would cover the White House over his dead body." Fortunately, it didn't come to that; Hochstein was persuaded that Knoll would be a credible, top-notch reporter. He was.

"A first-class pro," says Tom Johnson, deputy press secretary under Bill Moyers and George Christian. "Very conscientious, determined to get it right. I don't recall a situation where he produced a story that was off-base." Christian calls Knoll "a particularly intelligent reporter. He was highly suspicious of government, highly suspicious of the powers that be. Of course, from my point of view, he went overboard." Knoll was among some 40 or 50 reporters who regularly attended White House briefings. "He was a tenacious questioner," says Sidney Davis, a former member of the White House press corps. "His questions were usually very direct and persistent." "He was an aggressive reporter," agrees Reed. "No doubt about that."

The problem was, President Johnson didn't especially like

aggressive reporters. Soon after he was elected, Johnson leveled with a group of journalists: "If you play along with me, I'll play along with you. I'll make big men of you. If you want to play it the other way, I know . . . how to cut off the flow of news except in handouts." Knoll, for his part, admitted being daunted: "No matter how skeptical or alienated or disaffected you are, there is something about the power of that office that intimidates you. And it takes a lot of courage, especially in a public setting like on television, to get up and ask the President of the United States a nasty question."

In the fall of 1966, Knoll was among the reporters who accompanied Johnson on a 17-day, 31,500-mile trek through the Pacific, with stops in the Philippines, Australia, New Zealand, Thailand, South Korea, and Vietnam. Knoll played poker on the press plane, and filed daily dispatches via Western Union International. At Camp Stanley, near the demilitarized zone in South Korea, Knoll scribbled in his notebook as Johnson reminded the assembled soldiers that there were only 200 million Americans in a world of three billion people, "and they want to take what we got, and we got what they want, don't you think we haven't. And we don't ask for much, but what we ask for we're going to get, we're going to keep, we're going to hold." Knoll was so impressed by Johnson's words he checked his notes against a radio reporter's tape to make sure he got them exactly right.

"It was then, and it still is today, a perfect statement—short, concise, accurate—of what U.S. foreign and military policy has been all about since the end of World War II," Knoll later wrote. "There was no fancy rhetoric in Johnson's remarks about freedom, democracy, or the need to deter aggression. There was just the simple assertion of greed: We've got what the world wants. We're going to keep what we've got. This is the job of the military."

The first time Knoll met Johnson was on June 22, 1967, at a White House luncheon to which Knoll was personally invited—along with 130 other people, including two dozen reporters. A military aide stood on Johnson's left as he walked by a row of guests, pumping hands. As Knoll told the story, "The aide said, 'Mr. President, this is Erwin Knoll of the Newhouse National News Service,' and Johnson grabbed my hand with this huge hand of his and he stared at me and didn't blink for the longest time. It probably was half a minute or less, but it seemed like an eternity. Then he said, 'My Daddy always told me that if you looked deep into a man's eyes, you could change his heart.' I was absolutely petrified."

Knoll had several more close encounters with LBJ. Once Knoll was with Johnson when Lester Pearson, the prime minister of Canada, gave the President a small maple leaf pin. Johnson thought it was a lousy gift, and with a few choice vulgarities gave it to Knoll, who gave it to his neighbor Sheldon Tromberg, who has it still.

On January 1, 1968, just after Knoll accompanied Johnson on an around-the-world tour, the Knolls were invited to Johnson's ranch in Texas. Erwin and Doris arrived with their two young sons. The President greeted them, saying, "I want to show you the property." So the Knolls piled into Johnson's station wagon for a ride around the ranch. David, age eight, sat on Erwin's knees. Doris and Jonathan, age six, sat up front with the President, who sped off cheerily, briefly eluding his Secret Service agents. "He was wonderful down there," Erwin later said of Johnson. "He was a completely different person."

The kids liked it, too. Johnny proved the most precocious. As he was sitting beside the President, he suddenly said, "I saw a picture of you where you were pulling up your shirt to show a scar but it wasn't a scar it was a map of Vietnam"—a reference to David Levine's classic political cartoon that Knoll had hung in his office. (Johnson, at a press conference, had crudely raised his shirt to show off scars from an operation.) "Son," the President replied gamely, "there's a lot of pictures of me I don't see." Johnny got along famously with LBJ, and at the end of the visit remarked, "I wish he were my grandpa." Doris wrote the President a thank-you note, saying, she recalls, "I'm afraid our sons will now have a credibility gap of their own." He sent back a garish autographed picture.

But nothing Johnny said that day or any other stripped David of top honors in the Knoll family competition of "Kids Say the Darn'dest Things." His winning entry emerged late one evening while Doris and Erwin were entertaining guests, including Ben Wattenberg, a conservative Democrat who wrote speeches for Johnson. Young David, in his pajamas, appeared at the top of the stairs; he looked out at the assembled guests, inquiring, "Which one's the bloody war criminal who works at the White House?"

Erwin Knoll was, as time went on, becoming more sure of himself, and less willing to compromise. He was beginning to understand the power of taking a firm stand and not budging from it. He was becoming an absolutist. His old friend Mort Mintz, for one, found this hard to take.

In February 1967 it emerged that the CIA, as part of its efforts to co-opt journalists, had secretly given money to the Newspaper Guild; the revelation came just as the North Vietnamese had captured an American reporter. Muses Mintz, "If the Guild takes money from the CIA, why shouldn't reporters be regarded as spies?" Knoll's reaction was more extreme: He quit the union. Mintz is still appalled: "How can you do that? There's nothing the publishers would love more than to kill the Guild. If everyone followed Erwin's footsteps, that's what would have happened." In contrast, Mintz's response "was to mount a campaign—as far as I know I was the leader nationally—to pass a condemnation of what the leadership had done at the next convention."

Knoll maintained limited contact with his family in New York and New Jersey. He had served as best man at his cousin Norbert's wedding in 1958, and still saw him occasionally. His cousin Rita and her husband Saul Penn would visit the Knolls in Washington, bringing a bag of New York bagels. In 1965, the Penns moved to Washington, where Saul got a job in the defense industry—and into bitter quarrels with Erwin. "I don't remember Erwin having soft opinions about anything," says Saul. "He was not a seeker of truth. He came to conversation with set convictions, not an open mind." A few times a year, the Knolls would visit Erwin's father Carl in New York. David can still picture his grandfather, standing outside his print shop with his black hat and a *Yiddish Daily*: "He was definitely not into the Chinese-food-and-Polo-shirt brand of Judaism."

Around this time, Carl Knoll led an effort to reestablish a sense of family identity. He wrote histories of the Knoll and Diringer families, and arranged several large get-togethers, which Erwin and his family did not attend. Carl even began producing a newsletter, "The Knoll Diringer Family Circle Bulletin," that kept tabs on family members. In March 1966, Erwin contributed an essay to the newsletter—appropriately enough, on the subject of words, his preeminent concern.

"Words are the principal product of this world capital, and they are my stock in trade," he wrote from Washington. "I spend most of my waking hours speaking words or listening to them, writing words on one piece of paper or reading them off another. Lately I have had the feeling that the quality of words isn't what it used to be. Increasingly, it seems to me, words are being used to say the opposite of what they mean, or to obscure meaning altogether. In this city, it is customary for a Senator to address his most incompetent enemy as 'my distinguished friend.' Recently, I have heard generals refer to war as 'pacification,' or use the comfortably vague word 'interdiction' when they are talking about the ugly business of bombing. When a man is fired from his job he invariably 'resigns,' and when his departure has been eagerly awaited it is always received with 'regret.' A bill now pending in Congress to *reduce* the amount of milk given to school children is called—imagine!—the Child Nutrition Act of 1966."

In January 1967, the Knoll and Diringer families reunited at the Hotel Brewster in New York City. Erwin, in the newsletter on this event, is identified as one of the family "intellectuals." He and Doris attended from Washington, joining dozens of relatives from all over the world. A family that could trace its roots to a single village in Galicia now had members in Rumania, Argentina, Canada, the United States, and Israel.

That spring, around the time that Israel launched the Six-Day War against Egypt and Syria, Erwin Knoll bought and began riding a bicycle. He shed a few pounds, but remained a heavy smoker. Unlike others in his profession, though, Knoll never cared for intoxication, and rarely had more than one drink. Knoll's recreation of choice was a good game of poker. In Washington, he belonged to a group of players who met ten months a year—on Friday nights beginning at 8 or 9 and often going until 3 a.m. Organized by Knoll's friend and neighbor Sheldon Tromberg, a motion picture distributor, it was called the Harry S. Truman Memorial Poker Group, after the President/poker aficionado. ("Erwin was no fan of Harry Truman, but he went along," says Tromberg.) The game—and the group-owned green felt poker table it was played on—moved each month to a different player's house. Don Bacon, who sat in on some sessions, says Knoll was "an excellent player and loved the game. But more, I think, he enjoyed the male camaraderie that goes with it."

Sheldon Tromberg takes credit for Erwin's interest in three things: poker, radio broadcasting, and race horses. The two men would go to the track in Maryland or West Virginia several times each year, sometimes joined by fellow poker game members Al Shuster, then a foreign correspondent with *The New York Times*, and Bobby Goldhammer, a motion picture exhibitor. For a while, Knoll, Schuchat, and Tromberg even owned a race horse, named Sonic Beau. A horse of good lineage, Sonic Beau was acquired for what was deemed the bargain price of $3,000—plus the couple of hundred dollars a month it took to keep and race him. But Sonic Beau never won a race or finished in the money; after about a year, the partners unloaded him for $75.

Like the Knolls, the Trombergs moved to River Park so their children could attend Amidon, the experimental public school set up to implement District Superintendent Carl Hansen's educational vision of basic skills and core curriculum. (In 1966, the Knolls hopped within the neighborhood to 252 M Street in Carrollsburg Square; the Trombergs moved a few doors away on 4th Street.) The school received national attention, including a write-up in the *Saturday Evening Post*. But Amidon, the district's "magnet" school, drew mostly middle-class students, with about equal numbers of whites and blacks. Two other schools in the neighborhood were nearly all black. Inequities abounded; the library at Amidon had nearly twice as many books as the other two schools combined.

"Good education was being hoarded for middle-class kids and poor black kids were getting screwed," says Roger Wilkins, a black Amidon parent and Johnson Administration official who lived with wife Evie and daughter Amy a few doors away from the Knolls. "The school administration didn't look so good as it did before." And so, in the summer of 1966, the Trombergs, Knolls, and Wilkinses were among a handful of Amidon parents who joined forces with black parents from the other two schools to force a change in district policy, to put the three schools together. Beginning in February 1967, students in kindergarten through second grade went to Syphax school; a kindergarten class and grades three and four remained at Amidon; grades five and six went to Bowen. School officials opposed the idea from the start. "I can see nothing but educational disadvantage in the proposal and no reasonable expectation of achieving either racial or economic balance," said Superintendent Hansen. "It is predictable that the more affluent members of the community regardless of race will reject the proposal by moving out of the area or sending their kids to private schools."

According to Jessie Tromberg, school officials "deliberately withheld funds to make sure the tri-school plan did not work," just as the black parents from the two other schools feared would happen. Roger Wilkins says the officials "hated the idea of this tri-school and started punishing the kids of the leaders of that movement." When the Wilkinses felt that Amy's academic needs were being purposely neglected, they pulled her from the tri-school. "It's one thing to have ideals," says Roger. "It's another to make your kids suffer for them." Once Doris Knoll complained to the principal at Bowen that so little teaching was going on. His response: "Mrs. Knoll, if you care so much about your children's education, why are they in this school? This is a slum school."

Race relations in Washington were at an all-time low. Wilkins, then with the U.S. Justice Department, became "Johnson's point man on the riots" that erupted after the assassination of Dr. Martin Luther King Jr. on April 4, 1968. He spent that whole night at the Justice Department, then flew to Memphis as the President's representative. "When I flew back to Washington that night," he recalls, "the city was burning." The Schuchats and Trombergs fled to a hotel in Charlestown, West Virginia, where they stayed for a couple of days until things quieted down. "When we went out of town, we could see smoke going up in the sky; there were troops going into town," says Schuchat. "We were afraid they were going to burn down River Park."

So was Doris, but she was one of the very few who stayed behind. She and Evie Wilkins collected food and clothing for the people a few block away who had been burned out of their homes. Erwin was off covering the story, and Ben Wattenberg, the bloody war criminal who worked for Lyndon Johnson, called to offer Doris a White House limousine ride the hell away from there. No thanks, she told him: "If they want to burn my Steinway and my home, they have to do it right in front of me." The Knolls' home didn't have the luxury of federal protection, as did the nearby home of Supreme Court Justice Thurgood Marshall.

River Park did not burn down, and neither did Carrollsburg Square, but the riots lit a fire under the feet of white families who still sent their kids to the tri-school. When David Knoll was in the sixth grade, he was the last white student at Bowen. He was often chased and sometimes beaten. In early 1969, a policeman showed up at the Knolls' door. Erwin, who was then working at home, answered. "I wait every day till your son gets down this street and through those gates," the cop admonished. "Do you realize there are kids in that school who would like to kill him? I don't know what you're trying to do, but you're not proving anything." The Knolls pulled David from the school in February, and sent him to Burgundy Farm, the same private school in Alexandria, Virginia, that Amy Wilkins and Melissa Tromberg attended. Jonathan finished out the fourth grade at Amidon.

The Knolls were chastened in other ways as well. After the riots, Doris was walking through the neighborhood one day when she ran into Sam Jordan, a black neighborhood activist. "Sam put his arm around me, the same as you would to anyone," says Doris. "And a policeman with a rifle jumped out at him, pointed the rifle right at him. If I would have screamed, he would have shot him, I'm sure of it. I just kept saying, 'No, no, he's a friend!' That's when Erwin and I started to wonder whether we were more of a menace than a help."

President Johnson had himself reached a similar conclusion. On March 31, 1968, he announced that he would "not seek—and will not accept—the nomination of my party for another term as your President." This stunned the nation, but not Erwin Knoll; two weeks earlier, he had written a piece for Newhouse speculating that Johnson would throw in the towel. One of the chain's papers, the *Long Island Press*, proudly hailed Knoll's prescience in a front-page "You Read It Here First" splash.

As the Johnson regime ended, Knoll savaged the President in the pages of *The Progressive*. "He demonstrated in his years of Senate leadership that he was a master of the manipulative processes on Capitol Hill, but he came to the White House profoundly ignorant of basic aspects of American politics," Knoll wrote. "He failed to understand the critical problems of the cities, and mounted only feeble efforts to cope with them. For all his early experience with Mexican-Americans, the needs and demands of exploited minorities remained a mystery to him; he could not understand why the issue of Black Power should arise after he had named Thurgood Marshall to the Supreme Court. He was vexed by intellectuals, and reciprocated their hostility."

Knoll, in this article, made only passing reference to progressive legislation that passed under Johnson in such areas as higher education, civil rights, and social welfare; instead, he dwelt on "shattered hopes and unfilled promises." In later years, Knoll said of Johnson, "All the time he was in office I was frightened and angry that a man like this could be President of the United States. But, in retrospect, I'd have to say he was just about the best of the ones I've known."

Photo from Knoll's files, courtesy of Jonathan Knoll

Knoll (center, wearing bow tie) at the White House with LBJ.

CHAPTER SEVEN

A Writer at Large

On July 4, 1968, Erwin and Doris Knoll threw a party. It was inspired by the sudden popularity of U.S. flag pins among supporters of the war in Vietnam. As Erwin recalled, "We said, 'Bullshit, It's not their flag; it's our flag.' And so we made the Fourth of July a celebration of the Bill of Rights and especially the First Amendment." Erwin posted copies of the Bill of Rights and the Declaration of Independence to trees in his backyard.

The party became a family tradition, observed without fail every Fourth of July for the rest of Erwin Knoll's life. At one of these early parties, Johnny invited a young friend, who arrived with his father, a State Department official. As Knoll told the story, "He stood there looking at the Declaration of Independence, and he said to me: 'I was thinking about reading that to my kids this morning, but I read it first to myself. It's a pretty radical document. I decided not to read it to them.'" Knoll, telling this tale, would pause a moment, then his laugh went off like firecrackers: "Heh-heh-heh. Heh-heh-heh-heh-heh."

These early parties were also, to some extent, a celebration of Erwin Knoll's own independence—from Newhouse. In May 1968, Knoll quit the news service to become Washington correspondent for *The Progressive* and *The Capital Times*, a Madison daily. Editor Morris Rubin had offered the combination job—wherein each publication paid toward a meager salary—to his magazine's man in Washington, with the idea that he would be in line to someday take over as editor. Knoll, freed from his day job at Newhouse, would still have plenty of time to free-lance and work on longer projects.

It was ideal. Unfortunately, Rubin offered the job first to Knoll's friend and collaborator, Larry Stern.

Stern, after thinking things over, decided to stay in the fast track at *The Washington Post*. Knoll, whom Rubin asked next, leapt at the opportunity. For the rest of his life, Knoll felt as though he had traded fortunes with his friend. "I always said that if Larry had taken this job, and I kept doing what I was doing, I'd be dead now," said Knoll, leaning back into a chair at *The Progressive.* Stern, who died quite unexpectedly fifteen years before Knoll, went on to become the first editor of the *Post*'s new Style section; Knoll became a writer at large. They continued to collaborate, as Potomacus, on "The Word From Washington."

That *The Progressive* should make common cause with *The Capital Times* in hiring a Washington correspondent made perfect sense; the two publications' fortunes had long been entwined. *The Progressive* was founded as a weekly in 1909 by Wisconsin Senator Robert "Fighting Bob" La Follette; *The Capital Times* was founded in 1917 by William T. Evjue, who quit his job at the *Wisconsin State Journal* after the paper editorially condemned La Follette for opposing World War I. La Follette emblazoned his masthead with the words "Ye shall know the truth, and the truth shall make you free." Evjue's credo was "Let the people have the truth, and the freedom to discuss it and all will go well." When La Follette died in 1925, Evjue took what was then still *La Follette's Weekly*, renamed it *The Progressive*, and ran it out of his back pocket for the next fifteen years. The magazine consisted largely of recycled material from *The Capital Times*; circulation fell below the 5,000 mark. In 1940, Evjue was edged out of the editor's seat by La Follette's two sons—Phil, then governor of Wisconsin, and Bob Jr., then a U.S. Senator—and replaced by young Morris Rubin. Rubin became a member of *The Capital Times* board and a good friend of Miles McMillin, Evjue's successor. Both publications were represented by the Madison law firm of LaFollette & Sinykin, headed by Gordon Sinykin.

One of Knoll's first assignments in his new role was covering the Democratic National Convention in Chicago, where hundreds of hippies, Yippies, and Eugene McCarthy backers turned out to protest the party's embrace of Hubert Humphrey, a defender of the Vietnam war. "Erwin was rubbing his hands," says former neighbor and fellow free-lancer Ted Schuchat, who also covered the convention. "He was looking forward to it."

Knoll arrived in Chicago on August 24, several days before the main events. He stayed at the home of his friend, Dr. Sheldon Schiff, who had been best man at Knoll's wedding. Most of the time, Knoll hung around the Conrad Hilton, talking to political types and filing daily dispatches for *The Capital Times*.

On August 29, the final night of festivities, Schuchat was heading to the Chicago Amphitheater to hear Humphrey give his acceptance speech when he saw a police officer yell at a woman driver, then smash his night-stick down on the roof of her car, "giving her a $300 dent. I saw that and said, 'This place is going to explode.'" Knoll left the hotel at about 7 p.m. with his friend Stuart H. Loory, a Washington-based reporter for the *Los Angeles Times*. The two men noticed a small gathering across the street in Grant Park, and decided to check it out. Comedian/activist Dick Gregory was addressing a group of people. "Some were dressed in the style that we called hippies," Knoll recalled. "Some were very clean-cut. Black, white, a very mixed crowd." Gregory was saying that since the cops had denied the group permission to march to the Amphitheater, he was inviting everyone to his house. The problem was, Gregory's house was on Chicago's south side, near the Amphitheater. "We're going to test our constitutional rights," Gregory told the crowd. "We're going to see who in this town tonight can long endure."

The protesters, led by two dozen convention delegates and alternates, began marching off to 18th and Michigan, where the police had said they could go. There, Knoll related, they found "a rather formidable display of National Guardsmen and police. Blocking one street at that intersection was an armored personnel carrier which was parked crosswise in the street with machine guns mounted on it."

Gregory, after conferring with police, told the crowd through a bullhorn that "if you try to cross the street with me, you're facing an arrest situation." The National Guard had a bullhorn too, and essentially repeated this message: "All who intend to go in any direction except west will go to jail." No one went west. The protesters were arrested, one by one, and loaded into police vans. Knoll and Loory went to the arrest scene, wearing their clearly displayed press credentials. As they stepped off the sidewalk, a Guard officer announced, "The gentleman is with the press. Please handle him gently." Whereupon, Knoll was ushered off into a police van, packed with twenty bodies. Fellow arrestee Loory walked up to the first person in a long row, pulled out his notebook, and said, "I'm Stuart Loory of the *Los Angeles Times*, may I have your name please?" A voice came out of the dark, "Yes, I'm Tom Buckley of *The New York Times*. What are you doing here, Stuart?" Also in the crowded van was a Catholic priest from Pontiac, Michigan, who told Knoll, "This is probably old hat to you, but I've never been arrested before." Knoll said back, "Father, you may not believe this, but I've never been arrested before either." The priest: "Oh, I thought this sort of thing happened to you people [journalists] all the time." Knoll: "Only in Chicago, Father."

Knoll and Loory were taken to police headquarters, searched, fingerprinted and photographed. The cops confiscated and discarded Knoll's ballpoint pen and Loory's "Coolidge" button. Loory was incensed. Inside their jail cell, the two men could smell tear gas from nearby 18th and Michigan, where the cops had proceeded to rampage, sending protesters to hospitals. After being locked up for six hours, Knoll and Loory were brought before a judge, and released on bail. Only then were they allowed to use the telephone, to call their editors.

When the two reporters got back to the lobby of the Conrad Hilton at about 4:30 a.m., they were given a hard time by hotel security. The guards let Knoll through, on the basis of his press credentials, even though he wasn't a guest at the hotel. But Loory, who was a guest, was asked to show his room key, even though he also had press credentials. "There was a standoff and I began shouting," recalls Loory. "I was probably within a few seconds of being rearrested on the second disorderly conduct charge of the night. Erwin said, 'Stuart, you know what I think about you?' 'What,' I snapped, impatient that he should be butting in. 'I think you are becoming a hardened criminal, that's what.' I pulled out my room key and the crisis was over."

But not for everyone. As the two reporters made their way into the hotel lobby, young people were, by Knoll's account, "streaming out of the elevators, some of them hysterical, some of them injured, bruised, or bleeding, claiming that the police had just invaded the McCarthy suite downstairs and had beaten them." Youngsters continued to pour from the elevators, and sat in a circle on the floor. A few feet from Knoll, one officer, without the slightest provocation, lunged into the crowd and started beating a youth with his nightstick—right there in the lobby of the Conrad Hilton. Several other officers subdued him. All this made it into Knoll's story in the next day's edition of *The Capital Times*.

Knoll pled "not guilty" to the charge of disorderly conduct. But as the case headed to trial, *The Capital Times* lost its stomach for a fight. Gordon Sinykin, the paper's attorney, apprised Knoll that editor McMillan "feels strongly that you should accept the reduced charge of 'obstructing traffic' and plead guilty to it." That's exactly what Buckley of *The New York Times* did. But Knoll insisted on a fight; in early 1969, backed by the attorneys for the *Los Angeles Times*, he took his case to court—and won. He was even able to reimburse *The Capital Times* for the $25 bail bond money he had charged as an expense, minus $2.50 in court costs.

Sadly, Knoll's friendship with Schiff did not long endure. The problem wasn't that Schiff's car, which he lent to Knoll, was returned with a big dent in it from having been left on the streets of Chicago during the "police riot" that night. Rather, the two had a falling out over race politics. Schiff, co-director of Woodland Mental Health Center, a Chicago public-health agency, was accused of racism by several black associates. In March 1970, Schiff wrote Knoll asking for "a statement based upon your total experience with me" that he could use in his defense. Knoll wrote back that he was "troubled by your request and puzzled about how to respond to it." Although Knoll said he could readily "assert, affirm or swear that I have known you for almost twenty-five years and have never perceived in you any 'racist' attitudes or feelings," he felt that for Schiff to solicit testimonials from white friends "verges on the insulting." Knoll went on:

"The charge of 'racism' has been leveled (and will be leveled) at every white person now working in a field related to the black struggle. This is a tragic business, but I think we had better reconcile ourselves to it, for I'm certain it will continue until the nation makes some genuine progress toward racial justice. A racist society compels, in its victims, a racist response. . . . After hearing your account of the situation, I can understand—and respect—your determination to put up a fight. But I must add, in all honesty, that I think you're fighting the wrong battle at the wrong time and in the wrong place. And—to the extent that you see any merit in the collection of character references—most emphatically with the wrong tactics."

That was that. A friendship that traced back to Erasmus Hall High School fizzled, because Knoll refused to go along to get along. That same defiant tendency had brought about his most memorable moments—as a student editor who said he was ashamed of the university that graduated him; as an Army private who wouldn't let himself be labeled a security threat; as a young education reporter who refused to let his copy be compromised; as a union firebrand who led his Guild unit through contentious negotiations; as a White House correspondent who was more concerned about his integrity than with being liked. Now he was rebuffing an old friend, because he did not agree.

Knoll's arrangement with *The Capital Times* called on him to file a weekly column, "Erwin Knoll's Report from Washington," as well as frequent news stories. The paper, then as now, relished its rabble-rousing reputation, and Knoll was able to sharpen his reporting with an analytical edge. One example, from after the Democratic convention: "With enthusiasm that sometimes seems less than genuine and optimism that sounds suspiciously like whistling in a graveyard, the erstwhile supporters of Sen. Eugene McCarthy's candidacy are falling into line behind the Humphrey-Muskie ticket."

Meanwhile, for *The Progressive*, Knoll was cranking out feature-length articles virtually every month, in addition to frequent unsigned editorials and "The Word from Washington." Never again would the pages of *The Progressive* carry as much material written by Knoll as they did during the five years he served as Washington editor. Knoll wrote about Washington politics and politicians, the national media, Pentagon spending, the Nixon Administration, the Vietnam War, education, race relations, consumer protection, and more. One of his pieces, "Melvin Laird: Salesman for the Pentagon," about Nixon's Secretary of Defense, was reproduced for use in courses at The National War College in Washington D.C. Once at a Washington party, Erwin and Doris were talking to Laird, a guest of honor, as Erwin pulled out a newfangled elongated lighter he was then using to light his pipe. "Jesus, don't let him see that!" exclaimed Doris. "He'll want ten million for the military."

Another article, "The Education of Henry Durham," about the travails of a defense-industry employee who tried to blow the whistle on waste and fraud at Lockheed's plant in Marietta, Georgia, was optioned as a movie (but never made). Toward the end of his tenure as Washington correspondent, in early 1973, Knoll wrote "Homecoming in Vienna," about his return trip with Doris to the land of his birth. The piece appeared in *The Progressive*'s April issue and was excerpted in *The New York Times*. Knoll got mail about it from around the world.

This was also Knoll's most prolific period for other writing. In 1968 Knoll and William McGaffin, the head of the Washington bureau of *The Chicago Daily News*, co-authored a book about the Credibility Gap, a term coined in reference to the Johnson Administration, which used ever-shifting rationales to pull the nation deeper into a war in Vietnam. The book, published by G.P. Putnam's Sons, was called *Anything But the Truth: How the News is Managed in Washington*. One reviewer said it was "one of the best books on Washington reporting in many years." Another wrote, "Every thinker in America and perhaps the world should read this book and get mad."

That certainly was the Johnson Administration's reaction. "He was accusing us all of being liars," complains George Christian, Johnson's former press secretary, who is still irked. The book did accuse Christian and other Johnson administration officials of being liars, but it was nothing personal—the same charge was also leveled against the administrations of Kennedy, Eisenhower, Truman, and Roosevelt. It was like I.F. Stone's sage observation, which Knoll for many years posted on his wall: "Every government is run by liars. Nothing they say should be believed."

Knoll and McGaffin teamed up again on the 1969 Fawcett Gold Medal Book, *Scandal in the Pentagon: A Challenge to Democracy*, about the exponentially increasing power of the military-industrial complex. "The warning here is just as clear as that of Paul Revere," raved General David M. Sharp, former commandant of the United States Marine Corps. That same year, Knoll co-edited, with Judith Nies McFadden, a book called *American Militarism 1970*, a distillation of a conference attended by George McGovern, Richard Barnet, John Kenneth Galbraith, Herbert York, and others—on "the need to reassert control over the defense establishment." In 1970, the two co-edited *War Crimes and the American Conscience*, based on a conference prompted by the My Lai massacre.

During this time, Knoll free-lanced extensively, writing book reviews for *The Washington Post* and *New York Post*. He wrote for a magazine called *Change* and for a slick Paris-based newsweekly called *L'Express*, which translated his pieces into French. In March 1970, an article by Knoll on one of the nation's most powerful and least liked special-interest groups, the oil lobby, appeared in *The New York Times Magazine*. The piece packed a punch, and the oil lobby hit back, with an angry letter to the editor from Frank N. Ikard, president of the American Petroleum Institute. Knoll's published reply began: "Mr. Ikard's principal complaint about my article seems to be that it did not do what Mr. Ikard does so well—advance the oil industry's special pleading in behalf of its egregious privileges."

Knoll served as a consultant to the National Commission on Urban Problems and the Ford Foundation. From 1967 on, he delivered a 40-minute Washington commentary every other week for a radio station in St. Louis. He got to know writer Ben Bagdikian, then with *The Washington Post*. Bagdikian was impressed with Knoll's prescient understanding of how official appeals to national security were routinely misused: "It bothered him profoundly to know the Government was concealing things that shouldn't be concealed." Around this time, Bagdikian had his own encounter with this dynamic, when he received from Daniel Ellsberg a set of what became known as the Pentagon Papers.

Knoll also became friends with consumer advocate Ralph Nader. Once, after a press conference, Knoll offered Nader a ride. Nader looked at Knoll's subcompact British car and asked, "Do you mind if I ride in the trunk?" Knoll also became good friends with I.F. Stone, his idol as a teenager and mentor as a young reporter. The two would see each other often at Washington press events, and engage in long discussions about politics, journalism, and philosophy. Stone was a frequent dinner guest at the Knoll residence.

Erwin Knoll, in turn, helped guide and encourage many up-and-coming young writers. "He took me under his wing," recalls Jeremy

Rifkin, one of these writers. Knoll pushed hard for *The Progressive* to publish Rifkin's 1971 article, "The Red, White, and Blue Left," which traced the roots of American radicalism right back to the founding founders. Knoll predicted early on that Rifkin would play "a leadership role" on the Left. "At the time, I didn't think so," says Rifkin, who heads a Washington group called Foundation on Economic Trends. "Now it's thirteen or fourteen books later. Erwin gave me the confidence that I had something to say."

Rifkin remembers the Knoll household as a hotbed of activity, with media types and anti-war activists forever calling and stopping by. What was happening, Rifkin feels, is that Knoll was slowly shifting his professional focus, from reporter to advocate. He and Doris took their sons to anti-war demonstrations. Jonathan remembers being with his father watching angry Vietnam vets fling their war medals at the Capitol; he wondered whether the Government would recycle the medals, giving them to other soldiers.

But it wasn't all protests and rallies for the Knoll family. Jonathan remembers his parents taking him to a production of the musical *Hair*, naked dancers and all, when he was in fourth grade. The family went on strange vacations, once to a guest house on an island in South Carolina. There was nothing to do but take walks, and the island, says Jonathan, "was infested with alligators and snakes. My dad thought it was just the greatest thing."

By this time, most whites had left Southwest Washington. The Trombergs, the Knolls' friends and neighbors since they first came to River Park, in December 1970 moved into one of two adjoining new townhouses they bought on River Road in Northwest Washington; the other, they offered to the Knolls. But Erwin was determined to stay—until a few weeks later, when he and David, then eleven, were walking through the parking lot at Carrollsburg Square. Suddenly, a black youth ran past them, carrying a piece of meat he had just stolen from the grocery store across the street. An unmarked police car squealed into the lot. The officer jumped out, shouted "Stop or I'll shoot!" and then opened fire. David just stood there, ignoring his father's commands to drop to the ground. He says he didn't perceive he was in danger; his father saw it differently. That night, Erwin called Shelly Tromberg, asking if the house was still available.

In February 1971, the Knolls moved again, to 4202 River Road. The Trombergs had three young children, and these were fond times for both families. Now and then they'd go down to the waterfront and buy a big batch of crabs, which Erwin would cook as Shelly put on German music. Everyone, says Jessie Tromberg, "had a silly, grand old time."

Jonathan Knoll and the Trombergs' younger daughter Alicia would stage delightful little shows—song and dance numbers, or comedy skits—for the two families. Erwin continued to be a regular at Tromberg's rotating monthly poker game, and the two men still visited the track. One night, they drove to Charleston Racetrack in West Virginia, with instructions from their wives to: (1) be back by 11 p.m., and (2) not lose more than $100 combined. This should not have been a problem. "Erwin," notes Tromberg, "was not a big better. If he was going to bet $5 on a race, he wanted a partner." In fact, Knoll and Tromberg were partners on a $2 bet that won in an early race, giving them a chance to pick the finishers, in order, in a later race. Knoll suggested one combination; Tromberg noted that flipping the order would create much higher odds. It was a three-horse photo finish, and although Knoll and Tromberg could see that the horse they picked to come in first had won, they didn't know who was second until it was announced. Then Knoll made an announcement of his own: "I think I need a drink." Tromberg ordered him a double Scotch, and Knoll drank it down. They got home that night much later than expected. Jessie Thomberg came over from next door. Erwin, still groggy, asked Doris to make some coffee. "Why should I make coffee," she protested. "You're late. And I bet you lost money. How much did you lose?" Whereupon Erwin reached for his wallet, and counted off $1,700 in bills, split into two piles, as the two wives looked on in astonishment. Said Doris, "I'll get the coffee."

The crowning achievement of Knoll's years in Washington was his inclusion on Nixon's official enemies list. For Knoll, the revelation during the Watergate hearings in June 1973 that the President kept a list of more than 200 enemies to be discredited whenever possible and that his name was on it—along with Stuart Loory, Barbra Streisand, and Joe Namath—was like winning a Pulitzer Prize, drawing a royal flush and beating 30-to-1 odds at the track all on the same day. His family shared in the glory. Samson Knoll, a distant relative who met Knoll for the first time a few years before, remembers the excited call from his wife. "Think of it!" she exclaimed. "Erwin's on Nixon's enemies list!" Samson promptly wrote Erwin a letter of thanks "for upholding the family honor."

Before Nixon's list made the papers, the Knolls suspected that their phone line was tapped. Afterwards, they were sure of it. There were always clicks and disconnections, and once Jonathan picked up the phone to hear two other people talking. He said hello, and the others hung up. It got to be a running gag that Knoll and Tromberg wouldn't talk on the phone. One would call the other and say "Fuck communism," their password. Then they'd arrange to meet, usually on the sidewalks outside their doors.

From Doris's point of view, the family's Washington years were the best. Never again would there be so many good times, or such a diverse environment. But Washington could not hold Erwin Knoll. He again grew restless, and started sending out resumes. Knoll let one opportunity slide by in late 1971, when I.F. Stone offered to let him take over what was then *I.F. Stone's Bi-Weekly*. He declined, because he thought the publication was too closely identified with Stone for someone else to fill his shoes. Instead, Knoll bided his time, waiting for Rubin to step aside as editor of *The Progressive*.

During a visit to Madison in March 1973, Knoll was distressed by Rubin's mental state. Thereafter, he continued to get reports of Rubin's increasingly manic behavior from Griff Ellison, the magazine's business manager. On May 1, 1973, five years to the day after he signed on as the magazine's Washington correspondent, Knoll wrote to Gordon Sinykin, *The Progressive*'s chairman of the board.

"This is a difficult letter, and I have deliberated for the past couple of weeks about sending it," began Knoll, who noted that things had gotten so bad that Ellison was thinking of quitting. "I, too, am deeply concerned about the state of Morris's health, and about his capacity to continue managing the magazine's affairs. In my recent phone conversations with him . . . I can't help but be dismayed by indications that his memory is very bad, and that his attention wanders. His judgment, it seems to me, is still somewhat erratic. I could be mistaken about this last point—we have had our occasional disagreements in the past—but, to put it bluntly, I no longer have the full confidence in Morris that has governed our relationship over the past five years. I am apprehensive, for the first time, about what I may find in the next issue of the magazine." Knoll concluded with a not-so-veiled threat to break his ties to *The Progressive* unless something was done.

Something was. Sinykin, with the consent of Mary Sheridan, persuaded Rubin to step down as editor, while remaining *The Progressive*'s publisher and president. In August, the Knolls packed up to move to Madison; the Trombergs threw a farewell "Progressive Party," whose guests included nearly every journalist on Nixon's enemies list. For the first time in thirty-three years, *The Progressive* had a new editor.

CHAPTER EIGHT

Hello, Madison

In March 1921, Wisconsin Senator Robert Marion La Follette gave a speech in Madison. Friends counseled him beforehand that his opposition to the United States' entry into World War I—for which he was widely branded a traitor and almost expelled from the Senate—was a topic he would do well to avoid. But suddenly, in mid-speech, La Follette thrust his clenched fist into the air and thundered, "I do not want the vote of a single citizen who is under any misapprehension of where I stand. I would not change my record on the war for that of any man, living or dead."

The audience sat in silent amazement, then broke into deafening applause. A long-time political enemy was moved to tears. "I hate the son of a bitch," he said, "but my God, what guts he's got."

Above all, "Fighting Bob" La Follette was known for his courage. Throughout his decades of public service—as district attorney, member of Congress, governor, senator, and leader of the Progressive movement—La Follette left no doubt that he would rather imperil his political future than compromise his integrity. He held nothing dearer than his reputation as a man who could not be bought and would never give in. Principled obstinance was at the core of his being.

La Follette, a Republican, stood squarely in opposition to the powerful men and institutions of his time. He was appalled at the domination of government by special interests, and struggled to make government responsive to the rights and needs of those it was pledged to serve. His goal, he often said, was to make "the will of the people the law of the land." As governor of Wisconsin from 1901 to 1906,

La Follette pushed through a host of progressive legislation, including an anti-lobbying law, corrupt practices act, and a law restricting campaign contributions (to politicians like himself). He set up regulatory commissions for railroads, banks, and public utilities. He enacted industrial safety laws, child and woman labor laws, and the nation's first workman's compensation act.

The success of the so-called Wisconsin Idea provided a model for insurgent movements elsewhere and propelled La Follette into the national political arena. He served in the U.S. Senate for almost two decades, emerging as that body's foremost voice of progressive reform. "We must recognize that democracy is a life, and involves continual struggle," La Follette wrote. "It is only as those of every generation who love democracy resist with all their might the encroachments of its enemies that the ideals of representative government can ever be nearly approximated." He ran twice for president, in 1924 under the banner of the Progressive Party, polling one out of every six votes cast.

La Follette dismissed the corporate-owned newspapers of his day as the product of "hired men . . . whose judgments are salaried." But he had high regard for the muckraking journals that "strode like a young giant into the arena of public service." In this spirit, La Follette in 1909 founded *La Follette's Weekly Magazine*. Billed as "a publication that will not mince words or suppress facts, when public utterance demands plain talk," *La Follette's* became the vanguard of the insurgent movement. La Follette edited, wrote for, and pumped money into the magazine until his death in 1925.

Throughout his life, La Follette drove himself to the limit, repeatedly injuring his health. On one lecture tour, he spoke on 48 consecutive days, averaging, he recalled, "eight and one-quarter hours a day on the platform." He set a Senate record for filibustering 19 consecutive hours. Twice, he pushed himself to the point of nervous collapse. Still, he would not rest. A few years before his death, he wrote his son Robert, "When the last night comes and I go to the Land of Never Return, what an awful account of things undone I shall leave behind."

This was the legacy into which Erwin Knoll stepped. He became, upon arriving in Madison in August 1973, only the fourth editor in the magazine's history. His three predecessors—La Follette, William

T. Evjue and Morris Rubin—were all extraordinary men, known for their energy, integrity, and brashness of spirit. All were, to a degree, eccentric. La Follette's eccentricity was manifested in his endless striving for perfection—a trait his wife, Belle Case, encouraged—and his constant longing for approval, a void left by the death of his father when Robert was eight months old. When La Follette was thirty-nine, he had his father's remains dug up for reburial. Bernard A. Weisberger, in his book *The La Follettes of Wisconsin*, reconstructs the scene: "He took the skeleton out of the rotting coffin with his own hands and stood in the open grave amid the smells of corruption, trying to visualize the six-foot-three bearded giant who had sired him."

When La Follette announced his plans to start a weekly magazine, in addition to his political work and heavy speaking schedule, his friend Lincoln Steffens, the great muckraking journalist, was concerned. During a planning meeting for the new publication at the La Follette's home in Maple Bluff, just outside Madison, Steffens pulled his wife Belle aside and whispered, "You mustn't let Bob take on this terrible load. It will kill him." Her response, wrote Weisberger, "was a resigned laugh. Steffens knew as well as she did that nobody could stop Bob when his mind was made up." As it turned out, Belle shouldered much of the responsibility for the magazine, at one point chiding her husband for not being more involved.

Evjue was arrogant and irascible, and, toward the end of his life, senile. He was not so much the editor of *The Progressive* as its caretaker, recycling material from his daily newspaper, *The Capital Times*. His wife, Zillah, was a designer of women's clothes; she died in 1957. Bill Evjue lived until 1970, long enough to participate in a largely ghostwritten autobiography whose title, *A Fighting Editor*, played directly on the La Follette legacy.

Rubin and his wife Mary Sheridan ran the magazine as a team, but it was she who kept it going when her husband's bouts of depression drained his energy and clouded his judgment. Both put in bitterly long hours, for nominal pay. They never had children; they never had time. "This," Sheridan would say, referring to the magazine, "is my baby."

Erwin and Doris moved into a home at 6008 Winnequah Road in Monona, just along the Lake Monona shoreline from Madison.

For him, it was a welcome respite from the hustle and bustle of Washington. He relished being in what he always called the Middle West; he enjoyed his secluded home and his neighbors in Monona. "One of the things I was glad to leave behind in Washington was the delusion that Washingtonians entertain, which is that everything important in America happens there," he told a reporter writing a story for the *Chicago Sun-Times*' "Living" section in 1977. "Somebody in Washington recently asked me why we didn't move the magazine to Washington. My answer was, 'When the man comes to fix my furnace and I manage to spend 20 minutes talking to him about the state of the world, I figure I have had a political conversation at least as important as a political discussion the editor of *The New Republic* has when he has lunch with Teddy Kennedy.'"

For Doris, moving to Wisconsin was like being transported to some remote corner of the world—"beyond this is the edge and you drop off." She continued to play the piano, and to give lessons in her home. David, fourteen, attended Monona Grove High School. Twelve-year-old Jonathan was away at summer camp when the family moved. Erwin's college friend, Irwin Berkman, picked Jonathan up in New York and got him on a plane; the next day he started classes at his new middle school.

Each weekday, Erwin drove a few miles into the center of Madison. *The Progressive* was located in a nondescript two-story brick building about a half-mile from the spectacular state Capitol, where a bust of Bob La Follette is still on display. Knoll's starting salary was $20,000; he recalled making "50% more than that, more sometimes" in his five years as a Washington correspondent/free-lance writer. Knoll threw himself into his new job; he almost never missed a day of work and found it difficult to take vacations. He loved being editor of *The Progressive*. That left a big impression on his kids. "Work is where you're going to spent most of your time," David remembers his father telling him. "There's really nothing more important than finding work you enjoy."

Knoll scrupulously avoided urging his sons to follow his own or anybody else's footsteps. Neither showed much interest in journalism, although Jonathan did some writing for the Monona Grove school paper. On yellowing newsprint that Erwin for years stashed away, Jonathan began one article as follows: "Here at Monona Grove, there is an abundance of clubs and organizations which cater to the various interests of the students and faculty members. One of the more active groups which often stands out from the others is the French Club." David didn't see any value in the education he was getting and became, at age sixteen, a high-school dropout. His dad was disappointed, but did not interfere. David worked on cars—sometimes for dealerships, sometimes on his own—and hung out. "My interests leaned to getting stoned, getting laid, preferably both, and doing the things that adolescents do."

Madison is a pretty city of about 200,000 people built on an isthmus between two lakes. A narrow artery called State Street connects the city's two main attractions—the University of Wisconsin campus and the state Capitol—like weights on a barbell. The UW-Madison is renown as a major center of leftist thought, having given refuge to such historians as William Appleman Williams and Harvey Goldberg. In the late 1960s, Madison was also a national center of anti-war activity. But the local movement was shamed into near-oblivion in August 1970, when a fertilizer-and-fuel-oil bomb leveled a campus building used for military research, killing a graduate student who was working at the time. When Knoll came to Madison, he was heartened to see anti-war graffiti scrawled on downtown walls. By that time, however, it was so much dried paint.

Knoll's first major clash with "the Madison Left" occurred shortly after he came to town. WORT, a listener-sponsored community radio station, had recently gone on the air, and one of the station's volunteers announced plans to interview a spokesperson for the American Nazi Party. On the day of the intended broadcast, a crowd of demonstrators gathered outside the station, broke in, and smashed some equipment, preventing the interview. When Knoll heard this, he called the station and asked for permission to go on the air. When he arrived, "I found myself facing a young man from one of the self-designated 'revolutionary' groups on the University of Wisconsin campus, who said, 'The only answer to Nazi speech is a lead pipe to the skull.'" Knoll told the young man, and his radio audience, that "this was Nazi talk if ever I heard any."

A few years later, Knoll and *The Progressive* would just as vigorously defend the right of Nazis to march in Skokie, Illinois. Why? Part of Knoll's thinking was perhaps put best by Left intellectual

Noam Chomsky, who himself came under furious attack for objecting to the attempted muzzling of some crackpot who claimed that the Holocaust never happened: "It is a poor service to the victims of the Holocaust to adopt one of the central tactics of their murderers." Knoll also believed suppression was counterproductive—that lies and pandering to prejudice could be met more effectively with truth and appeals to reason. It was by far his most radical conceit, for it meant that it was within the power of people like himself to change the world.

Not that it would be easy. *The Progressive*, in terms of its human and capital resources, was not much more substantial an operation than this low-watt community radio station. The magazine had fewer than a dozen people on staff, including Rubin as publisher and president, Mary Sheridan as managing editor, and John McGrath as associate editor. Shortly after Knoll was hired, the magazine's business manager, Griff Ellison, left for a job at *Harper's* magazine. He was replaced by Ron Carbon, a Vietnam War veteran, eight-time college dropout, and ex-disc jockey who had been fired from a commercial Madison radio station for talking politics on the air. Carbon's parents had subscribed to *The Progressive* for years. "The magazine was congruent with my politics, but it seemed so sedate," he later said. "I was much angrier. *Ramparts* was more my thing." McGrath, with the magazine since 1947, was a raconteur and tipler who, like Rubin, had seen better days. When Knoll became editor of *The Progressive*, his father said to him: "You'll be a good writer and editor, but I don't think you'll ever be a good manager. You won't fire people who need firing." Knoll, recalling this, chuckled. "He was right. I don't do that."

Knoll liked the people he worked with and developed friendships with many of them. One day in 1974, Carbon, knowing nothing of Knoll's taste for poker, happened to remark, "We need a poker game." As he says, "The rest is history." Knoll would belong to this poker group, which met every other Wednesday, for the next twenty years.

Knoll's closest and most enduring work relationship was with Teri Terry, who came to the magazine in May 1974 at age twenty-seven, in response to an ad for a bookkeeper. "I knew not a thing about this magazine, not a thing about Erwin Knoll," says Terry, who went on a job quest when the dentist she worked for could no longer afford a receptionist. When she arrived for an interview, there was Mary Sheridan, one of the dentist's patients. Terry interviewed twice with Ron Carbon, and then met with Knoll, who had the final say. "We talked for five minutes and he said, 'You're hired, as far as I'm concerned.'"

From the start, Terry was in awe of Knoll's intellect, his precision with language. "Some of the words he was using I didn't even know," she recalls. "I mean, that's where I started from." Knoll, in turn, had high regard for Terry's fastidiousness. "I was never off a penny, and he respected that. If I was off a penny, I found a penny." Over time, Knoll would become Terry's most important teacher—about language, about politics, about taking stands on principle. "I grew up in Baraboo," she says. "I got my education at *The Progressive*."

Around this time, Knoll also became friends with Samuel H. Day, editor of *The Bulletin of the Atomic Scientists*, a Chicago-based journal devoted to nuclear issues. One day in the spring of 1974, Day received a fund-raising appeal from *The Progressive* that included a letter from Carbon to Knoll, detailing the magazine's dire financial condition. "I said to myself, 'Holy smoke, this magazine is about to go out of business,' " recalls Day, who sent in a check with a personal letter expressing his sorrow at this bitter turn of events. "Erwin wrote me back. 'Don't worry,' he said. 'This is our standard letter.'"

The two editors met for the first time in 1975, at a conference in Chicago sponsored by the Ford Foundation. Knoll spoke, and Day was impressed. "Erwin had a good perspective, an analysis of the state of the world from a non-liberal, non-Democratic perspective, with lots of examples thrown in." Afterwards, the two started a correspondence, and agreed to critique each other's magazines. Day, the South African-born son of a U.S. diplomat, had previously been editor of a weekly newspaper in Idaho. Knoll was glad to hear Day's criticisms regarding *The Progressive* and he welcomed Day's story suggestions, particularly those regarding nuclear or scientific issues. "Erwin always felt a bit inadequate with respect to science," says Day. "I thought he had a bit of an inferiority complex when it came to this area." Likewise, Day found Knoll's criticisms of the *Bulletin* enormously useful. In 1976, Day paid Knoll's airfare to Boston to meet with the *Bulletin*'s board. "Your writers sound like they're talking to each other," Knoll told the board. "As a reader, I feel uninvited."

Throughout much of his tenure at the *Bulletin*, Day was embattled. The board's chair, physicist Hans Bethe, launched a national campaign to defend nuclear power, and was none too pleased when Day ran an article from a group of scientists who took a dissident view. "Erwin," says Day, "provided good moral support. He appreciated the battle. He had been through all those battles himself."

At *The Progressive*, Knoll and Rubin agreed on most matters, including their support for the creation of a Palestinian state in the Middle East. "Morrie estimated that by the time I came out here this position had cost *The Progressive* at least a million dollars. And my guess is that in the 20 years since then it's cost $2 million more. This magazine is heavily dependent on contributions as well as subscription income, and when you talk about contributions to Left causes in America you're talking about predominantly Jewish money." Where the two men diverged most sharply is on the issue of electoral politics.

Rubin considered himself a liberal, and like many of his fellows tended to support whoever happened to be the most liberal among the Democratic candidates. Knoll, disgusted by the choices he faced at the polls, came to see wisdom in the old Wobbly slogan that if voting were a way of changing things, it would be against the law. He also started to see liberals and liberalism as part of the problem. In particular, Knoll hated Hubert Humphrey, who in 1968 had accepted his party's nomination while Knoll sat in a Chicago jail. Humphrey's entire political career, in Knoll's opinion, was "one long exercise in the abandonment of principle for the sake of political expediency." Rubin was inclined to endorse Humphrey, his personal friend for many years. "But," as Knoll told the story, "Rubin's oldest friend and closest colleague on the magazine was Milton Mayer, and Milton and I separately and without consulting each other wrote to Morrie in the week after Humphrey won the Democratic nomination, saying we felt we could no longer write for the magazine if it supported Humphrey." No endorsement was made. Said Knoll, "It was very painful for Morrie."

In 1972, the magazine supported Democrat George McGovern in his bid against Richard Nixon. The prospect of this endorsement did not prompt a threatened rebellion, but neither was Knoll persuaded that the magazine should be supporting anybody for President. In his two decades as editor, it never did.

Knoll strove constantly to find fresh perspectives, to push the debate in a more radical direction. When everyone around him clamored for the resignation or impeachment of Richard Nixon, Knoll refused to go along. "In recent months, it seems to me, the President has rendered a heroic (if unintended) service to the American people by substantially undermining their faith in the Government—and particularly in the Presidency," he wrote to one correspondent who invited him to board the band wagon. "I wonder if it would not be preferable to keep him in the office for another three and a half years, so he can continue to discredit it. Our principal problem, after all, is with the monstrous power invested in the Presidency—not with the particular transgressions of Mr. Nixon, which differ only in degree from those of his recent predecessors."

In May 1975, Rubin wrote Knoll a lengthy memo criticizing *The Progressive*'s lack of attention to national electoral politics: "I suspect this may be nothing but a reflection of your cynicism in the political process. But other people *are* interested and concerned, and I have not been to a cocktail party or dinner party or whatever in the past few months when the conversation did not turn to, or stay for a long time on, what lies ahead politically in 1976. These are mostly egghead types, but then much of our readership resides in that class, as our survey demonstrated." Rubin proposed a new department, "Politics," to deal with these issues; he even offered to write it.

A few days after Rubin gave this memo to Knoll, an emergency meeting was held at the offices of Rubin's psychiatrist, Dr. Gene Abrams. It was a Sunday morning, June 8. Present were Rubin, Abrams, Knoll, Sheridan, and Gordon Sinykin, *The Progressive*'s chairman of the board. At issue was Rubin's increasing activity, his torrent of letters and his hiring of temporary stenographers to help crank them out. The psychiatrist, Dr. Gene Abrams, said Rubin had entered a critical phase—"hypermanic" was the word he used. Rubin said he had been unaware, until the meeting was called at Sheridan's request, that people around him felt the situation was out of hand.

Knoll said the magazine's staff was uniformly upset by Rubin's behavior and that it was "essential to remove Morris from the offices of *The Progressive*." Sheridan objected, saying that while her husband was having problems, Erwin's diagnosis of the situation was "an exaggeration" and his prescription "unfair." It was agreed that Rubin would take a month off to seek treatment. But Knoll, recording these events in a memo written later that day, told Sinykin, "I am even more firmly convinced than I was this morning that it will not be possible for Morris to return to the office after a month's 'leave of absence'—or at any other time."

The following week, Rubin was in the office much of the time, and by Knoll's account "seemed quite high." He told Knoll he wanted to get in touch with one of the magazine's artists because he had an idea how they could "make a lot of money" collaborating on a book about sharks. Knoll, appraising Sinykin of these events, set forth:

"1. The experience we have been going through has completely undermined my confidence in Morris's ability to exercise responsible judgment in the affairs of *The Progressive.* 2. My personal and professional relationship with Morris has been impaired to a degree that I believe to be beyond repair or reversal. 3. I am convinced his return to the office and to an active role in the magazine would have a profoundly negative effect on staff morale and the efficiency of our operations. 4. I am, therefore, unwilling to accept *any* arrangement that involves his renewed participation, in however limited form, in the editorial or business work of *The Progressive*." Knoll proposed a generous severance package: full salary for one more year, until Rubin turned sixty-five, "and appropriate compensation thereafter."

Knoll also sent Sinykin a memo based on his conversation with Milton Mayer, who had met with Rubin in Madison on June 11. According to which, Rubin "regrets having relinquished direction of the magazine, believes it was unnecessary for him to do so, and a mistake. He particularly resents my [Knoll's] remarks last Sunday morning about my obligation to give first priority to the welfare of the magazine. He also resents your [Sinykin's] role, complains that you are telling lies about him." Mayer, said Knoll, felt that Rubin's condition would only get worse. "He's unable to separate his own identity from that of *The Progressive*," said Mayer. "He feels he has to live forever and he has to run *The Progressive* forever."

Rubin would do neither. He was forced to step down as publisher and president. In the end, though, Knoll couldn't bear to fire anybody, not even the boss. In November 1975, after Rubin had been away three months, Knoll invited him back, "on a part-time basis," to take on some editorial duties and attend to other projects and tasks. But problems persisted. In August 1976, just after Rubin's 65th birthday, Knoll sent a note: "Morris, I have been increasingly concerned for a couple of weeks about your health. There is mounting evidence, in my judgment, that you are again moving into a period of excessive activity and impaired judgment." Rubin retired for good the following month, after leaving a detailed memo regarding projects in progress. He remained on the masthead as "Editor and Publisher Emeritus"; more importantly, he remained on *The Progressive*'s board of directors.

Knoll also faced battles from below. Business manager Ron Carbon, still the angriest man at *The Progressive*, began slacking off at work, prompting a terse letter from the boss. "Your performance—or rather lack of it—has reached the point where it is a disruptive and demoralizing force in this office," Knoll wrote. "Please decide *immediately* whether you want to continue to have a job here. If you do, I will expect you to act accordingly, all the time."

Carbon stewed a while before responding in December 1976 with a blistering handwritten letter beginning with his critique of *The Progressive*, as follows: "This magazine sucks. It's dull, pompous, moralizing, abstract, aloof from nitty-gritty movement change." Knoll thanked Carbon for his letter, and then ripped it to shreds, beginning with, "This magazine does not suck. It isn't as good as it could be, as it should be, as I hope it will be. But it definitely does not suck." He went on, "I don't even know what 'nitty-gritty movement change' means, so you are obviously right when you charge that the magazine is aloof from it." Carbon wrote back that it was pointless to argue. But he stayed with the magazine for another six years.

Knoll's next big blowout was with the board, and this time Gordon Sinykin was emphatically not on his side. It occurred over *The Progressive*'s placement of an advertisement in the *Madison Press Connection*, a daily newspaper published by striking workers of Madison Newspapers Inc. Sinykin, like Rubin, was on the board of directors of *The Capital Times*, one of the two newspapers put out by MNI, which had spurred a walkout by all five of its plant unions by announcing layoffs and salary cuts for one group of union members. That *The Progressive*, an unabashedly pro-union magazine, should side with the workers and not the bosses in such a dispute made abundant sense—except to Gordon Sinykin. On the evening of November 6, 1977, the day the ad appeared, Sinykin called Knoll at home. Knoll, in a letter to Sinykin the following day, said "I cannot recall when I was last subjected to such a torrent of verbal abuse." Sinykin had said the board would demand Knoll's resignation if "anything like this" happened again. Knoll defended the ad, which had been paid for by Associate Editor John Buell, not the magazine, and apprised Sinykin that while the board could fire him "I will not submit my resignation, voluntarily or on demand, on such grounds. My conscience is a severe taskmaster, and I accede to *its* demands. But in this matter, my conscience is clear."

Sinykin responded with an equally indignant note, calling Knoll's letter "an unconvincing bit of rationalization." He went on to berate Knoll some more: "I can't understand how you could have been so thoughtless. . . . You should have known—you must have known—of the embarrassment [the ad] would be to Morris and to me. . . . *The Capital Times*, Evjue and [successor Miles] McMillin have been staunch friends and supporters of the magazine from its beginning, many years before your association with it. The paper has a long record of support—far better than any other daily paper in this state—for progressive principles, for the underdog and for unpopular causes. It deserves more than a blind stab in the back from those who should be its friends."

Knoll fired back: "In my opinion, [*The Capital Times*'] conduct in the current labor dispute is directly contrary to its tradition. I do not expect you to agree with me, but you should recognize that I have no personal interest in reaching that conclusion, and don't see how it constitutes 'a blind stab in the back.'" That same day, a majority of *The Progressive*'s board of directors approved the following resolution: "No one is authorized to use the name *The Progressive* in any ad in the *Press Connection* or in any other publication with respect to the strike." The staff was furious, but Knoll refused to further fight. "I'm not going to die in that ditch," he told them.

Back at *The Bulletin of the Atomic Scientists*, Sam Day's clock was rapidly approaching midnight. He was in trouble with his board again, and he put out feelers to Knoll. Day had already proven his value to *The Progressive*, helping senior editor Sidney Lens research "The Doomsday Machine," a 24,000-word treatise on the nuclear peril that appeared in *The Progressive* in February 1976. Knoll, says Day, considered Lens's piece "one of the most important magazine articles ever written by anybody." Publication of the article stirred public sentiment against nuclear weapons and led to the creation of Mobilization for Survival, a national anti-nuclear group. "Erwin," says Day, "recognized the need of *The Progressive* to get on top of scientific issues, particularly in the nuclear field." So when Day expressed his availability to *The Progressive*—and his willingness to fund-raise his own salary—Knoll said yes.

The rest was about to become history.

CHAPTER NINE

The H-Bomb Secret

During the last fifteen years of his life, it happened all the time. Erwin Knoll would be introduced to someone as the editor of *The Progressive*. A look of vague recognition crossed the person's face. Then came the inevitable question, "Isn't that the magazine that tried to tell people how to build their own nuclear bomb?" Sometimes, before patiently clearing up his questioner's every last misunderstanding, Knoll would answer, just for fun, "No. *The Progressive* isn't a hobbyists' magazine. We don't teach people how to build things. You must be thinking of *Popular Mechanics*."

The controversy over *The Progressive* magazine's determination to publish an article divulging what the United States Government considered to be secret information about hydrogen bombs was the pivotal episode of Erwin Knoll's life. It thrust him into the national limelight, and secured his place in history. Yet for every person who came to side with *The Progressive*, many more never got beyond the barrage of misinformation put out by the U.S. Government when it moved to block publication in March 1979. The spin in those early days was that the suppressed article by free-lance writer Howard Morland contained information that might make it easier for terrorists and Third World despots to build hydrogen bombs. This claim was specious, as even the federal judge who popularized it soon admitted. Even so, Judge Robert W. Warren, for the first time in U.S. history, censored a publication on grounds of national security.

For six months and nineteen days, *The Progressive* and its editors were prohibited, under the 1954 Atomic Energy Act, from "publishing or otherwise communicating, transmitting or disclosing" the restricted information in the H-bomb article. The case immediately took on Kafkaesque tones. Information about nuclear weapons, no matter whence it derived, was deemed "secret at birth." Affidavits submitted by both sides were censored by one side: the Government. Censors blocked out references to articles that had appeared in magazines and encyclopedias. Letters about the case from U.S. citizens to members of Congress were classified. Knoll and other defendants could not even see many of the affidavits submitted on their behalf. They were subject to court decisions they could not read, based on proceedings they were not permitted to attend.

Despite these constraints, unprecedented in the history of American jurisprudence, Knoll seized his every opportunity to defend "The H-Bomb Secret: How We Got It, Why We're Telling It," saying the article contained information vital to informed debate on nuclear weapons and nothing not already in the public domain. The real secret about the hydrogen bomb, he said, was that there is no secret; the real purpose of U.S. nuclear secrecy is to keep the American people from knowing what the Government is doing with their tax dollars and in their name.

The Government's contention that a tiny magazine in the Midwest had discovered an otherwise well-kept "secret" of H-bomb design began self-destructing almost from the start. The prosecution, in trying to hold the pieces together, was compelled to constantly expand, ultimately to absurd lengths, the boundaries of what was considered secret. By September 1979, it seemed likely that Warren's decision would be overturned, creating a precedent that would make it harder for other judges to impose prior restraint. Then, just days before an expected federal appellate court ruling, the Government took advantage of a fortuitous development to drop the case. *The Progressive* declared victory, but in fact was denied the decisive win that seemed imminent. It published the article, but the constitutional impact of its fight against the Government was rendered ambivalent. And the great majority of citizens—people whom Knoll hoped would someday participate in informed debate on nuclear weapons policy—remained ignorant about the case, as he was so often reminded.

More than a million words have been published about *The Progressive*'s H-bomb controversy. It's the subject of two books, a stage play, and the script for a Hollywood film; the case is still discussed in law schools and journalism classes. But the concepts at issue were never easy to turn into soundbites, which is what Knoll and his co-defendants at times had to do. This complexity always put them at a disadvantage, especially given the constraints imposed on what they could say and even know. The Government's alarms about a grave threat to national security—steeped in the language of Cold War paranoia—were for many people, including Judge Warren, persuasive. *The Progressive* was up against the full force of the U.S. Government at a time when official claims about the vital importance of nuclear secrecy were widely accepted. Still, Knoll and *The Progressive*, with some unintended assistance from the Government, managed to turn public opinion around. Insofar as the Government's self-serving decision to drop the case permitted, the defense prevailed.

There are stories that have not been told, about the battles behind the scenes as Knoll and other players bumped into each other like subatomic particles. There are Government bureaucrats who bungled their way into committing genuine breaches of national security and scientists who put their careers on the line in defense of the truth. There are tales that were for many years kept secret, by people who justifiably feared criminal prosecution. There are shocking records about the U.S. Department of Energy's internal response to the case that have in recent years been pried into the public domain, through persistent Freedom of Information Act requests.

But the primary unexplored avenue for understanding *The Progressive*'s H-bomb case has to do, aptly enough, with theoretical physics—specifically, two principles of quantum mechanics. The first is that there is within the seeming order of the universe an essential, fundamental element of randomness; the second, that the process of observation alters the phenomenon that occurs. In the H-bomb case, randomness ruled, and the eye of the media—alternately credulous and incisive—held powerful sway over the course of events. Much of what happened happened, like countless scenarios one can imagine for nuclear catastrophe, by quirk and circumstance—in short, by accident.

It was an accident—actually, a series of accidents—that led to *The Progressive* crossing paths with Howard Morland. In the spring of

1978, Sam Day arrived in Madison with the title of managing editor (replacing Mary Sheridan, who became book editor) and the mandate from Knoll to make nuclear issues a main focus of the magazine. That April, he spoke at a meeting of a local peace group in Crawfordsville, Indiana, an invitation he'd accepted a few months earlier, when he was still editor of *The Bulletin of the Atomic Scientists*. Day arrived to find himself pitted in a debate against one of the U.S. Government's highest-ranking nuclear officials—Charles K. Gilbert, deputy administrator of the Department of Energy, which runs the nation's nuclear weapons program. The debate was amiable enough; afterwards, the two men went out for a beer. Day expressed his desire to tour the nation's nuclear factories and Gilbert readily agreed, directing Day to call Jim Cannon, the department's director of public affairs, to set it up. Day, thrilled by the prospect of doing a story on the nation's vast nuclear-weapons complex, relayed these developments to Knoll.

In preparing for his travels, Day called some old contacts in Washington, including his friend Dave Johnson at the Center for Defense Information, a peace outfit run by ex-military personnel. Johnson mentioned an anti-nuclear activist in New Hampshire who had put together an interesting slide show on nuclear weapons that was being used as an organizing tool by the Mobilization for Survival. The activist's name was Howard Morland.

As he headed to Washington to begin his DOE-approved tour, Day met with Morland on June 25, during a one-hour layover at Logan International Airport in Boston. The two men shared a deep disdain for nuclear secrecy, which they saw as destructive to informed debate. Earlier that year, Morland had presented his slide show at a University of Alabama dormitory in Tuscaloosa. Toward the end he asked, mostly in jest, whether anyone there knew the secret of the hydrogen bomb. To his surprise, one student stood up and said, as Morland recalled in his book, *The Secret that Exploded*, "I have a friend who knows somebody at Oak Ridge, and he said the secret of the H-bomb was in the gamma rays—that the gamma rays from the fission trigger set off the fusion part of the bomb. The inside of the bomb casing is a lot of very highly machined reflecting surfaces. That's what they do up at Oak Ridge, they machine the inside of the bomb casing to make it reflect gamma rays."

Morland was skeptical. He had grown up in Chattanooga, Tennessee, ninety miles downriver from Oak Ridge, and he never heard anything about it being a nuclear-weapons factory. But when he hit the backroads on a return visit, he found himself gazing at Oak Ridge's sprawling Y-12 Plant, one of the seven major U.S. weapons facilities that Day had DOE permission to visit. The Y-12 plant had produced the Uranium-235 in the bomb that devastated Hiroshima and was still churning out nuclear-bomb components. Morland, whose "bones had been nourished by the diluted discharge" from the Y-12 Plant, got to thinking about all the other weapons factories in the backyards of people who didn't even know it and yet were, due to their proximity, likely to be among the first victims of an all-out nuclear war. Each of these factories was performing some essential task whose significance could be gauged only in reference to a total picture that only the bomb makers were allowed to see.

"I was impressed with the intensity of his interest in trying to figure out the dynamics of the nuclear-weapons program," says Day. "He felt you couldn't understand nuclear weapons until you understood how they were made. He had done all the reading he could, and had put together some sketches. I was just fascinated. I said to myself: This is very important."

A former Air Force pilot with movie-star good looks, Morland had flown transport missions from California to Vietnam, going over with soldiers and supplies, returning with bodies in aluminum boxes. In 1969, he was honorably discharged from the service for reasons of mental disability: the military called it a schizophrenic reaction; he called it an aversion to the war in Vietnam. Morland traveled the world, working as a commercial pilot and carpenter. In 1974, he moved to Hanover, New Hampshire, to attend graduate school at Dartmouth College, but dropped out without receiving a degree. Next he tried and failed at a sidewalk business of selling homemade whole-wheat bread. In 1976, Morland got involved with the Clamshell Alliance, an ad hoc environmental coalition opposing the planned construction of a nuclear power plant in Seabrook, New Hampshire. The next year, he was arrested in a protest at the construction site and locked up for twelve days in National Guard armories. During his stay, he met a fellow activist who had put together a slide show called "Global Terror." This Morland borrowed and eventually bought to create his own slide-show presentation on the ties that bind nuclear power and nuclear bombs. He added some slides and a bibliography, and soon found his presentation in demand. Morland became, in his words, a "traveling salesman of disarmament."

In this capacity, Morland soon saw that public ignorance about nuclear-weapons production kept people from making obvious connections. Anti-nuclear-power activists like those at Seabrook often did not deal with the issue of nuclear weapons, because they didn't understand how nuclear power and nuclear weapons were technologically entwined. Part of the reason for this ignorance was the Government's posture of official secrecy with regard to nuclear issues. But part also owed to people's tacit acceptance of the whole notion of secrecy, reinforced through such Cold War object lessons as the 1953 execution of Ethel and Julius Rosenberg for allegedly giving away vitally important atomic secrets and the 1954 stripping of security clearance from J. Robert Oppenheimer, the chief scientist of the Manhattan Project that built the first atom bombs, for alleged disloyalty. Among those testifying at Oppenheimer's inquisition before the Security Review Board was the military's former top atomic official, General Leslie Groves, who captured the essence of the proceedings with this frightening admission, itself kept secret for nearly three decades: "I think the data that went out in the case of the Rosenbergs was of minor value. I would never say that publically. [It] is something [that] should be kept very quiet, because irrespective of the value of that in the overall picture, the Rosenbergs deserved to hang, and I would not like to see anything that would make people say General Groves thinks they didn't do much damage after all." It was not the last time the U.S. Government would knowingly exaggerate the danger of nuclear disclosures.

"The Oppenheimer hearings were used," says Morland, "to create a new status group: security clearance. The issue now was, 'Are you right-wing enough to get full citizenship?' "

Most people weren't, thus any discussion about the direction of the nation's nuclear weapons program took place, as historian Herbert York noted, between hawks and superhawks. Since 1945, this closed system had spawned 60,000 nuclear warheads of 71 types for 116 different weapons at a cost to the U.S. taxpayers of $789 billion (an amount likely to be exceeded by the cost of ongoing efforts to mitigate their environmental harm). The United States had the ability to obliterate 100 cities the size of New York and still have more than 90 percent of its warheads in reserve.

There remained, in public references to nuclear-weapons design, one great secret: the precise nature of the so-called Teller-Ulam Idea of 1951. This was the joint achievement for which physicist Edward Teller later became known as "the father of the hydrogen bomb." Actually, he was more aptly its mother, since he brought to fruition a suggestion implanted by mathematician Stanislav Ulam, the bomb's real dad. That such a secret still existed, providing a false pretext for shutting off public access to all kinds of information about nuclear weapons, was egregious to Morland. As he wrote in *The Secret that Exploded*:

"I began to get the idea that the Teller-Ulam trick that made the H-bomb work was an arch-secret of greater weight than all others and was encrusted with a heavier patina of tradition and seriousness, if only because it was the last of the bomb secrets. Apart from my personal pique at the Government for denying me this information, I felt that the H-bomb secret stood symbolically for all secrets, and that its revelation by an outsider would puncture the bloated sanctity of the weapons priesthood." Day was on the same wavelength: "We wanted to shock the nuclear-weapons establishment."

It was resolved, at that first meeting in Boston and a subsequent one on July 3 in Chicago, that Day would seek DOE permission to let Morland tour some of the seven weapons facilities to which Day had been promised access. Morland would gather material for a larger story about the workings of the nation's nuclear-weapons complex, with an eye toward discovering what Day called "the Government's deepest, darkest secret" about the hydrogen bomb. Day himself visited three plants, writing a piece on the culture of nuclear-weapons work that appeared in the magazine's October 1978 issue under Knoll's memorable headline, "The Nicest People Make the Bomb."

Although Knoll signed off on the assignment, he doubted whether the thirty-year-old Morland—whose entire journalist career consisted of a few articles in *Flying* magazine—had the chops to pull it off. Day, however, saw Morland's lack of journalistic training as an asset: "I felt it was too bold a story for an ordinary writer."

Knoll didn't need to be persuaded of the story's merits. He, too, had developed a passionate disdain for official secrecy. In the late 1960s, when Knoll was a reporter in Washington, he wrote several articles on Project Sanguine (later Project ELF), a massive electromagnetic communications link with nuclear submarines. One day a legislative aide asked Knoll to stop by the office of Senator Gaylord Nelson of Wisconsin, where ELF is based. "We've got something interesting to show you." There, in the Navy's file on Project ELF, which Nelson had obtained, were clippings of Knoll's widely published articles. Each had been stamped "SECRET." Knoll had seen often enough how Government officials used claims about secrecy to evade accountability and cover up their own abuses. Knoll took an especially dim view of nuclear secrecy—predicated on the historically disproven notion that, were it not for seditious breaches, "they" might not figure out how to build "our" bombs. Five nations independently mastered this achievement, with no help from the Rosenbergs; and there was no indication that India, the only nation to have A-bombs but not H-bombs, was hampered by a lack of technical know-how. The Big Lie that nuclear proliferation hinged on access to some sort of secret (rather than policy choices made by hawks and superhawks far from public view) was, as Knoll saw it, responsible for nearly all of political repression—the spy scares, the witchhunts, the loyalty purges—that had confounded progressive change in Cold War America. Knoll, revolted by all of this, leapt at his chance to boldly challenge the nuclear secrecy mystique.

In a letter to *The Progressive* dated July 7, 1978, Morland laid out his strategy for the story. After seeking out experts in the Boston-Washington area, he would tour at least several major nuclear weapons facilities to deepen his understanding of how the bomb was built. "Some of the needed information is classified, of course, and holes in the story will have to be filled by educated speculation. It is important that this speculation be as close to the truth as possible in order for the narrative to be credible to knowledgeable readers," he wrote, "Without revealing military secrets I should be able to describe a hypothetical warhead containing the known components of warheads in some plausible configuration and thereby tie the production plants to their products."

Morland immediately began meeting with scientists, mostly academics, to inquire about nuclear weapons. Most, at first, were not very helpful; they either didn't know much about H-bombs or else were tight-lipped, citing security-clearance restrictions on what they were allowed to say. Morland plunged into the public literature, unearthing detailed illustrations of H-bomb concepts accompanying articles by Edward Teller in the *Encyclopedia Americana* and physicist Ralph Lapp in *World Book*. Morland, who had seen the outer casings of real H-bombs during his days as a U.S. Air Force pilot, used these scientists' illustrations to make various deductions about shape, materials, and configuration. One obvious disclosure in the Teller diagram is that an H-bomb consists of two parts: a primary, or atomic (fission) bomb, and a secondary—a hydrogen (fusion) core that the primary ignites. Morland got many more clues during his DOE-approved tour.

On July 14, 1978, Morland met with the DOE weapons chief Gilbert and spokesperson Cannon at the department's bomb division headquarters in Germantown, Maryland. Gilbert, who had agreed to let Morland fill in for Day, revealed that bomb casings were made at the Bendix plant in Kansas City, from which Morland deduced that bomb casings did not necessarily contain Uranium-238, as he had thought, since the Bendix plant does not handle uranium. But Gilbert's most significant disclosure came toward the interview's end, as Morland in his book relates: "He volunteered that there was more to building an H-bomb than merely knowing how. Even an H-bomb blueprint by itself would not be very useful, he said; a sizeable technological base was required. Still, he thought that weapons secrets should remain secrets as long as possible."

Why? Gilbert, Morland wrote, "delivered himself of a bizarre simile. Weapons information was obscene; it was like pornography, except worse, in that a picture of a naked woman never hurt anybody, while a picture of a bomb could." Sam Day got a kick out of this analogy, remarking that only the bomb-makers got to see pictures of naked bombs.

At this same meeting, Morland and the DOE worked out the ground rules for his visits. He could meet with plant officials, but not see any bomb-making in progress. Since Morland, untrained in either science or the vagaries of Government classification, could not possibly know what information was classified and what was not, he would be allowed to ask any question, and it was up to the person he asked to decide what if any answer could be given.

Morland began his tour July 24 with a visit to the Mound Facility outside Dayton, Ohio, where Monsanto Corporation made detonators for nuclear bombs. From there, Morland drove to a town near Cincinnati called Fernald, where the Feed Materials Production Center processed raw uranium for use in weapons. Morland, who did not have DOE permission to visit this plant, settled for a snapshot of the plant gate through the window of his car. At a roadside fruit stand he met a former plant worker who warned ominously against his stated plan to look for work. "The jobs pay well," the man told him, "but eventually the radiation gets you. You don't know what's going on until you get on the inside, and then you're sworn to secrecy and you can't tell about it."

Morland returned east, staying with his brother in Washington while he pored over the transcripts of hearings held before the Congressional subcommittee charged with overseeing weapons procurement. He kept contacting scientists, pressing them for information. One of the most helpful was Ralph Lapp, the physicist whose article on H-bombs had appeared in *World Book*. Lapp, a crusading scientist who in the 1950s sounded the first alarms about the dangers of atmospheric H-bomb testing (which led to a measurable increase in radioactivity in every living thing on the planet), was himself muzzled by official secrecy. In 1955, the Atomic Energy Commission classified an article Lapp had written on H-bombs for *The New York Times*, even after he provided paragraph-by-paragraph documentation of the story's public sources. Lapp told Morland he didn't know how H-bombs worked, but pointed to an article he had written in 1956 for *The Bulletin of the Atomic Scientists*. Called "The Humanitarian Bomb," the article took issue with the U.S. military's claim that the latest H-bombs, which entail nuclear fusion, were "clean" bombs in terms of radioactive fallout. The article said this wasn't true because H-bombs are not pure fusion bombs. They required a fission-bomb trigger, and wore a "jacket" of fission material that contributed greatly to their explosive power. From this Morland concluded that the bomb was spherical in design, involving an atom-bomb core surrounded by lithium-6 deuteride, a fusion material, covered by a layer of U-238.

In August, Morland issued a progress report to *The Progressive*, as he was required to do to receive the second half of a $1,000 advance. This promised total fee, seemingly stingy for a major investigative project, was in fact five times the magazine's going cover-story rate. Morland's report—a collection of fragmentary writings on various aspects of his research to date—was received with great disappointment. "It was literally incomprehensible," recalls Day. "I showed it to Erwin and Erwin just groaned, 'That's that.' " But although the second $500 payment was not immediately forthcoming, *The Progressive* wasn't ready to give up on Morland. Day wrote back, advising Morland of his need to find "some sort of strong, journalistic, investigative focus."

Morland kept at it, resuming his contacts with nuclear experts and buying a two-week bus pass to continue his tour of nuclear facilities. In early September, he took the Greyhound to St. Petersburg, Florida, to visit General Electric's Pinellas Plant, which used tritium to make high-voltage devices for initiating a fusion reaction. His next stop was DuPont's South Carolina Savannah River Plant, which pumped tritium into high-pressure containers to be released in bombs. These two visits provided the basis for an article about the safety and environmental hazards of tritium that Morland wrote for *The Progressive.* This article—which after considerable rewriting was deemed fit for publication in the magazine's February 1979 issue—went a long way toward mitigating the bad impression Morland had made with his progress report. As Day recalls, "It helped Erwin take Morland more seriously, as a guy with potential." It still didn't free up the second $500.

By this time Morland had become a nuclear nomad, bouncing around the country like a stray electron. He stayed with relatives, with friends, with people in the peace movement sympathetic to his cause—wherever he could find someone to put him up. Throughout these many months of H-bomb research and for some time afterwards, Morland was, as a matter of fact, homeless. Morland sold his car for $500, continuing his quest in a dilapidated VW squareback he had gotten for free. He contacted more scientists, showing them his diagrams of various hypothetical H-bomb designs. George

Rathjens, a DOE consultant who teaches at the Massachusetts Institute of Technology (MIT), looked at one drawing and said, "I don't think this will work." He wouldn't elaborate, but referred Morland to a colleague who turned him on to more information in the public domain. Shortly thereafter, Morland drove his VW—which sucked in exhaust fumes from holes in the floorboard—to Lynchberg, Virginia, to get a few slide-show photos of Babcock and Wilcox, a company that makes nuclear fuel for the U.S. Navy. As he took a few pictures from his car, Morland was accosted by a security guard who confiscated his film. All of Morland's pictures were, on official review, deemed secret; he never got them back.

In late September 1978, Morland finally visited the bomb factory whose discovery had launched his quest: Union Carbide's Y-12 Plant in Oak Ridge, Tennessee. He was greeted, his head throbbing from exhaust fumes, by a delegation of eight high-ranking plant officials. By this time, Morland knew the right questions to ask. Pointing to a photo of a particular piece of equipment in the plant booklet, he inquired whether it "is used to press lithium-6 deuteride powder into a shaped, ceramic-like material for later machining." After a long, shocked pause, one of the scientists answered "Yes." Morland was finding that the more he knew, the easier it was to obtain information. He had mastered the nomenclature, learned the secret handshake. He respected the expertise of weapon makers, the precision they brought to their craft; they in turn responded to his sincere desire to know. The ground rule that Morland could ask any question he wished proved enormously useful.

In November, on his way to Kansas City for a DOE-approved visit to a plant operated by Bendix Corporation, Morland caught a *Progressive*-paid plane to Madison to meet, for the first time, with Erwin Knoll. Morland, who in his book called Knoll "a portly middle-aged man with a fretful manner," says he and Knoll agreed that it was a good idea to write about how nuclear weapons were made, and to get such an article into print before the Government moved to prevent its publication. (The DOE had on several recent occasions blocked publication of research papers dealing with nuclear topics.) It was a friendly meeting. Knoll's interest in Morland's story increased.

Morland took a bus from Madison to Kansas City to visit the Bendix plant, which made almost all the nonnuclear parts for U.S.

nuclear warheads, and the Harry S. Truman Library in nearby Independence, where he looked up Truman's address to the nation on August 9, 1945, and came across these frightful words: "The world will note that the atomic bomb was dropped on Hiroshima, a military base. That is because we wished, in this first attack, to avoid, insofar as possible, the killing of civilians. But that attack is only a warning of things to come." What was to come was a massive push to acquire the power to destroy the planet in order to dominate it.

After a bus ride to Denver, Morland sought DOE permission to visit the Rocky Flats plant, but department spokesperson Cannon turned thumbs down, because Day had already been there. Morland got into the plant anyway, in the company of his friend, Louise Franklin-Ramirez, a seventy-four-year-old peace activist who presented herself at the plant gate saying she was a senior citizen making a grand tour of the nation's nuclear weapons plants and could she come back the next day with a friend? The pair, after shaking up a Rocky Flats Plant representative with their probing questions, rode a bus to the birthplace of the bomb—Los Alamos, New Mexico. There, Morland met with a disaffected former weapons worker who led him, by degrees, to another former Los Alamos worker in Santa Fe—a fellow Morland in his book referred to, pseudonymously, as Vernon Kendrick. From Kendrick, Morland thought he got what he had been seeking: the H-bomb secret.

It happened toward the end of a long interview with Kendrick, one of the many footsoldiers in the Manhattan Project. Morland decided to show Kendrick the diagrams that accompanied Edward Teller's article in the *Encyclopedia Americana.* He asked Kendrick how the four diagrams in the series could be made clearer. Kendrick, who apparently had not seen these diagrams before, got to the third one and said, "Of course, you'd need something in there to keep the neutrons off the secondary."

This was, for Morland, a Eureka moment. He remembered what the student at the University of Alabama in Tuscaloosa had said—that "the secret of the H-bomb was . . . that the gamma rays from the fission trigger set off the fusion part of the bomb." He also remembered a section on radiation pressure in his college physics textbook. It all made sense. Gamma rays and x-rays are the fastest moving products of an atomic blast; both travel at the speed of light. These rays comprise only a small part of the blast, but because the blast is so huge and their speed so great they create the kind of intense pressure needed to produce a fusion reaction.

"So," Morland stated as calmly as he could, "it's radiation pressure that compresses the fusion fuel." "Yeah," said Kendrick, still looking at the Teller diagram.

Morland was suddenly sure that radiation pressure was the key that unlocked the Teller-Ulam Idea—and equally sure the DOE was catching on to him. In one respect, he was right: The DOE was starting to worry about Morland. "I don't know what he's up to, but he's no ordinary reporter," the DOE's Cannon told Day. "Even the questions he's asking are classified." Morland and Franklin-Ramirez rode on to Albuquerque, where there was a message waiting for him from a local DOE official. When Morland called back, the official complained, "I hear you've been asking a lot of questions about classified information." Morland responded by saying he had Chuck Gilbert's permission to ask any question he pleased. "Well, just be careful," the official said. Franklin-Ramirez and Morland continued on to Berkeley, where Morland in mid-November conducted more interviews and worked on his H-bomb sketches. Morland went on alone to Los Angeles, where he stayed with friends in Echo Park. There he found that the DOE had responded to a series of detailed questions written by Morland and submitted on Oct. 24, 1978, by U.S. Representative Ronald Dellums (D-California). The DOE informed Dellums that none of the questions could be answered and that *the list of questions itself* had been classified. Even to ask was now forbidden.

Toward the end of his H-bomb research, Morland went to Hawaii to work on a grass-roots campaign against the U.S. Navy's nuclear-weapons storage facilities at its West Loch base alongside Honolulu International Airport. (He learned of this opportunity through a classified ad in *The Progressive*.) After two weeks, he went back to Berkeley, and then to Boston, where he spent the last two weeks in December scratching out new H-bomb drawings and captions. He showed these to a number of scientists for comment, but was careful about giving them out. Morland declined to leave his bomb schematics with Ron Siegel, a former graduate student of Rathjens at MIT, for fear they might fall into the Government's hands. Siegel agreed to discuss the diagrams from memory with Rathjens, and later got back to Morland with some points of clarification. Morland gave a set of H-bomb stretches to Randall Forsberg, an MIT grad student who would rise to national prominence as the founder of the Nuclear Weapons Freeze movement. Then he was off to New York and Washington, where, armed with bomb schematics and a story outline, he pitched his H-bomb piece to *Scientific American* and *The Washington Post*, neither of which was interested.

When Sam Day saw the same materials, he was excited. He urged Morland to begin the article by declaring its intention to reveal nuclear "secrets" as a way of attacking the secrecy mystique. In mid-January, Day and Morland rendezvoused at an anti-nuclear conference in Santa Cruz. Morland gave his slide-show presentation and freely showed off his H-bomb schematics. By this time, Morland's article was about half-written, in long hand; he spent much of the conference in an empty classroom, grinding out the rest of what proved to be a twenty-four-page manuscript. Day returned to Madison, H-bomb article in hand.

Morland stayed in California, bouncing back and forth between cities. In late January, on his third return trip to Davis, he finally managed to meet with Stanislav Ulam, the mathematician whose suggestion helped Teller build the bomb. Morland used his real name but falsely claimed he was collecting information about nuclear weapons for a study on the SALT treaty. Ulam looked at Morland's sketches and said he couldn't comment.

"You know," Ulam told Morland, "at one time all of this was secret." Asked Morland, "You mean, it's not classified anymore?" "No," Ulam clarified. "It's still highly classified. It used to be *secret*."

Meanwhile, back at *The Progressive*, Day undertook the task of rewriting the mess of a manuscript Morland had given him in Santa Cruz. He tried to blend the article's two themes, weaving the technical material into a larger narrative focused on the politics of nuclear secrecy. A dramatic Editor's Note advised: "The following report contains 'secret/restricted data.' "

Around this time, Day received "the first signal of our impending crisis"—a call from Randy Forsberg, the MIT grad student to whom Morland had given copies of his diagrams. While Forsberg had, in her contacts with Morland, strongly supported his goal of "demystifying the H-bomb program," she now saw publication as potentially dangerous. She told Day that fellow grad student Siegel had persuaded her of this danger, and urged Day to get in touch with him.

Day, delighted to learn that Morland's H-bomb speculations were close enough to the mark to cause concern, did more than that. In early February, he sent copies of the edited version of Morland's article, including diagrams, to Forsberg and Siegel, as well as to four scientists at the Argonne National Laboratory, a DOE-funded nuclear facility. Through his work at *The Bulletin of the Atomic Scientists*, Day had become friends with Theodore A. Postol, yet another MIT grad. Postol, in addition to being a physicist and nuclear engineer at Argonne, was also a member of the Chicago Committee for a Nuclear Overkill Moratorium, or NOMOR. When Morland traveled to Chicago the previous July 3 for his second meeting with Day, the three men went swimming in Lake Michigan. Day also introduced Knoll and Postol, who in 1978 collaborated on an article, "The Day the Bomb Went Off," which described the effects of a twenty-megaton nuclear bomb that exploded "a few feet above street level at the corner of LaSalle and Adams" in the Chicago Loop. It was only natural that Postol should be among the first to see Morland's article.

The problem was, Day's colleagues at *The Progressive*, who were also getting their first look at the edited piece, were underwhelmed. "The story left me cold," remarked Ron Carbon, the publisher of *The Progressive*. Associate editor John McGrath found it "much too dull and technical." John Buell, the magazine's other associate editor, attached a memo: "I am afraid that some of the significance of this piece is lost on me. He has dug up some information on how the hydrogen bomb is put together. In the process, he illustrates the thesis that there can be no real long-term atomic secrets. But the piece gets so bogged down in technical detail that its major thrust is lost. By the time he gets back to his major theme, most readers will have lost the thread." Morland, receiving the rewrite in Los Angeles, where he was staying with friends, was also displeased, feeling that Day had "butchered" his work.

But Knoll, while agreeing that the story needed another rewrite, grasped its significance—and understood his responsibility. On

February 12, Knoll came over to Day's west-side Madison home and, with Day on the other line, placed a call to Morland in California. The two editors wanted to make sure—absolutely sure—that Morland was not working with purloined material. If the secret of the H-bomb had come to him via improperly obtained information, the story's whole point would be lost. Knoll grilled Morland: Had he ever seen any classified documents? Had anyone given him information after receiving a promise of confidentiality? If he were under oath in court and asked to name everyone he talked to, would he be able to? Morland answered no to all three of Knoll's questions. While he had not promised anyone confidentiality, he feared that naming some of his sources in a court proceeding might expose them to repercussions, and he was not willing to do that. In particular, Morland was worried about the former Los Alamos worker he called Vernon Kendrick. Morland, while showing proper journalistic fortitude in refusing to disclose a source, was never quite sure if he violated journalistic ethics by sneaking into the Rocky Flats Plant or lying about being a graduate student of nuclear engineering in his visit to Ulam.

Morland, in his book, says Knoll responded with glee to the prospect that the Government might move to block publication: "That would put us on the front page of every newspaper in the country." According to Morland, the editors also assured him that money would be available for a First Amendment fight. Day demurs, calling these representations "either figments of Howard's imagination or misplaced from other contexts." Morland stands by his account: "I had very clear memories about that."

That this issue should be a point of dispute is no surprise, for it strikes at the nerve center of the H-bomb case. Did *The Progressive* actively court a confrontation with the Government? Did it goad the DOE on? Morland's belief is that it did. He would later brand the controversy over the article's publication "largely a publicity stunt, as cynical critics have charged." Knoll was acutely sensitive to this charge—says Day, "It made us look masochistic, asking the Government to spank us"—and steadfastly denied it. Day says neither he nor Knoll seriously believed the Government would seek to suppress publication, although this notion appealed to their defiant spirit. At best, they thought the Government might be coaxed into making some public statement that would call attention to the piece. "We wanted to get the story noticed. We hoped to get the Government saying, 'For God's sake, don't do that.' This would make our point for us."

Morland was "horrified" to learn, in this same call, that Day had sent copies of his rewritten article and diagrams to the MIT scientists. He distrusted Siegel in particular, and had been careful not to let the diagrams fall into his hands. Morland got off the phone angry—not for the last time—with Knoll and Day.

That same day, February 12, Randy Forsberg wrote a letter to Day regarding Morland's manuscript. She urged that *The Progressive* run only an "edited version" of the story, which she thoughtfully provided. Unless the magazine agreed to these "precisely defined and limited" deletions, she said, the article might help the governments of South Africa, Israel, South Korea, Taiwan and possibly Brazil more quickly master the concepts needed to build thermonuclear weapons. "I urge you in the strongest possible way not to publish the unedited version, and to get further, competent (physicists') views on the potential usefulness of what you are publishing to countries that might not otherwise get H-bombs." Forsberg said she planned to "go over the edited version" with Professor Rathjens that day.

Knoll was unmoved by Forsberg's letter. He thought it preposterous that Morland, untrained in either physics or journalism, could in six months come up with anything beyond the reach of a committed foreign government which already possessed the tremendous resources needed to build an ordinary atomic bomb. And even if the information in Morland's piece were somehow useful to a government interested in building bombs, Knoll saw such proliferation as inevitable, and of lesser immediate concern than the fact that five irresponsible nations already possessed thermonuclear weapons, in quantities sufficient to annihilate life on the planet.

After Day's second rewrite, Morland's piece was in much better shape. It now began: "What you are about to learn is a secret—a secret that the United States and four other nations, the makers of hydrogen weapons, have gone to great lengths to protect. The secret is in the coupling mechanism that enables an ordinary fission bomb—the kind that destroyed Hiroshima—to trigger the far-deadlier energy of hydrogen fusion. The physical pressure and heat generated by x- and gamma radiation, moving outward from the trigger at the speed of light, bounces against the weapon's inner wall and is reflected with enormous force into the sides of the carrot-shaped 'pencil' which contains the fusion fuel. That, within the limits of a single sentence, is the essence of a concept that initially eluded the physicists of the United States, the Soviet Union, Britain, France, and China; that they discovered independently and kept tenaciously to themselves, and that may not yet have occurred to the weapon makers of a dozen other nations bent on building the hydrogen bomb."

The article goes on to ask, "Why am I telling you?" and answer, "I am telling the secret to make a basic point as forcefully as I can: Secrecy itself, especially the power of a few designated "experts" to declare some topics off limits, contributes to a political climate in which the nuclear establishment can conduct business as usual, protecting and perpetuating the production of these horror weapons." It concludes: "We have less to fear from knowing than not knowing. What we do with the knowledge may be the key to our survival."

This version of Morland's story, which was not again to undergo significant change, benefited significantly from the input of Ted Postol and the other Argonne scientists. Although they disagreed with the article's purpose, they improved its technical discussion. Day asked Postol how useful the information in Morland's article might be to an H-bomb-coveting foreign government. "Any well-grounded physicist," Postol replied, "could have come up with what Morland did. The information is available to any nation-state that really wants it."

Did that mean *The Progressive* need not fear the U.S. Government's response? Quite the contrary, Postol explained: "The drawings are very damaging to classification, although not to national security. There is not much doubt at all that classification has been penetrated. I think the shit may hit the fan."

He was right. The H-bomb story was about to explode, putting *The Progressive* on the front page of every newspaper in the country. On February 15, George Rathjens of MIT placed a call to Sam Day. Rathjens had "apprehensions" about Morland's piece; Day was polite but unpersuaded. "I may be all wrong," Day says Rathjens admitted. "Perhaps this is all in the public domain."

The next day, Rathjens's secretary called to tell Day that Rathjens was turning his copy of the article over to the DOE. Day protested, saying Rathjens did not have the magazine's permission to do this. Rathjens called back later that day and spoke to Erwin Knoll. The deed, he said, had been done; the article was on its way to John A. Griffin, the DOE's director of classification. "In that case," Knoll told Rathjens, "we have nothing more to discuss."

CHAPTER TEN

"Let's Have a Lawsuit"

Gordon Sinykin's involvement with *The Progressive* traced to 1940, when he became, at age 30, the magazine's unpaid part-time business manager. Philip La Follette, the son of the magazine's founder, had just nudged Bill Evjue from his custodial tenure and turned the magazine's reins over to a new editor, Morris Rubin. With Sinykin in charge of the business end, Rubin and his wife Mary Sheridan ran the magazine for the next thirty-three years, until the reins were pried from Rubin's knuckles and handed to Erwin Knoll. Nineteen forty was also the year young Erwin and his father reunited with his sister and mother in New York City. And it was the year that Phil La Follette was resoundingly defeated in his bid for a fourth term as Wisconsin's governor. As nine-year-old Erwin entered public school and began learning English, Bob La Follette's son wallowed in despair so profound he never again sought office; Sinykin, who had run Phil's campaigns and served as his legal counsel, called this "just a tragedy."

After the bombing of Pearl Harbor in 1941, La Follette and Sinykin enlisted in the military; toward the end of the war they jointly served on General MacArthur's staff in the Pacific. There, in Manila in early 1945, the two first discussed opening a law practice. Sinykin returned to Madison from his slightly longer tour to find, in an office across the street from the state Capitol, the law firm of LaFollette & Sinykin, which bonded their futures. In 1946, Phil's brother Robert M. La Follette Jr. also suffered a career-ending political defeat, losing his U.S. Senate seat of more than two decades to a virtually unknown Republican primary rival named Joseph R. McCarthy.

The law firm and the magazine were now the last vestiges of the La Follette legacy; Sinykin saw his obligations to both as a sacred trust. As *The Progressive*'s lawyer and chairman of its board of directors, Sinykin stayed true to the magazine even after Robert Jr. killed himself with a handgun in 1953 and Phil developed a greater interest in alcohol than the law firm long before his death in 1965. Sinykin remained loyal to Rubin, even after participating in the decision to bring Knoll to the magazine as editor.

At the time of the H-bomb case in 1979, *The Progressive*'s board of directors consisted of four individuals: Sinykin, Rubin, Sheridan, and Knoll. From Knoll's point of view, this was not an ideal arrangement. Rubin, shut out of influence at *The Progressive*, had begun meeting with Sam Day, the new managing editor, ostensibly to pass on story ideas but transparently to percolate about Knoll. "It became quite apparent to me that Morris had a very strong dislike of Erwin—an almost pathological dislike," recalls Day. "He regarded him as an interloper." Rubin, through Day, got Knoll to accept a monthly critique of the magazine. But Rubin's criticisms, says Day, were nitpicking and unconstructive, and after a couple of months "Erwin got the point across that he was not interested in Morris's opinions. Morris got chilled out on that."

But the sharpest conflict was between Knoll and Sinykin, who had clashed mightily over *The Progressive* magazine's support for the *Madison Press Connection*, the newspaper published by striking workers of Madison Newspapers Inc. Sinykin and Rubin also served on the board of *The Capital Times*, an MNI paper, and had vehemently objected when *The Progressive* ran an ad in the strike paper in November 1977. Knoll, after being ordered not to let the magazine's name be used in this fashion again, published an article about *The Press Connection* cowritten by John Junkerman, a leader of the local strike-support group, and Alex Kotlowitz, a former editorial intern at *The Progressive*. (Junkerman would later receive an Academy Award nomination as a documentary filmmaker; Kotlowitz went on to the *Wall Street Journal* and to write the 1991 bestseller, *There Are No Children Here*.) Associate Editor John Buell says this article prompted "extremely bitter exchanges between Gordon and Erwin." Knoll would come away from these encounters persuaded that Sinykin's close ties to *Cap Times* editor Miles McMillin had "skewed his political judgment and made it more conventional." Around this time, Sheridan quietly arranged for McMillin to contribute an otherwise unmemorable book review to *The Progressive*. "It was Mary and Morris's symbolic slap at Erwin," says Buell. "I found it amusing."

It was this troubled history on which Knoll reflected, likely without amusement, following George Rathjens's February 16 call. It is not every day, after all, that an editor is told that an article he plans to publish has been turned over to Government security officials. Sinykin and other board members needed to be apprised.

Knoll put off apprising Sinykin until February 21—curiously the day after Rubin and Sheridan left for a ten-day vacation in Mexico. That morning, *The Progressive*, having heard nothing from the Government, mailed Howard Morland's diagrams and captions to DOE spokesman Jim Cannon, along with Day's note: "I enclose a copy of some material—entitled 'How a Hydrogen Bomb Works'—which has been submitted for publication to *The Progressive*. Since this is a subject on which the Department of Energy has authoritative information, we would appreciate your verifying the accuracy of the material."

Day and Knoll knew the DOE had a long-standing policy—inherited from its predecessor in nuclear weapons work, the Atomic Energy Commission—against confirming or denying the accuracy of information about nuclear arms. Still, they hoped the DOE might be drawn into making "an outraged response" to the article, which would help prove its point—that the Government was wedded to pretensions about what information was "Secret." Says Day, "We knew we were pulling the tiger's tail." Knoll also thought that sending the diagrams to Cannon would establish that the magazine, however naively, regarded this as an area into which the media had a right to inquire.

That afternoon, Knoll and Day stopped by the offices of LaFollette & Sinykin for a meeting with the senior partner. They told Sinykin about Rathjens's call, and indicated that the magazine might have a problem. Sinykin did not seem terribly concerned, but he did ask to see a copy of Morland's article. That night, as he read it, alarm bells went off. Was the technical information in Morland's piece correct, or would its publication make the magazine look foolish? Was what

Morland found a real secret and, if so, was the Government's classification system breached? Who was Morland anyway; where did he come from; how much did Knoll and Day know about him? (Not much, it emerged.) But the clincher was when ex-military man Sinykin reached for his copy of the *U.S. Code* and looked up the Atomic Energy Act of 1954. The phone rang at Knoll's house at 9:30 p.m.

"Do you know what's in this law?" Sinykin demanded, proceeding to explain. The Atomic Energy Act of 1954 declared that all information about nuclear weapons or nuclear power was automatically restricted, no matter whence its origin. Anyone who "communicates, transmits, or discloses" this information "with intent to injure the United States or with intent to secure an advantage to any foreign nation" is subject to a $10,000 fine and ten years imprisonment. "You'll be glad to know," Sinykin wryly advised Knoll, "that the death penalty no longer applies."

Sinykin, in his official capacity as the magazine's legal counsel, said it was essential that *The Progressive* establish its innocence of criminal intent. It was arguable that the Atomic Energy Act was overreaching and unconstitutional. Way back in 1958, a Congressional committee declared, "However well-intentioned, however loosely or intelligently enforced, such a law is a latent danger to the life of this democracy." But the law had never been subjected to a constitutional challenge. Sinykin felt the magazine would be on firmer ground to prevail in such a fight if it made some show of deference to the DOE's authority. "If there was going to be a lawsuit," Sinykin later reflected, "I would much prefer restraint to criminal sanctions." Since the version of Morland's story Rathjens had sent the DOE was not the same as the one *The Progressive* intended to publish, Sinykin urged Knoll to send the latest version to the DOE.

Knoll did not take well to this suggestion. It was one thing to provide diagrams and captions in an attempt to check facts, which good journalists are supposed to do, and quite another to submit an entire article to the Government—or, for that matter, to anyone—for prepublication review, which was abhorrent to Knoll's instincts as the editor of a leftist magazine. Knoll said he needed to talk to Day; together, they stalled.

On the morning of February 26, a Monday, they could wait no longer. *The Progressive*'s April issue would be going to press the following week, and if there was going to be a problem with their plan to use Morland's piece as the cover story, they needed to know. As a precaution, Knoll spent the weekend writing "Oh Promised Land," an alternative cover story based on his recent travels to Israel; the last page fell from his typewriter that Monday at 3 a.m. Day called Cannon at the DOE's bomb division headquarters in Germantown, Maryland. Cannon knew nothing about the diagrams and captions, or Morland's article. The letter Day had sent February 21 by certified mail would, due to a massive snow storm in the Washington area, take eight days to arrive. Day told Cannon to expect another mailing, via Federal Express.

Knoll and Day, faced with having to dispatch diagrams to Cannon again, assented to Sinykin's advice, and included the final version of Morland's article. The enclosed note advised the DOE of the magazine's imminent publication deadline. The next afternoon, Cannon returned Day's phone call to say that he had received these materials and passed them on to "our technical people." Day said *The Progressive* needed a response by March 1; Cannon, a former Associated Press writer well liked by the press, said he would try. Then Cannon apprised Day, newsman to newsman, of his concern about articles that "get into areas that are classified," as Morland's seemed to do. He told Day a story about a television reporter whom, when told by Cannon that the matters about which he was inquiring were classified, promptly backed off. "Now I know you're not dumb, and you seem to know what you're doing," Cannon said. "But I hope you're familiar with the Atomic Energy Act and its penalties."

Day recorded these remarks in a memo to Gordon Sinykin, noting Cannon's suggestion that, the next time the two men spoke, it might be on less friendly terms. Sinykin received news of this communication with great concern. But the magazine's editors had done as he had asked, and now there was nothing left to do but wait.

Knoll and Day never knew whether the Government's decision to seek prior restraint was based on the manuscript it got from Rathjens, or the one it got from them. Were dozing DOE officials prodded to action by the sheer persistence of the editors of *The Progressive* in calling the story to their attention? Knoll and Day never knew, but a document produced by the DOE in 1987 and pried into the public domain eight years later reveals that the DOE's top officials—

including Secretary James R. Schlesinger—met on Saturday, February 17, the day after Rathjens turned over the article, and decided "to attempt to stop publication."

At the time, though, all *The Progressive*'s editors knew was that the DOE had still not gotten back to them. On Thursday, March 1, at 10:30 a.m., Day called Cannon and reminded him of the magazine's fast-approaching deadline. "How long can you wait?" Cannon asked. "Until noon tomorrow," Day said. "Thanks," said Cannon. "That will help me spur them a little." Day told Cannon that since the magazine had not heard from the DOE, it was operating under the assumption that its article posed no security concerns. "I wouldn't necessarily read it that way," Cannon replied.

Day immediately typed a memo to Sinykin, advising him of this conversation. At ten minutes past noon, Day got a phone call from Lynn R. Coleman, the DOE's general counsel; Knoll joined the conversation on his turquoise-blue phone. Coleman stated that the article by Howard Morland had been read by himself and other DOE attorneys, by several assistant secretaries, and by Schlesinger. Their conclusion was that the article and diagrams contained "Restricted Data" as defined by the Atomic Energy Act and that its publication would injure the United States, give an advantage to foreign countries seeking thermonuclear weapons, and undercut the Carter administration's stated commitment to curbing proliferation. "We have to ask you to refrain from publishing the article in its current form," Coleman said.

"Is the department prepared to tell us which portions of the article contain 'Restricted Data'?" Knoll inquired. "No," replied Coleman. "But our people could sit down with you to work out an article." If the magazine intended to proceed with publication, Coleman said, "I have no alternative" but to seek an injunction against it. Knoll said he would discuss the matter with the magazine's lawyers and get back to the DOE later that afternoon.

Knoll and Day scheduled an emergency meeting at LaFollette & Sinykin and typed out memos about their conversation with Coleman. They also called the printer to delay the April issue for a week and move forward with plans to substitute Knoll's story on Israel. The atmosphere at *The Progressive* was, by Day's account, electric: "The Government of the United States had made its move—

decisively and massively. Whatever happened from this point on, whenever and however it was published, the Morland article would serve its principal purpose—to draw public attention to the problem of nuclear secrecy and its impact on public policy. I felt a surge of excitement, Knoll an immense sense of relief."

At 2 p.m., Knoll, Day, and publisher Ron Carbon were taking an elevator up to the third-floor offices of LaFollette, Sinykin, Anderson and Munson. They were in high spirits, viewing the possibility of a battle with the DOE with great enthusiasm. "I love it!" exclaimed Knoll.

Sinykin, as expected, insisted that *The Progressive* hear the Government out. Knoll and Day should offer to fly to Washington that night to meet with DOE officials the next morning. Day, from the law office, relayed this offer to Coleman's assistant, who told him not to bother; a delegation of DOE and Justice Department officials were planning to fly to Madison the following morning.

The Progressive's editors and attorneys could only guess what was happening in Washington. In fact, alarm bells were sounding in the Carter White House. DOE Secretary Schlesinger, formerly director of the CIA under President Nixon and Secretary of Defense under President Ford, had dropped the matter on the desk of U.S. Attorney General Griffin B. Bell. "No Cabinet secretary in my tenure," Bell recalled in his book, *Taking Care of the Law*, "ever pushed us harder to move in court against a defendant." But Bell "needed no prodding" to accept at face value the claim that the article threatened national security.

Walking the five blocks from their lawyers' office to *The Progressive*, Knoll, Day, and Carbon were stopped by two reporters for the *Madison Press Connection*. One of them was John Junkerman, whose pro-*PC* article in *The Progressive*, his first published piece, had bent Sinykin's nose out of joint. Junkerman said he had heard that *The Progressive* was about to publish a sensational article about the hydrogen bomb. (The *Press Connection* was tipped off to the story, although Bob Mong, the editor who passed the tip on to Junkerman, no longer remembers the tipster—possibly a well-known local lawyer of anarchistic bent who later committed suicide.) Knoll said he could not discuss the matter, but he took down the reporters' home phone numbers, and promised to call them when he could.

Because *The Progressive*'s cramped office—then located in a dismal brick building at 408 West Gorham Street near the UW-Madison campus—was deemed no place to greet an official U.S. Government delegation, the meeting was scheduled to take place that morning at the relatively regal offices of LaFollette & Sinykin. Fog in Chicago delayed the flight, and the meeting did not begin until nearly 2 p.m. The six-member delegation was headed by assistant DOE secretary Duane C. Sewell, the nation's top nuclear weapons administrator. Also present was Sewell's technical assistant, William C. Grayson Jr., two members of the DOE's legal team, and two attorneys from the Justice Department's civil division. On hand for *The Progressive*: Knoll, Day, Carbon, and attorneys Sinykin and Brady Williamson.

Sewell restated Coleman's charge that the article contained "Restricted Data" that "we definitely feel" would be useful to other countries interested in building hydrogen bombs. Sewell, like Coleman, declined to identify what data was restricted, but did say it involved all of the diagrams and captions and about 20 percent of the text. He also confided that, while there were "some inaccuracies in the technical portion" of the article, "in the overall context they are not substantial."

Knoll and Day were thunderstruck, and for the first time scared. The Government's top nuclear official had just violated a thirty-five-year-old policy against confirming or denying the accuracy of information about nuclear weapons. It was a serious tactical blunder—the first of many—and it meant that, from this time forward, the Government had to do everything it could to block the article's publication. ("My God!" exclaimed Morland, when told of Sewell's confirmation. "I didn't really know until now.") Sewell, in making this disclosure, evidently assumed that *The Progressive* would assent to the Government's demands that the magazine let it rewrite the piece, removing the Restricted Data. "That was his whole history with the media—the media had always backed away when somebody mentioned classified information," says Day. "He didn't know us."

Sewell admitted that the DOE's planned rewrite would "certainly take a lot out of the article." But the piece's politics and meaning, he professed, would be unchanged. The process would take several days, and the DOE would be willing to discuss its deletions and substitutions. Unless the magazine agreed to these terms, the Justice Department was prepared to move to block publication. "We are ready to act if necessary," said civil-division attorney David Anderson, implying that the delegation was prepared to walk the four blocks to the federal courthouse in Madison to file for an immediate injunction.

It was. On this day, March 2, Attorney General Bell wrote a memorandum to President Jimmy Carter, apprising him of plans to seek an injunction if the editors of *The Progressive* did not accede to the DOE's demands. The memo says the article by "Howard Moreland [sic] . . . contains a useful and informative presentation of at least two of the basic concepts of thermonuclear weapon design that remain classified as 'Restricted Data' under the Atomic Energy Act of 1954." The attempt to seek prior restraint, Bell noted, will present "difficult constitutional and statutory issues. In the unsuccessful case against *The New York Times* to enjoin publication of classified material, the Supreme Court pointed out that there the Executive Branch was seeking a prior restraint on the press without any authorizing legislation. Here, we do have a statute, part of the Atomic Energy Act, specifically authorizing injunctive actions to prevent disclosure of such information."

The message of this memo was clear: This time we have a chance to impose prior restraint and get away with it. President Carter jotted down his response: "Good move. Proceed. J" For years afterwards, the Justice Department sought to suppress this memo, blacking out huge portions of it. Now, the Department claims to have lost the memo altogether; a 1995 Freedom of Information Act request for this and other H-Bomb case documents was denied on grounds that DOE records custodians have been unable to locate the box. An undeleted copy, however, did turn up in Jimmy Carter's presidential library.

Knoll spoke up, telling the Government delegation he was "incredulous that a writer with Morland's limited background . . . could so readily penetrate what you are describing as perhaps the most important secret possessed by the United States. If this were really the case, it would constitute a national security scandal of horrendous proportions." Sewell replied that he didn't understand what had happened, and pledged an investigation: "We are concerned there may be a fault in our system." After about an hour, *The Progressive* side retired to Sinykin's office while the Government officials finished the sandwiches and cookies ordered by their hosts. Knoll, to his attorneys, expressed his response to the Government's offer to rewrite the piece "in a few blunt expletives." Sinykin, to the Government delegation, translated that while Knoll found this offer "more than objectionable," the magazine wanted time to ponder it. The magazine's lawyers would reply to Coleman by 6 p.m., March 6. In the meantime, the Government had his and the magazine's assurance that the article would not go to press. The Government agreed to these terms, and the two sides complimented each other on their "lawyer-like" approach.

There was another reason for waiting until Tuesday before responding to the Government's offer. Sinykin insisted that any decision with such potentially grave consequences be made by the magazine's board of directors. And two of its four members—Morris Rubin and Mary Sheridan—would not return from their Mexican vacation until late Monday night. Knoll, preparing for this meeting, wrote a memo to Sinykin outlining what he hoped would be the magazine's official response—that the editors had upon careful consideration concluded that submitting the piece to Government rewrite would "violate the ethics of a free press and independent press and, in our opinion, undermine the guarantees of the First Amendment." Knoll said the magazine would be willing to postpone publication of Morland's article to give the Government time to seek to restrain publication through the Federal courts. Day, with the help of his friend Ted Postol, began to compile a list of scientists who might be willing to testify that Morland's article contained nothing not already in the public domain. Postol himself was not sure he could do this, for fear it would cause problems at his DOE-funded workplace, Argonne National Laboratory.

The morning after their night flight to Madison, Rubin and Sheridan received a call from Gordon Sinykin. There was a problem at the magazine, an article that might involve litigation. How quickly could they get down to the office? Soon after, the jet-lagged couple was inundated with information about Morland's article and the Government's ultimatum, with its rapidly approaching 6 p.m. deadline. They heard that defiance of the Government could subject the magazine to a protracted and costly legal battle. They heard the editors defend the story both on First Amendment grounds and as a calculated challenge to nuclear secrecy. They looked at Morland's lengthy article, with its detailed diagrams and technical information, and pleaded for another day to read the piece and make up their minds. *The Progressive*'s lawyers obtained an extension on the magazine's promised final decision until 3:30 the next afternoon.

The visitors left, and the mood at *The Progressive* turned somber. Rubin had questioned the propriety of publishing what the Government considered to be restricted information. Sinykin had been, as Day put it, "tense and uncommunicative." To Knoll, however, Sinykin made his feelings clear. "He did not want that article to run; he did not want it to run," recalls Teri Terry, Knoll's secretary. Elaborates Carbon, "He felt we were jeopardizing the future of the magazine [by going up against] the overwhelming power of the Government. He felt we'd just get squashed."

The next morning, *The Progressive's* board of directors met at Sinykin's office; Day was also present. Rubin, after pontificating at length about the article's faults—it was too long, too boring, too technical, not political enough, and definitely not the sort of thing he would have accepted for publication at *The Progressive*, he said, looking coldly at Knoll—stood by the article on First Amendment grounds, as did Sheridan. Knoll was elated.

That afternoon, Gordon Sinykin placed a call to Coleman, as promised. *The Progressive*'s top lawyer told the DOE's top lawyer that, after careful consideration, the magazine's editors had decided the Government's "position against publication is untenable. We decline your request not to publish the article, and we do not believe it is proper to permit the Department to rewrite it." The two lawyers exchanged legal information; the call lasted eight minutes. Afterwards, Sinykin and colleagues Brady Williamson and Earl Munson conferred with clients Knoll, Day, and Carbon. Sinykin said all anyone needed to hear: "If we're going to have a lawsuit, let's have a lawsuit—and a good one."

Photo by Jon Biever, *The Milwaukee Journal*

Leaving the Federal Building in Milwaukee in March 1979.

CHAPTER ELEVEN

Prior Restraint

There was, until 1979, only one occasion in the entire history of the United States of America in which the federal Government sought to insist that something not appear in print. It happened on the other end of that same decade, in 1971, when the Nixon Administration moved to block publication of the Pentagon Papers by *The New York Times* and *The Washington Post*. In that case, *New York Times Co. v. United States*, the Supreme Court promptly voted 6-3 to reject the Government's censorship attempt, with Chief Justice Warren Burger declaring that "prior restraints on speech and publication are the most serious and least tolerable infringement on First Amendment rights."

In reaching this decision, the court rejected the contention advanced by Attorney General John Mitchell that publication of documents exposing the tragedy of errors behind the nation's war in Southeast Asia fell within the narrow First Amendment exception carved out by the Supreme Court's 1931 ruling in *Near v. Minnesota*. In that decision, the court rebuffed efforts to censor a malicious local scandal sheet. But in the course of doing so, Chief Justice Charles Evans Hughes noted that some restrictions do apply: "No one would question but that a government might prevent actual obstruction to its recruiting service or the publication of the sailing dates of transports or the number and location of troops." It was this loophole the Nixon Administration sought, without success, to widen in the Pentagon Papers case. In *The United States of America v. The Progressive, Inc., Erwin Knoll, Samuel Day Jr. and Howard Morland*, the Carter Administration tried again.

Heading into what promised to be another landmark battle, *The Progressive*'s editors and attorneys believed they would prevail. That was before the media and public responded to news of the story with almost uniform hostility, creating a political climate in which losing was a real possibility. Perhaps Gordon Sinykin, who had been the least willing to draw the magazine into a First Amendment fight involving nuclear "secrets," best understood what terrible force the federal Government could bring to bear against a tiny leftist magazine in Madison. It's a wonder—and in large part, an accident—that *The Progressive* didn't get squashed.

On March 7, just after Sinykin announced his desire to "have a good [lawsuit]," the phone rang at his office. It was Teri Terry, calling to say that Howard Morland had arrived at the Madison airport and she was off to pick him up. ("How will I recognize you?" asked Terry, ever-practical. "Trust me, you'll know me by my scruffy appearance," said Morland. She did.) Morland, at Knoll's request, had flown in from Hawaii, where he was involved in a federal lawsuit brought by local activists against the U.S. Navy. The Navy had built "igloos" capable of storing up to 1,200 nuclear weapons near the Honolulu airport. Morland, a former U.S. Air Force pilot, was allowed to testify about the possibility of a plane crash into the igloos, but the judge would not let him discuss whether the bombs might detonate, since he was not an expert in nuclear weapons. At this same proceeding, a Department of Energy classification specialist testified that the Navy could not provide an environmental impact statement or comment on the possible dangers these weapons posed, because to do so would violate the Atomic Energy Act of 1954. The judge sided with the Government, and dismissed the suit.

Morland arrived in Madison in peak form, about to have his moment in the mushroom cloud. "Howard was a star," beams former Associate Editor John Buell. "A little boy with a unique toy." When Knoll, Day and Carbon got back from Sinykin's office, Morland was holding court at *The Progressive*. Knoll and Day pulled their H-bomb whiz kid aside, to debrief him on the day's events. But first, Morland took his turn at show-and-tell. He produced typewritten notes from his phone interview a few days earlier with Dr. Edward Teller. "Things which can be communicated in simple language are not secret and cannot be secret," Teller told him. "Any aspect of technology which can be communicated in simple language should be declassified. This includes the technology of nuclear weapons and thermonuclear weapons." Morland then pulled from his backpack a T-shirt onto which a copy shop in Honolulu had printed his diagram of a hydrogen bomb. Knoll told Morland that while LaFollette & Sinykin would represent him for now, he might later need his own attorney. He also asked Morland to stay out of sight for the next few days.

At first, Morland stayed at Sam Day's house. Kathleen Day, whom Morland in his book describes as "the long-suffering mother of three grown sons and Sam's indulgent companion through his years of tilting at windmills," took Morland aside and warned him not to let Sam and Erwin talk him into anything that might land them all in jail. That night, unable to sleep, Morland stayed up until 4 a.m., writing a poem "in which the sequence of events in the detonation of a hydrogen bomb was presented in disguised form, as though in a riddle or an oracle." It wasn't a very good poem.

After two nights, Morland was shuffled off to more permanent lodgings, at the lakefront home of John Buell and his wife, Susan. Morland met with the magazine's attorneys; Knoll waited for the other shoe to drop. At the ready was a statement from Knoll responding indignantly to the Government's action, with a space left to type in whatever that action was as soon as it became known. That evening of March 8, the sun set for the last time on *The Progressive* magazine's obscurity.

At 8 p.m., Frank Tuerkheimer, the U.S. Attorney for the Western District of Wisconsin, placed a call to the home of court clerk Joe Skupniewitz, advising him of his immediate need to see District Judge James E. Doyle. A half hour later, Tuerkheimer, an assistant, and two lawyers from the U.S. Justice Department met Skupniewitz, who was waiting in his car in front of Doyle's west-side Madison home. The five men filed into the judge's living room and presented Doyle with a stack of papers that bore the title, *United States of America, Plaintiff, v. The Progressive, Inc.* Doyle didn't read any further. He told his visitors he could not become involved in the case due to his ties with the magazine. Doyle, an alumnus of the LaFollette & Sinykin law firm, was friends with Sinykin and Rubin.

Rebuffed by Doyle, the four lawyers drove back to Tuerkheimer's office. Tuerkheimer called Earl Munson at LaFollette & Sinykin, obtaining reassurance that the magazine was not about to publish the article. The article they had taken to Judge Doyle's home. The article that was now. . . . "I thought you had it." "I thought *you* did." The lawyers rushed to the street, where they retrieved the article from Tuerkheimer's unlocked car. This crisis contained, they pondered their options. Doyle was the Western District's only judge, so they had to try the Eastern District, in Milwaukee. But they were unable to reach any of its three federal judges that night. The next morning, March 9, Skupniewitz of Madison notified his clerk-of-court counterpart in Milwaukee that a "high-visibility" case was on its way. And, barreling down the seventy miles of interstate that separate the two cities, it was.

The jurist it connected with was Judge Robert W. Warren, a conservative Republican whom Nixon had named to the bench just days before resigning in disgrace. Warren was a former Wisconsin attorney general, and in that capacity had overseen state efforts to monitor student opposition to the Vietnam War. If any judge was going to stand up to the full authority and might of the United States Government, he was not the one.

That morning, Warren was presented with a lengthy complaint outlining the Government's case against *The Progressive*. The article, it claimed, contained secret Restricted Data as defined by the Atomic Energy Act of 1954; publication of this information would result in "grave, direct, immediate, and irreparable harm to the national security of the United States and its people."

These adjectives were selected to meet the precise criteria for prior restraint set forth by the U.S. Supreme Court in the Pentagon Papers case. The Government's bid for a restraining order also advanced the argument that, even if some of the data in Morland's article and diagrams represented "an original work product" it would still be restricted because, under the Atomic Energy Act of 1954, all information about nuclear technology was deemed "classified at birth"—that is, born secret—regardless of its origin.

The Government's complaint was accompanied by both versions of Morland's article—the one from Rathjens and the one from *The Progressive*—and nine affidavits. Sewell, in a public affidavit, stated that Morland's article contained Restricted Data whose disclosure would clearly, immediately, and irreparably harm the national interest. He also submitted an affidavit *in camera* (under seal to the court) contending that the article revealed "the secret of the H-bomb." Similar contentions were advanced in affidavits submitted by DOE Director of Classification John Griffin, Assistant Secretary of State Thomas R. Pickering, and Charles N. Van Doren, head of the Non-Proliferation Bureau of the Arms Control and Disarmament Agency. Van Doren's affidavit was especially powerful: "Of all the manuscripts purporting to be unclassified that I have reviewed in my twelve years in this field, this one, if made public, appears to be the most flagrant example of deliberate dissemination of sensitive nuclear weapons design information, and the most likely to damage U.S. interests in preventing the spread of nuclear weapons capabilities."

Knoll, of course, knew this was nonsense. So, too, by degrees, did Frank Tuerkheimer, the U.S. Attorney in Madison. (Tuerkheimer, a former Watergate prosecutor named by Carter to the U.S. Attorney's post, says the Justice Department attorneys at one point asked him to take over the case, but he declined. "There was something about it that bothered me. I told them, 'You guys do it.' ") On Friday morning, as the lawyers from Washington headed for Judge Warren's court, Tuerkheimer for the first time read Morland's article. "I was really shocked," he recalls. What shocked him wasn't the article's content but the Government's deletions. "I saw things in the boxes marked off as 'censored' that I had known in high school, when I was interested in nuclear physics. Things like, you need a fission trigger for a fusion bomb." That weekend, Tuerkheimer visited the physics library on the UW-Madison campus, photocopying parts of textbooks and articles that contained some of the same information the Government wanted to keep from appearing in *The Progressive*. On Monday, he sent these materials on to the Justice Department attorneys handling the case; four days later the Government reduced the amount of "Restricted Data" it said was in Morland's article by 40 percent, from 2,190 to 1,322 words.

The ninety-minute hearing before Judge Warren began at 2 p.m. *The Progressive*'s attorney Earl Munson argued, so softly he could not be heard in the back of the courtroom, that Morland's article contained nothing that was not already in the public domain. Justice Department attorney Thomas Martin contended that "the manuscript contains the essential principles of the operation of the hydrogen bomb." Judge Warren, heedless of the possibility that both statements were true, sided with the Government. "I'd like . . . to think a long, hard time before I gave the hydrogen bomb to Idi Amin," Warren stated, invoking the ill-fated Pentagon Papers case. "I can't help feeling that somehow or other to put together the recipe for a do-it-yourself hydrogen bomb is somewhat different than revealing that certain members of our military establishment have very poor ideas about how to conduct a national effort in Vietnam."

Then, after stating that "any prior restraint on publication comes into any federal Court with a very heavy presumption against its validity," Warren launched into an extraordinary assault on the First Amendment, taking off directly from the *Near* decision: "No one would question but that a government might prevent actual obstruction of its recruiting service or the publication of the sailing dates of the transports or the number and location of troops. So on similar grounds the primary requirements of decency may be enforced against obscene publications, the [security] of the community life may be protected against incitement of actions of violence and the [overthrow] by force of orderly government. The constitutional guarantee of free speech does not protect a man from an injunction against uttering words that may have all the effect of force. . . ."

Warren granted a temporary restraining order against the article's publication, in effect for ten days, until a hearing could be held on the Government's request for a preliminary injunction.Knoll and Day emerged from the packed proceeding to face the microphones, then raced back to Madison ahead of the restraining order. When the Federal marshals arrived late that afternoon, *The Progressive*'s tiny office was crammed with reporters. Knoll, savoring the moment, asked Teri Terry to make the marshals wait: "Tell them I'm in a meeting." After a time Knoll emerged from his office to receive the papers, as cameras whirred and clicked.

This was a battle Erwin Knoll was born to fight—one that combined his two preeminent concerns, militarism and the First Amendment—and he was ready for it. His whole lifetime of experience had taught him one overriding lesson: Do not trust the Government. Now the Government that had participated so eagerly in nuclear proliferation—always leading the way, and escalating when matched—was concocting fables about its interest in nonproliferation in order to assert dominion over what *The Progressive* was allowed to publish. Knoll was outraged, and believed he could persuade others that it was outrageous. In his first round of interviews and from that time on, Knoll stressed that Morland's article was garnered entirely from public sources and that the Government's reaction proved the story's point: that official secrecy served "to deprive the American people of access to essential information."

But Knoll and *The Progressive* were at a keen disadvantage. Officials of the U.S. Government—under Jimmy Carter, the most liberal president since Johnson—were making what seemed to be authoritative statements about the danger this information posed to a public that, by and large, didn't know the first thing about hydrogen bombs. Nor could Knoll do much to educate. He and other defendants were prohibited from "communicating, transmitting or disclosing" the Restricted Data in Morland's article and even from knowing what parts of it the Government considered secret. And, to some extent, it didn't matter *what* Knoll said: The evening news and morning headlines were destined to be shaped by Warren's soundbite about having to "think a long hard time before I gave the hydrogen bomb to Idi Amin"—a statement that exposes Warren's ignorance of the issue at hand. Even the Government was not claiming that Morland's piece would spur proliferation in the Third World, merely that it might speed the development of this technology in such nations as Israel and Pakistan. Asked at the press conference about Judge Warren's remark, Knoll replied, "I'd think long and hard before I gave the bomb to *anybody*."

That night, on the "NBC Evening News," David Brinkley described *The Progressive* as a "socialist" magazine that wanted to print instructions for anyone "who might like to build a hydrogen bomb in his garage." At *The Progressive*, Buell was turning the TV dial and happened to catch MIT physicist Henry Kendall, chairman of the anti-nuclear Union of Concerned Scientists, making a statement on the case. He called to Day, who had identified Kendall in his note to the magazine's lawyers as someone who might testify on behalf of the defense. "Tremendous!" shouted Day, rushing into the room. "But you don't understand," Buell said. "Kendall has come out against us." *The Progressive*'s would-be defender called the planned publication of Morland's article, which he had not seen, "an act of appalling irresponsibility."

The media and scientific community's intensely negative initial reaction—which left more lasting impressions than any that came later, after the Government's claims were scrutinized—was no accident. The night before the hearing in Judge Warren's court, the Department of Justice had put out a press release suggesting the magazine was about to publish a blueprint for the bomb. By the time Knoll reached into his pocket for the phone number of *Madison Press Connection* reporter John Junkerman, to whom he had the week before promised an exclusive on the story, the whole world knew.

Secretary of Energy James R. Schlesinger personally contacted *The New York Times, The Washington Post* and the *Los Angeles Times* to discourage them from rallying to *The Progressive*'s defense. Secretary of Defense Harold Brown paid personal visits. It worked. *The New York Times* withheld judgment, while the other two papers came out strongly against *The Progressive*. *The Washington Post,* Knoll's alma mater, was especially hostile: "As a press-versus-Government First-Amendment contest, this, as far as we can tell, is John Mitchell's dream case—the one the Nixon Administration was never lucky enough to get: a real First Amendment loser." Knoll, after nearly two weeks, responded with a letter to the editor. "Somehow," it concluded, "*The Washington Post* has become John Mitchell's dream newspaper. How did that ever come to pass?"

On Sunday, March 11, *The Progressive* received a telegram from the Federation of American Scientists, a group founded in 1945 (as the Federation of Atomic Scientists) with impetus from former Manhattan Project scientists, including Leo Szilard and Albert Einstein. These scientists were horrified by the atomic monster they had helped create and took strong stands against the secrecy that served to protect it. "The SECRET stamp is the greatest weapon ever invented," observed Szilard. Einstein, in 1947, was more profound: "Through the release of atomic energy, our generation has brought into the world the most revolutionary force since prehistoric man's discovery of fire. This basic power of the universe cannot be fitted into the outmoded concept of narrow nationalism. For there is no secret and no defense; there is no possibility of control except through an aroused understanding and insistence of the peoples of the world. We scientists recognize our inescapable responsibility to carry to our fellow citizens an understanding of the simple facts of atomic energy and its implications for society. In this lies our only security and our only hope—we believe that an informed citizenry will act for life and not death."

But in 1979, the Federation of American Scientists was all for keeping nuclear "secrets." "Your effort to publish an article whose draft title was, 'How a Hydrogen Bomb Works' is not in the interest of nonproliferation but quite the reverse," declared director Jeremy J. Stone and two other Federation officials who hadn't seen the article. "A great deal of the damage may now be irreversible since there is a possibility that some other press organ will secure and reprint any deletions you might make. And the unfortunate precedent of Government restraint of freedom of the press is in the process of being made."

That Jeremy Stone was the son of journalist I.F. Stone, Knoll's mentor and long-time friend, made this missive especially hard to bear. But a far more crushing blow awaited him. A few days later, Knoll and publisher Ron Carbon were in Washington, D.C., making contacts regarding the H-bomb case. They had lunch at the Great Wall, a Chinese restaurant then on 19th Street, with Stone, Morton Mintz and wife Anita, and Walter Pincus, *The Washington Post* reporter to whom Morland had earlier shown his diagrams. There, Knoll learned that his friends—Stone included—were united in their opposition to the article's publication. "Why do you want to do this?" Stone demanded, telling about a time during World War II when he declined to print sensitive military information that had come his way. Stone glared across the table at Knoll, whom he had earlier asked to be his successor, denigrating his determination to print Morland's article. "He thought it was stupid," says Mintz. "He was quite affirmative and astringent about it."

Carbon concurs with this account. "Stone said that the First Amendment may be absolute, but on this issue you're foolish and irresponsible to exercise it. He urged Erwin not to print the thing." Stone's harsh reaction "caused Erwin a great deal of angst," says Carbon. "It was as though Izzy had forgotten who Erwin was." Later,

Stone came to express support for the story even as his son Jeremy continued to inveigh against it. Knoll would help bring about many more such transformations, as public sympathies shifted from the Government to the defendants. But there were some people—including Mintz and Pincus—whom Knoll would never win over.

Knoll, for reasons that shall remain his own, never mentioned his traumatic experience of being stoned by Stone to others at *The Progressive*, or even to Doris, his wife. She, in turn, kept a secret of her own. It was about her encounter with Mort Mintz, sent by *The Washington Post* to cover the case. She was happy to see this longtime friend among the packed throng at a legal proceeding, but barely had time to say hello before Mintz demanded to know whether Erwin had lost his mind. She has never forgotten how Mintz looked that day, how angry he was. And she remembers her retort, "Even if you have a Cuisinart, Mort, you can't build the thing in your damn kitchen." But she never told her husband "what Mort had done."

Jonathan Knoll, then eighteen, says his father "forewarned me that he was going to be in the news." Still, it came as a shock to see him be the center of attention, fielding the constant phone calls. "I knew there were other kids who didn't get to meet the President," says Jonathan. "But until that time, I never thought of my dad as a public figure." To David Knoll, who that month turned twenty, the whole idea of the U.S. Government taking a keen interest in "the short, dowdy bunch of well-intentioned and essentially benign people" who produced *The Progressive* seemed funny. John McGrath was a boozer; Buell brilliant and nerdy; Day recklessly fearless; Carbon a former Marine, ex-DJ and practicing substance abuser. "The only person in the office not an odd duck in any quantifiable way was Teri Terry."

Shortly after the H-bomb story exploded into public view, Erwin and Doris went away for the weekend, leaving David to dog-sit at the Knolls' latest home, a 100-year-old farmhouse in McFarland, a Madison bedroom community. That evening, a man telephoned for Mr. Knoll, a title David was "just arrogant enough" to claim. The caller started in about how angry he was that Knoll intended to divulge nuclear secrets and, since the Government seemed to be pussyfooting around, he would be coming to Knoll's house to take direct and forceful action.

"I'm afraid you have the wrong Mr. Knoll," David responded. "You want Erwin Knoll the pacifist, the editor of *The Progressive* magazine. You've got his older son. Since you have the phone number, I assume you have the address. I'm here with a Winchester Model 70 .338-magnum elk rifle and about 200 rounds of ammunition, and would be delighted to entertain you. I will be home all weekend. Please feel free to stop out." David wasn't fooling; he had the weapon in his car for target shooting.

Anger was also directed at *The Progressive*, where the staff could not as readily threaten violence in a pinch. "One Saturday we were working and an old lady from Madison came in and started yelling and screaming," remembers Teri Terry. "I told her she was totally inappropriate and had to leave." In the middle of the night, somebody ripped open the garbage bags behind the magazine's office and went through its trash. Local television crews used their access to the office to rifle through desks. Harshly critical letters flowed in. "I hope the Government wins its case, as the First Amendment was never meant to cover irresponsibility of this kind," wrote one reader. Another correspondent called the suppressed article "a craven effort to gain publicity and subscribers. If I had a subscription, I'd cancel it." Knoll wrote back, commiserating with the man's misfortune: "It's always a good idea to subscribe, so you won't be caught in that predicament." In fact, the H-bomb story had little positive effect on *The Progressive*'s circulation. But it did make the magazine a more interesting place to work.

"It was so exciting," says Terry. "We worked seven days a week, hating to leave at night and rushing to get back the next morning. Erwin, Ron, Sam: They were in their glory. They all just fed on that kind of stuff." Knoll led the PR assault. "He'd give two speeches a day and really turn people around," says Terry, who often served as Knoll's driver, so he could write his speeches on the way. Knoll relished the attention, and he started to realize how good he was at handling it, having spent much of the last three decades as a reporter, asking other people questions. And Knoll was, under the glare of the cameras, a sight to behold, as Junkerman recalls: "He looked a bit like Arafat, with his goatee, his bad taste in ties, his wheezy voice, chain-smoking in-your-face New York attitude." He left quite an impression.

Morland, who during this time produced affidavits for the defense, wrote an op-ed column for *The New York Times* and a "My Turn" column for *Newsweek*, grew resentful of Knoll's efforts to grab the spotlight. Morland had been "appalled" by how Knoll had come across—defensive, equivocal and imprecise, he thought—during his initial spate of television appearances. Knoll's pronouncements, in "a public-speaking voice that seemed always to quiver with suppressed alarm," struck Morland as too sweeping, as when Knoll accused the Government of having a much larger agenda "to intimidate and throttle all news media and prevent informed discussion of urgent public questions."

Knoll, says Buell, felt that Morland "owed him more deference." Morland, in his own words, felt "this is *my* story." Knoll thought Morland would in time have ample opportunity to tell his part of the story. But while *The Progressive* faced the threat of an unprecedented injunction against publication on national-security grounds, Knoll did not want Morland to be speaking for the magazine. Knoll, saying Morland was unavailable, snatched Morland's invitation to appear live on "The Tom Snyder Show." Dan Rather of "60 Minutes" made tentative plans to fly to Madison for an interview that Saturday with Morland, but the segment was dumped when colleague Mike Wallace landed an interview with Yasir Arafat.

Morland's short leash in hand, Knoll took the lead in defending the magazine's public image. "The Government's assertions are demonstrably absurd," he wrote in an opinion column that appeared in *The Washington Post* and other papers. "The contention that an enterprise with *The Progressive*'s pathetically limited resources can penetrate the 'secrecy' of the nuclear establishment is, on its face, preposterous." He complained bitterly about the Government's censorship of affidavits, chastising its stated preference for the word "deletions": "I don't care if the Government calls it banana cream pie. It's still censorship." Knoll also responded publicly and privately to the article's critics, almost all of whom had not read it. He took especially strong exception to a column by James J. Kilpatrick, in which the syndicated arch-conservative warned that *The Progressive*'s First Amendment battle could lead to "a Supreme Court decision that will place judges in our pressrooms in disturbing new ways."

What Kilpatrick was really saying, Knoll surmised in reply, was that 'we had better not try to exercise our First Amendment rights lest his be jeopardized. I want to assure you that we are not prepared to take such a cavalier attitude toward Kilpatrick's First Amendment rights; we are prepared to defend them to the death." Elsewhere, Knoll railed against commentators who claimed that, given the current adverse climate, *The Progressive* ought not push the boundaries of press freedom, lest those boundaries be further constrained. "It never occurs to them, apparently," he wrote, "that their rhetoric is feeding the 'adverse climate' about which they profess to be concerned."

The U.S. Justice Department, meanwhile, was doing its best to create an adverse legal climate for *The Progressive*. On March 13, the prosecution obtained a protective order barring the defense from showing Morland's article to anyone who did not have a Government security clearance; the magazine would have to submit, at least 24 hours in advance, the names of any non-cleared scientist who wished to read the piece. Even *The Progressive*'s attorneys had to receive clearances before they could see documents submitted *in camera*. *The Progressive*'s editors refused to submit to clearances—as did several scientists from whom the defense sought affidavits—and consequently could not see these filings.

By that Friday, March 16, the Government had filed nine new affidavits, including three from Cabinet secretaries: James Schlesinger (DOE), Cyrus Vance (State Department), Harold Brown (Department of Defense). This batch of filings also included the first affidavit from Jack W. Rosengren, a nuclear consultant hired by the DOE. In this affidavit, which was put into the public record, Rosengren contended that "The Morland article goes far beyond any other publication in identifying the nature of the particular design used in the thermonuclear weapons in the U.S. stockpile." This design, he said, "is far superior in efficiency and practicality to any other known type of design." This hyperbolic (and untrue) contention not only violated but did violence to the Government's erstwhile policy of not commenting on the accuracy of information about nuclear weapons.

The Government's attorneys, in a memorandum seeking to counter the anticipated argument that the Atomic Energy Act is overly broad, made a key concession: "If the data [in Morland's article] were already available and in the public domain and well-known in the scientific community, it is difficult to see how the defendant could have reason to believe disclosure would injure the United States."

Knoll seized on this language, saying the data in Morland's article clearly fell in this category. Morland was charged with compiling a record of public-domain sources from which he drew information. Day set out to find scientists willing to read the piece and file affidavits. At first, Day encountered a wave of refusals. Then Ted Postol, his friend at the Argonne National Laboratory, led the way for other scientists with an affidavit declaring that any physicist who saw a copy of the diagram accompanying Edward Teller's article in the *Encyclopedia Americana* would arrive at the ideas and information in Morland's article "not within years, but within hours."

Day took a copy of Postol's affidavit on the road with him, as he met with scientists and academics who had agreed to read the article. But even though Day had given the Government the names, dates of birth, and Social Security numbers of the persons needing security clearances more than 24 hours in advance—long enough for a competent physicist to discern the secret of the H-bomb from a drawing in an encyclopedia—the clearances were not processed in time. Day found himself standing in the homes and offices of people who had agreed to read the article but lacked the security clearances that would make this legal. One evening, as the clock edged toward midnight and there was still no word from the Justice Department, Day showed the article to two California State University scientists in violation of the court order. Knoll, he says, approved of this breach, but it did little good, since the scientists could not refer to the article's content in their affidavits.

Day's trip did net one key affidavit, from a scientist who already had all the clearances needed: Hugh DeWitt of the Lawrence Livermore Laboratories, a major nuclear-weapons facility. Day gave DeWitt a sealed copy and watched him walk off into a sun-room and close the door. Three hours later DeWitt emerged ashen-faced, as Day recalls: "He said, 'This is the most damning story I can conceive of. You've totally violated national security and I can't give you an affidavit except to that effect.'" Day implored DeWitt to also read Postol's affidavit; two hours later, DeWitt handed Day a statement that powerfully affirmed the article's contention: that "after more than 25 years the H-bomb secret is not so secret anymore."

Like many scientists conducting research in restricted areas, DeWitt knew what information was secret; what he hadn't realized, until he saw Postol's citations of public-domain material, was how much secret information had become public knowledge. DeWitt's affidavit was the first to contend that, were Morland's article suppressed, it would not be long before some other reporter came across the same material. Other supportive affidavits, prepared with the help of the American Civil Liberties Union, soon issued from three of Postol's colleagues at Argonne National Laboratory. They said Morland's article would be "negligible or at most of minor consequence to the speed with which additional nations could succeed in developing thermonuclear weapons."

The most powerful defense testimony came from Ray E. Kidder, a top-ranking physicist at Livermore. Day, at DeWitt's instigation, met with Kidder on March 20, leaving him with a copy of Morland's article and the affidavit from DOE expert Jack Rosengren. On March 23, just three days before Judge Warren was to rule on the Government's request for a preliminary injunction, Day returned to collect Kidder's affidavit. Actually, Kidder had two affidavits, both of which he placed face up on a desk at the Livermore lab, showing just the signature lines to Day and a hired notary public. One of the affidavits, Kidder announced in a loud voice as a security guard looked on, contained classified information. He could sign the documents and then seal them in an envelope.

"That's it," the guard barked into a telephone. "He's turning over classified information!" The lab's security chief soon appeared and pointed out that Day was not authorized to carry classified information. This spurred a 24-hour standoff as attorneys in Washington and Madison bickered about how the affidavit might be returned to Madison in time for Monday's court hearing. In the end, it was decided that the classified affidavit could return to Madison accompanied by a security-cleared volunteer courier: Hugh DeWitt. He and Day caught the weekend's last plane back to Wisconsin.

Kidder's affidavits were devastating to the Government's case. He contended—and as a nuclear weapon's designer, he ought to know—that nothing in Morland's article would be of significant help to a nation desiring to acquire thermonuclear weapons. He also stated that Rosengren's public claims about the dead-on accuracy of Morland's H-bomb design were "misleading" and "factually in error." Kidder, in his *in camera* affidavit, said he didn't know of any weapon in the U.S. nuclear stockpile that works the way Morland's device is intended to work.

As it turned out, the Government censored parts of *both* Kidder affidavits, meaning that only *The Progressive*'s security-cleared attorneys—but not Knoll or the other defendants—could see them. The affidavits were, however, made available to Rosengren and DOE technical adviser William C. Grayson Jr., who that day responded with an affidavit attacking Kidder's contentions. The Government likewise suppressed large portions of affidavits from Postol, DeWitt, and Morland. Also censored were four of Morland's forty-seven exhibits of previously published material because these exhibits, including Morland's college physics textbook, contained underlining that the Government felt gave too much away. Morland had to go back over these textbook pages, whiting out his earlier transgressions.

The extension of censorship to such lengths was telling, in that it underscored a shift in the prosecution's approach. The Government was now contending that, even if all of the information in Morland's article could be found in public sources, its publication would still violate the Atomic Energy Act, because the article brought together more of this information in one place than had been done before. U.S. Attorney Tuerkheimer, one of a dozen Government lawyers signing filings in the case, refused to go along: "My signature never appears on any brief where that theory was advanced."

Officials at the DOE, meanwhile, quietly advanced another theory: that the disclosures in Morland's article smacked of sedition. At the core of this canon were prosecution affidavits submitted *in camera* by Rosengren and Grayson. These two names, Morland later mused, "would echo together throughout the case like those of Rosencrantz and Guildenstern throughout *Hamlet*." The pair set out to suggest, as well they could without any evidence, that Morland had unacknowledged access to Restricted Data. In a March 23 filing, Rosengren and Grayson argued that the fragmentary nature of Morland's narrative and the unexplained detail of his diagrams meant he must have had "a great deal of guidance from a person or persons with access to secret design information."

The Government topped off its case with an affidavit from renowned Cornell physicist Hans Bethe, the board chairman of *The Bulletin of The Atomic Scientists* whom Day had crossed swords with a few years before. Being on the Government's side came easy for Bethe. In 1950, the Atomic Energy Commission arrived at the offices of *Scientific American* just as its April issue containing an article by Bethe on atomic bombs went to press. AEC officials, having threatened legal action to block publication, destroyed the plates and burned 3,000 already-printed copies of the magazine. The DOE demanded four deletions in Bethe's piece, which had been previously cleared for publication. Three of these bits of information, it later emerged, had been previously published in *Scientific American*; the fourth was deliberately false technical data that Bethe put into the piece to throw the Russians off track. Gerald Piel, the magazine's publisher, was angered by the DOE's intrusion, but Bethe did not protest. In 1954, Bethe wrote a history of nuclear weapons development in which he called the hydrogen bomb a "calamity" and urged a global ban on testing and development. The AEC, upon review, stamped the piece "Secret" and suppressed it for decades. Bethe again raised no objection. He had, Knoll later wrote, a "sorry record of pusillanimous acquiescence in such blatant acts of political (not military) censorship."

By now, the public commentary on the case began to shift in favor of *The Progressive*. This, too, was no accident. In addition to the magazine's almost daily press releases and steady stream of opinion columns, Knoll and Carbon took a cue from the Government and sought to manipulate opinion behind the scenes. They journeyed to the Big Apple for a meeting with members of *The New York Times* editorial board, accompanied by attorney Floyd Abrams, who had defended the *Times* in the Pentagon Paper's case. That next Sunday, March 25, the lead editorial in the nation's newspaper of record came down squarely on *The Progressive*'s side, calling the Government's charges "lame in both logic and law. The shouts of alarm are more dangerous than the danger they describe.

"The Government," the editorial continued, "is doing its best to intimidate the Milwaukee judge and to incite the public against the magazine." The *Times* ridiculed the Government's claims that the article posed a threat to national security, as well as Judge Warren's worries about giving the H-bomb to Idi Amin: "The Ugandan dictator does not own the requisite atomic bomb; if he did, and for some unimaginable reason needed a hydrogen bomb too, he would presumably find it easy to recruit his own Howard Morland." The case against *The Progressive*, said the *Times*, "turns out to be a case against the national interest—against free speech and free inquiry." It stated—just as Knoll had argued, to Morland's distaste—that the Government was really seeking to vastly expand the parameters of its power: "[The Carter Administration] asks that all thought and discussion bearing on nuclear weapons be forever in its control, whether or not the information emanates from Government files and laboratories." The editorial praised *The Progressive*'s attempt "to prove that once-significant secrets no longer exist—and that Government controls aim to monopolize only policy judgments." The embarrassment and inconvenience this disclosure may cause the Government "plainly do not justify suspending the First Amendment."

On March 26, a second hearing was held at the federal Courthouse in Milwaukee. It was so crowded that Doris Knoll could not get inside. (Erwin had a reserved seat.) Howard Morland—fresh from an appearance that morning on the "Today" show—arrived at Judge Warren's court wearing the T-shirt he had printed in Honolulu, with its graphic depiction of a naked bomb. He wore it under a white dress shirt and tweed coat, and, just to be on the safe side, inside out, "so that even if I had my outer clothing torn off by a deranged groupie, I would still not have been guilty of violating the injunction that was likely to be issued."

Knoll and his co-defendants sat back in their seats and watched the drama play out. The essence of the two sides' cases was in the affidavits that had been submitted. Warren, one way or another, had already reached his decision. The hearing was mere theater.

Judge Warren began by acknowledging that he had on this issue gratefully received "all sorts of advice from lots of good Americans." He rattled off the names of various affiants—high-ranking Government officials on one side, dissident scientists on the other. Then he gave each side one hour to summarize its case.

Assistant Attorney General Thomas Martin represented the Government, as he had at the March 9th proceeding. He argued that the defendants wanted to publish information of the sort the Government had "always attempted to withhold"—albeit not always successfully. Under the Atomic Energy Act, Martin said, any information that the Government wanted to be secret was considered secret, no matter how easy it was to come by. Martin, in closing, urged Warren to err on the side of secrecy: "If the Government is wrong, this article will be delayed for another issue. If the Government is right and the injunction does not issue, the harm to the country will be staggering."

Next up was Earl Munson, for the defense. In comparison to the young, bearded Martin, the balding, owlish Munson seemed downright square. Holding up a volume of the *World Book* encyclopedia set that belonged to his nine-year-old daughter, Munson flipped it open to an article entitled, "How the Hydrogen Bomb Works." It was one of the unquestionably public sources from which Howard Morland had derived information. "And if Morland can find it, then by no stretch of the imagination" can its publication entail a catastrophic security breach, said Munson: "Sure as we are standing here, somebody else will duplicate what Morland did."

Munson argued that the Atomic Energy Act posed an unconstitutional constraint on freedom of thought and expression. He called the DOE's censorship "capricious," citing its decision to nearly halve the amount of Restricted Data it alleged to be in Morland's piece and its purging of affidavits from the public record. He charged that the Government had interfered with the magazine's defense, by requiring and then not processing security clearances. But the Justice Department, he asserted, was starting to realize the enormity of its mistake: "This is not John Mitchell's dream case. This is the Schlesinger-Brown nightmare. By placing its stamp of authenticity on Morland's article, the Government has called far more attention to the piece than *The Progressive* ever could have hoped."

After a round of rebuttals and a brief recess, Warren declared his intention to side with the Government—again. He felt the Government had "met the test" set by two justices in the Pentagon Papers case—namely, that publication would cause "grave, immediate, and irreparable harm." Warren conceded his comments at the March 9 hearing were overblown: "Does the article provide a do-it-yourself guide for the hydrogen bomb? Probably not." Building a hydrogen bomb requires "a large, sophisticated industrial capacity" and a "coterie of imaginative, resourceful scientists and technicians"—for starters. Still, the judge found that the article "*could possibly* provide sufficient information to allow a medium-sized nation to move faster" in building a bomb, because it "*could* provide a ticket to bypass blind alleys." He stated that "A mistake in ruling against the United States *could* pave the way for thermonuclear annihilation for us all." (Emphasis added.) Finally, Warren quarreled with *The Progressive*'s editorial judgment: "This court can find no reason why the public needs to know the technical details about hydrogen bomb construction to carry on an informed debate on this issue."

In fact, Warren's series of "coulds" showed he was ignoring the standard set in the Pentagon Papers case by Justice Potter Stewart, who said that only publication that "will surely result in direct, immediate, and irreparable damage" can be subject to prior restraint, and Justice William Brennan, who emphatically disallowed restraint "predicated upon surmise or conjecture that untoward consequences may result."

What Warren did was return to *Near v. Minnesota*'s narrow national security exemption—that the Government could in times of war curb First Amendment freedoms with regard to tactical information. And he found a way to blow this narrow exception wide open. "Times have changed significantly since 1931 when *Near* was decided," the judge observed. "Now war by foot soldiers has been replaced in large part by war by machines and bombs. No longer need there be any advance warning or preparation time before a nuclear war could be commenced." In other words, *Near*'s extremely narrow exception to the rule against prior restraint was, in the age of nuclear weapons, in place all the time.

For Knoll, this was always one of the case's key lessons—how the narrowest exception was interpreted as giving the Government sweeping powers. For him, it confirmed the wisdom of taking an absolutist position on the First Amendment. "When it comes to matters of fundamental freedom—and the First Amendment is our most fundamental freedom—even the narrowest of exceptions is too broad," Knoll would later say. "And when that narrow exception is based on claims of possible adverse effect on 'national security,' the likelihood of abuse is so great that it becomes unavoidable."

Judge Warren gave *The Progressive* one last chance to submit to voluntary censorship, by letting a mediation panel decide what information should be cut. The judge, in seeking to force this resolution, noted that the magazine did not have "the blessing of the entire press" to continue its fight: "Many elements of the press see grave risk of permanent damage to First Amendment freedoms if this case goes forward."

Warren called a recess to let the defense think things over. Sinykin urged his clients to think carefully; to pursue the case further would mean, at the very least, monumental legal bills. Knoll argued, persuasively, that any agreement to compromise would undercut the magazine's ability to raise funds for a serious First Amendment fight. The court reconvened, Earl Munson "respectfully" declined the mediation offer, and Judge Robert W. Warren issued his edict: *The Progressive* and its "agents, servants, and attorneys" were henceforth barred, pending further litigation, from "publishing or otherwise communicating, transmitting, or disclosing in any manner any information designated by the Secretary of Energy as 'Restricted Data.' " They were also ordered, within five days, to round up or otherwise account for all known copies of Morland's article. It was, in Warren's words, "the first instance of prior restraint against a publication in this fashion in the history of this country." He said he did not covet the "notoriety."

Knoll and Morland liked the notoriety fine. They burst from Warren's courtroom to meet the press. Morland says he had just assumed his rightful place before a phalanx of cameras and was about to mention he was wearing a forbidden H-bomb drawing on his T-shirt "when Knoll appeared at the other end of the steps, and the whole crowd of reporters abandoned me for him." Knoll knew just what to say: "When the Founders framed the First Amendment they did not put it out for mediation. . . ." From Erwin Knoll's point of view, the battle was just beginning. Now, more than ever, he was certain he would win.

Photo by Glenn Trudell, courtesy State Historical Society of Wisconsin.

Facing the microphones with Howard Morland; looking on, Bruce Ennis.

CHAPTER TWELVE

It Blows Up

"The presumption against prior restraint is so strong, there are very few cases on the subject," wrote Ellen Alderman and Caroline Kennedy (the daughter of JFK) in their 1991 book, *In Our Defense: The Bill Of Rights In Action*, which featured *The Progressive* case in its discussion of the First Amendment. "In the rare instance where the Government does seek to impose a prior restraint, the case is hurried through the judicial process in an uncharacteristically feverish fashion, leaving important issues in somewhat of a blur." And how.

In *Near v. Minnesota*, the U.S. Supreme Court tried to show how hard it was to justify prior restraint and ended up giving Government a tool it would use in *United States v. New York Times Co.* (the Pentagon Papers case) to seek suppression of information on the war in Vietnam. In that case, the Supreme Court emphatically declared that the Government's desire to avoid embarrassment did not justify prior restraint. Still, even this ruling's extraordinarily high threshold—that prior restraint could be imposed only if publication "will surely result in direct, immediate, and irreparable damage" to the national interest—was soon taken by the Government and affirmed by Federal Judge Robert W. Warren of Milwaukee as allowing the Government to censor even the "original work product" of an amateur H-bomb researcher who had no access to classified information.

Before *The Progressive* case was over, the Government would exercise—and seek to expand—this newfound authority several more times, in alternately frightening and comical ways. As its case began to self-destruct, the Government sought to contain the blast. But these efforts served mainly to reflect attention back to the core of its problem—the weakness of its case. The media and scientific community redirected this destructive power inward long enough to create an even more powerful—and embarrassing—explosion of events.

In the end, the Government was forced to abandon its case—like Nixon his presidency—in disgrace. Still, the liberal Carter Administration proved that prior restraint could be done. As the case progressed, the Government's prosecutors imposed ever-more-onerous constraints on the defense. It was a bare-knuckled, high-stakes fight, and although he emerged from it with his right to publish intact, Erwin Knoll for the rest of his life wished he had done things differently. He wished he had defied his attorneys and asserted his right to publish by publishing, not by filing affidavits in federal court. "For those six months and nineteen days," he said, "I allowed myself to be stripped of my First Amendment rights and I would never do that again."

Knoll was between the rock of his beliefs and the hard place of his promises: Having pledged early on to respect the authority of the courts, he couldn't very well declare that authority illegitimate now that a federal judge had twice ruled against him. And yet, as a First Amendment absolutist, Knoll firmly believed that no judge had the right to tell him what he could or couldn't print. Although he successfully resisted the urge to engage in defiance that might undermine the magazine's defense, Knoll found the experience of being a censored man agonizing. "The lawyers were right," he later said. "They advised us correctly. My error was in following their advice."

But as he left Judge Warren's courtroom on March 26, 1979, Knoll needed to focus on a more immediate concern. That Monday was, by chance, the production deadline for *The Progressive*'s May issue. The magazine had readied reams of copy from the public portions of the court record, printed commentary, and letters to the editor. But only one longer article was ready. It had been edited, fact-checked, illustrated, set in type, proofread and laid out on page boards. It was Morland's story, the one that couldn't run.

The 68-page May issue went to press, a few days behind schedule, filled with articles about the Government's suppression of Morland's article. Knoll wrote the lead story, "Born Secret," which laid out the history of the case. "We intend to resist the Government's attempt at censorship," Knoll announced. "We will appeal Judge Warren's preliminary injunction to the Court of Appeals and, if necessary, to the U.S. Supreme Court. We will somehow find the resources to sustain our struggle. And we will win." Morland and Day wrote about their respective roles—Morland mapping out his H-bomb odyssey, Day examining the scientific community's alternately hostile and supportive response. The magazine published strong testimonials from Ralph Nader and Ramsey Clark. "Our present policy of secrecy is a fatal abdication of founding principle," wrote Clark, formerly U.S. Attorney General under President Johnson. "It is only a matter of time before proliferation leads to destruction. Failure to understand this leads to reliance on secrecy rather than development of international systems of prevention and control based on law."

Things were looking up for *The Progressive*. Most of the nation's newspapers now supported the magazine's right to publish. *The New York Times* came down like a ton of Uranium-235 on Warren's ruling of March 26, calling it "not only unconstitutional but also unnecessary, arbitrary, and ill-informed," and on Judge Warren: "He yielded in the end to the authority of distinguished Government witnesses whose policy judgments he felt too ignorant to dispute. He thus became just one more victim of a system of secrecy that permits the cry of 'national security' to overwhelm our most precious safeguards against suppression of speech. . . . Is it too much to expect the courts to see through the scare-talk?"

The Progressive's PR battle got another, less welcome boost March 28, when the Three Mile Island nuclear power plant in Pennsylvania experienced a near-catastrophic accident. Here was further proof that Government assurances about nuclear technology were frightfully unreliable. As the catastrophe unfolded, members of the Federal Nuclear Regulatory Commission met in secret to decide what, if anything, to tell the people in the area whose lives were in danger. As the mood turned to near panic, the commission chair announced, "Which amendment is it that guarantees freedom of the press? Well, I'm against it."

Despite Knoll's confidence, winning before the Seventh Circuit of the U.S. Court of Appeals in Chicago was no sure thing. The Government continued to have vastly superior resources, and the defense still labored under unprecedented constraints. For both reasons, the offer of the American Civil Liberties Union to get involved in the case was eagerly accepted. It was agreed that defendants Knoll and Day would be represented by the ACLU, Morland would keep his own attorney, and *The Progressive* would still be represented by LaFollette & Sinykin. "I consider [this] to be one of the most significant free-speech cases of the decade," declared ACLU Legal Director Bruce Ennis in an April 4 letter to his clients, detailing the defense's strategy. "[It's] the most important case on the docket of the national ACLU."

Ennis's dense, nine-page letter also discusses whether the defense ought to take an absolutist position with regard to the First Amendment. This, he noted, was a risky thing to do, since the Appellate Court is bound by decisions of the Supreme Court, which had in both *Near* and *New York Times* recognized exceptions to the rule against prior restraint. "I understand that both of you [Knoll and Day] would feel comfortable in taking the absolutist position, but that you would both also be willing to forego that position if we, as your attorneys, conclude that it would be tactically unwise." If the case did go to the Supreme Court, which has free reign to reexamine earlier decisions, taking an absolutist position might be advisable. For now, Ennis wrote, the defense would argue that "the Government has not made a case for prior restraint even under the exception mentioned in the Pentagon Papers case."

Knoll was happy with his new attorneys, and wouldn't have minded terribly if the old ones went away. Earl Munson, says Sam Day, became extremely territorial, at one point remarking, "I'll be damned if the ACLU is going to run this case from the Georgetown cocktail circuit." Sinykin also insisted that his law firm stay involved, in part because of his distrust for Knoll. The ACLU, like Morland's attorney, worked *pro bono*, with the defense reimbursing actual costs. LaFollette & Sinykin represented *The Progressive* first for $65 an hour, then $50 an hour, about half its usual rate. Still, the legal bills added up, by Knoll's calculator, to a grand total of $248,000. For years afterwards, as *The Progressive* paid off its debt to LaFollette & Sinykin at the rate of $2,000 a month, there was resentment within the magazine over the law firm's costly involvement.

That spring, Morland's resentment of Knoll was reaching critical mass. Knoll continued to take what he felt was his rightful role in defending *The Progressive* and the First Amendment. Morland was starting to feel used. He had spent more than $2,000 of his own money running down the story of how H-bombs are made. He had been paid only $500, half of what was promised. Knoll and Day used his article, he believed, to goad the DOE into a confrontation, the point of which had little to do with how H-bombs are made. And now Knoll was trying to crowd him out of the glory.

On the morning of April 17, Morland met with Knoll and Ron Carbon in New York City. Morland had gotten an agent, and was in town to pitch the idea of his writing a book. Knoll and Carbon were also hawking a book proposal, and they wanted Morland to write part of it. Morland complained that *The Progressive* had left him to fend for himself, and hadn't even paid him fully for the piece. Knoll, unaware that the magazine still owed Morland money, promised that this matter would be promptly resolved. (It was.) He also offered Morland the use of the magazine's agent for booking speaking gigs. But now it was time to get going.

"Where?" Morland asked. "To the ACLU." Morland tagged along to the ACLU's East 40th Street office, where the trio met with Charles Sims, one of the attorneys on the case. Morland was talking with Sims as everyone got on the elevator to leave. Knoll asked Morland where he was going. Morland said he'd just keep tagging along. Knoll directed him back upstairs to talk to Ennis. Morland later learned where the group had gone—a "Conference on *The Progressive* Case" sponsored by the prestigious Alicia Patterson Foundation. Among the twenty-nine participants: media heavies John Chancellor of NBC, Ben Bradlee of *The Washington Post*, and Lewis Lapham of *Harper's*, as well as former Rear Admiral Gene LaRocque, Hodding Carter III of the U.S. State Department, and Pentagon Papers attorney Floyd Abrams. Bradlee found his place among the article's critics, which is where he still stands. "Here was Erwin's problem," he says. "He was hustling this [article] as a great revelation involving national security. His defense was that it wasn't. He couldn't have it both ways."

Also giving Knoll a hard time at the conference was *The Washington Post*'s Walter Pincus, who recounted how *The Progressive*'s editors sent the diagrams, and later Morland's article, to the DOE.

"They were *asking* for the Government to do something," he said. "This was a series of provocations that led to prior restraint." Knoll disputed this interpretation: "We did not ask for permission to publish this article." And he warned that if the Government prevailed in its case against *The Progressive*, "every editor at this table can expect all too soon to be subjected to similar constraints."

Morland, who would have "traveled a thousand miles" to be a spectator at this event, learned he would have been welcomed as a panelist, had the organizers known he could attend. When the trio returned, Morland asked where they had been. Carbon presented him with a list of conference attendees; Morland "felt like punching him in the face." Six days later, Knoll and Carbon were back in New York, and met with Morland. He declined to cooperate with the proposed book, which he felt focused on "how they got a dumbshit reporter to do the job for them just to show how easy it was." He also again decried his exclusion from the Patterson event. Knoll said nothing. Afterwards, Morland learned that the *The Nation* magazine was hosting a forum on the case that very night. The organizers were happy to include him but, as before, hadn't known he was available. Six days later, the American Society of Newspaper Editors held its national convention in New York; Knoll accepted an invitation to speak; Morland wasn't told about it.

"Fame," Morland reflects. "Erwin loved it. He and I both got addicted to it and there wasn't enough of it to share." Carbon feels this is too simplistic, that "different perspectives" and "substantive issues" separated the two men. Day says all the media attention "went to Erwin's head and Howard's head and Ron's head. They were just exulting too much in the publicity. They were not sufficiently humble or matter-of-fact about it." This, says Day, became a source of discord within the magazine: "We showed a lot of human foibles during that time."

So did the Government. That April, the DOE produced a "psycholinguistic" analysis of Morland's article, diagrams, and captions. Various experts concluded, with varying degrees of certainty, that Morland had outside help in preparing these materials. The experts, in studying word choices and style, found clear evidence of multiple authorship. In fact, multiple authorship of articles was and is a common practice at *The Progressive*, except there they have another name for it: editing. Had the Government bothered to ask, the magazine would have admitted that Morland's article was extensively rewritten by Sam Day, with additional tinkering by the whole editorial staff. The experts also garnered from these collectively written materials insights into Morland's "personality traits." "There are elements of grandiosity and concreteness in his thinking," wrote one expert, whose name is blacked out. "His reasoning style is loose, repetitive, coercive, not fully controlled nor cogent, and suggestive of innuendoes and indirect allegations." All of these internal speculations were classified as Restricted Data. They first came to light in 1988, in response to Knoll's request under the U.S. Freedom of Information Act.

Morland, who perhaps coincidentally fit much of this expert's description, already had plenty to worry about in Judge Warren's order that the defense collect or account for all known copies of Morland's work. Knoll had pointed out the Government's apparent lack of concern about this material, which it claimed was so sensitive the defense could not show it to anyone lacking a security clearance. This was a fine argument for Knoll to make, since the magazine's copies were safely in hand. But Morland, prior to Warren's restraining order, had been "distributing copies to all and sundry like autumn leaves." Morland, after calls of apology, provided the Government with a list of recipients; soon FBI agents showed up at their homes. But many people who relinquished the article also replicated it. To not covet possession of such a secret is against human nature. The Knolls kept their copy page-by-page in Doris's book of sheet music for Beethoven's *Moonlight Sonata.* Music books, she explains, won't shed hidden documents when shaken—something the Knolls suspected might happen in their home.

The hardest leaves to collect were those blowing across the continent of Australia, the homeland of Dr. Helen Caldicott, an antinuclear physician who had crossed paths with Morland in Honolulu. Two U.S. Government officials, including William Grayson of the DOE, were dispatched to the Land Down Under, rakes in hand. One copy had been given to an Australian newspaper, prompting an urgent communication from the DOE to the Criminal Investigation

Division of the FBI. The U.S. Government asked that publication be suppressed, and the Australian government complied. The Carter Administration was exercising censorship on a global scale.

Copies of Morland's articles and diagrams (including the one he had printed on a T-shirt) were locked up, along with defense affidavits deemed too sensitive for the defendants to see, in file cabinets at LaFollette & Sinykin. In late April, the Government said this was not good enough; thereafter, all documents (and T-shirts) containing Restricted Data in the law office had to be kept in a special safe, wired to a private security firm. Was the office maybe "wired" in other ways as well? "From my point of view, I couldn't care less," says attorney Munson. "We were arguing that everything was open."

Everything was. *Milwaukee Sentinel* reporter Joe Manning spent a week researching nuclear weapons, using only materials available in public libraries in Milwaukee and Waukegan, Illinois. His findings were published on April 30 and May 1, under the respective headlines, "H-bomb's secrets are few" and "H-bomb material readily accessible." The latter article referred to recent speculation, in a magazine called *Fusion*, about the nature of that Great Secret, the Teller-Ulam Idea. "Teller and Ulam," Manning wrote, "may have come up with some sort of arrangement that would compress the fuel through the use of soft x-rays from the atomic bomb blast reflected off the bomb casing wall." The DOE privately concluded, in a letter to the Justice Department requesting an FBI probe, that Manning obtained access to this information "either by reviewing parts of the Morland article or from another source familiar with the *in camera* documents subject to [Judge Warren's] Protective Order." In reaching this conclusion, the DOE ignored Manning's stated and credible explanation—that he got this information from reading *Fusion* magazine.

The article in *Fusion*'s March 1979 issue ran with an editor's note anticipating that DOE Secretary James Schlesinger would declare its contents classified, and perhaps prosecute. The point of this article, like Morland's, was that none of these things was really secret. In 1976, *Fusion* reported, distinguished Russian physicist L.I. Rudakov gave lectures at several U.S. laboratories about topics that could not be publicly discussed by scientists in the United States.

Rather than question the wisdom of maintaining official secrecy toward ideas discussed freely by scientists of the nation the United States most wanted to keep secrets from, the DOE responded by classifying Rudakov's work in the United States, and even confiscating a blackboard on which he had written.

Fusion was the organ of the Fusion Energy Society, a right-wing outfit that believed only the conspiratorial hand of Government impeded progress toward a future of unlimited fusion energy too cheap to meter. The group would provide a friend-of-the-court brief in support of *The Progressive*. An even stranger bedfellow was Lyndon LaRouche's lunatic fringe U.S. Labor Party, which contended in a press release that *The Progressive* case was a hoax plotted by the U.S. Council on Foreign Relations "to further stifle scientific research and development by increasing scientific classification" with the aim of destroying technological progress and paving the way for global war. The release also said the Council "deliberately sabotaged" Three Mile Island to give nuclear power a bad name.

Knoll, during this time, traveled extensively, speaking about the case. He got better at it as time went on, says *Madison Press Connection* reporter John Junkerman. "Erwin realized he could editorialize, extemporaneously, with a great deal of verbal relish and insight. He knew Washington, he knew the media, he knew how the world operated, so he knew how to cut to the quick."

As *The Progressive* case was being appealed to the Seventh Circuit in Chicago, arguments and evidence continued to be filed in Judge Warren's District Court. An affidavit from DOE classification chief John Griffin claimed the Morland article revealed three highly secret H-bomb concepts: separate stages (of fission and then fusion reactions), what Morland called radiation pressure (actually radiation coupling), and compression (of the fusion fuel). The security-cleared defense team set out to show that each of these concepts was already in the public domain. To this end, it submitted the articles from *Fusion* and *Milwaukee Sentinel* and the Teller diagram as it appeared in *The New York Times* and *The Washington Post*. The Government blocked these filings—available in most public libraries—from the public record.

Despite such exertions, the DOE was proving far more adept at spilling secrets than keeping them. On April 25, the four Argonne National Laboratory scientists who had filed briefs in support of *The Progressive* wrote a letter to U.S. Senator John Glenn, the chair of a subcommittee overseeing national security. In it, the scientists—Ted Postol, Alexander DeVolpi, Gerald Marsh, and George Stanford—complained about the Government's own inconsistency and negligence in letting Restricted Data into the public domain. First, the Government allowed Postol's affidavit to make specific reference to the diagram accompanying Edward Teller's 1976 *Encyclopedia Americana* article, which resulted in the publication of this diagram in newspapers throughout the land. The censors also let DOE consultant Jack Rosengren contend, in a public affidavit, that Morland's article revealed "the nature of the particular design used in the thermonuclear weapons in the U.S. stockpile"—a conspicuous departure from the Government's age-old policy of not commenting on speculations regarding nuclear weapons.

"We believe that this deplorable mishandling or misuses of secured information should be investigated at the Congressional level," the scientists wrote. "The Government's confirmation of the general accuracy of the Morland article might be a conscious attempt to influence the outcome of the case by increasing the apparent sensitivity of Morland's information in hopes of establishing a legal precedent for prior restraint." The scientists, for a full month ignored by Glenn, scattered copies of their letter like Morland's autumn leaves.

On May 8, a twenty-three-year-old Harvard student named Dimitri Rotow found, on the shelves of the Los Alamos Scientific Library, a declassified report known as UCRL-4725. A year earlier, Rotow had stumbled upon another sensitive document at the library, prompting a security review. Now, at Morland's suggestion, the ACLU hired Rotow to try his luck again. This time he struck the jackpot: UCRL-4725 gave research data about the yield, weight, and configurations of actual H-bombs. And it had been, for nearly four years, on the shelves and in the card catalog of a public library that had, during just the last two years of this document's availability, received 590 foreign visitors from 52 countries. The DOE immediately shut down the library to launch a document-by-document search of the shelves.

How significant a disclosure was UCRL-4725? Rotow, an amateur H-bomb designer, in mid-May told the *Chicago Sun-Times* that the 29-page report was more revealing "by a factor of 100" than the suppressed Morland article: "There is even a description here of how to fill the empty spaces of the bomb canister with foam." "We have egg on our faces," admitted Joseph K. Brattan, head of the DOE's nuclear weapons program. Rotow had sent copies of the report to the ACLU, *The Progressive*, and two newspapers. One of the papers, *The Washington Star,* refused the DOE's demand for this document, giving it instead to Senator Glenn, who was horrified by the breach and ordered a high-level probe.

The UCRL-4725 leak badly undermined the Government's case. The defense filed a motion asking Judge Warren to reconsider and vacate his earlier decision in light of this new evidence. More scientists came forth to deny there was anything secret about the concepts the DOE was seeking to suppress. The media scoffed at the Government's position, and briefs in support of *The Progressive* flowed in from major newspapers and media groups. More embarrassing still, the Government's own attorneys sought to abandon ship. Frank Tuerkheimer, the U.S. Attorney for Western Wisconsin, laid out his arguments for doing so in a May 25 letter to U.S. Attorney General Griffin Bell. The Justice Department, in response to an FOI request, says this document has been destroyed.

Bell disregarded Tuerkheimer's advice, purportedly making disparaging remarks about Tuerkheimer in the process. Shortly thereafter, Bell relates in his book, "the entire team of Justice Department lawyers assigned to *The Progressive* matter, with the backing of Deputy Attorney General [Benjamin R.] Civeletti" also urged him to drop the case. Bell refused. "Our case is now weakened, but . . . the public interest and Atomic Energy Act require that we do our best," he wrote on June 3. "By going forward, even if we lose, we support the national security, the law (i.e., the Atomic Energy Act), and we enhance the First Amendment by keeping it from being used as a suicide provision—as the great majority of the media recognize. There is sometimes honor in taking a weak position."

It was maybe not just honor but also his hide that Bell was seeking to protect by pressing forward with a badly wounded case. For years, there were ongoing disputes between the Justice Department, which was vested with the sole authority to litigate on behalf of Government agencies, and those agencies, especially the DOE, which craved autonomy in this area. For Attorney General Bell to spurn DOE Secretary James Schlesinger's forcefully presented litigation demand would have been tantamount to a declaration of inter-Cabinet war.

As it happened, the DOE was deeply frustrated by its inability to persuade the FBI—an agency not known for its vigilance in protecting civil liberties—to go after Morland, Knoll, Day, DeWitt, Manning, and Chuck Hansen, a nuclear-weapons buff who had begun expressing his views on the case in letters to members of Congress. On May 29, the DOE appealed directly to FBI Director William M. Webster, sending along its psycholinguistic analysis of the article "allegedly prepared by Howard Morland." But the FBI would not get on board.

Hansen, a thirty-two-year-old employee of a California aerospace firm that built communications satellites, had for years been scouring public sources to learn what he could about nuclear weapons. When *The Progressive* case broke, he read through the public filings, looked up the referenced public-domain literature, and, just as the Argonne scientists had indicated could be done, pieced together a coherent if not exactly correct understanding of the concepts underlying H-bomb design. Hansen concluded, as had *The Progressive*, that the DOE was misusing claims about nuclear secrecy.

Curiously, records of DOE involvement released years after the fact indicate that the Government spent far less energy rounding up copies of UCRL-4725 than it did trying to contain the next outbreak: the letter that the four Argonne scientists had sent to Senator Glenn. On May 25, after the Rotow revelation made the issue fashionable, Glenn wrote Postol, saying he was passing the scientists' letter to the DOE with a request that it formally respond. It did—by classifying the letter. But by this time the letter had been sent to newspapers across the country. DeWitt, a security-cleared scientist, had sent Hansen a copy just hours before learning the letter had been classified. This accidental breach led to a letter of reprimand being placed in DeWitt's file and a request from his boss at Livermore that the FBI investigate DeWitt for "probable illegal activities." The FBI declined, and DeWitt later got the letter removed from his file. Hansen also gave a copy of the letter to his representative in Congress, Republican Paul N. McCloskey, who issued a statement saying that "absolutely nothing in the letter is confidential and there is no imaginable justification for classifying it."

The DOE had more imagination—and, ultimately, more egg on its face. During the week beginning Monday, June 11, the agency sent stern letters to *The Progressive*, the ACLU, and a half-dozen newspapers from the *San Jose Mercury News* to *The Washington Post* that had received the Glenn letter, warning that it contained Restricted Data and that "criminal penalties" attached to its "unlawful dissemination." All copies were ordered returned to the DOE or placed in "proper storage." Then, on June 13, the Glenn letter was published by *The Daily Californian*, a Berkeley student paper. It would soon be reprinted in college newspapers across the land.

The Progressive case had become a First Amendment *cause célèbre*. Knoll and Morland were in hot demand; the day the Glenn letter was printed, they appeared together on "The Phil Donahue Show." Knoll's family watched excitedly from their McFarland home. Other media began running thoughtful articles on the case, and Knoll was quoted often. "The mystique of secrecy is something they protect more jealously than the secrets themselves," he told the *Columbia Journalism Review*. "So long as we have that mystique, it is possible for a tight little group—the guardians of secrets—to make policy in this terribly important area and to exclude the rest of us from having a say in that policy. To say the secrets aren't secret is to say the emperor has no clothes."

Even if the emperor was buck naked, he still had Warren in his court. The judge on June 15 denied the defense's motion to vacate the injunction, overlooking overwhelming evidence that the three secret concepts identified by the DOE were all in the public domain. Knoll and the other defendants were not allowed to attend the hearing held on this issue, nor could they read the decision it produced. Both were deemed secret.

Warren, to this day, thinks he did the right thing. He says that, throughout the case, "I wasn't sure where the truth stood" and "didn't trust either side in terms of what they were saying." Wasn't it apparent that the Government's claims were overblown? "I think the Government did overstate its case," says Warren, admitting that, as a "hick judge from Wisconsin" (his term), he had been especially impressed with the affidavit from Dr. Edward Teller, who he remembers meeting way back when. (Warren may be thinking of Hans Bethe; Teller did not file an affidavit in the case.) Now, he realizes, "I didn't get a straight showing of the cards by the Government. Apparently, some of that same stuff was in that library down in Los Alamos." But Warren nonetheless sided with the Government. The fate of the case now rested with the Court of Appeals.

On Friday, July 13, the defense submitted its brief to the appellate court. That evening, a capacity crowd of 3,000 gathered at the UW-Madison Stock Pavilion for a fund-raiser and rally in support of *The Progressive*. The event, organized in cooperation with the *Madison Press Connection*, featured folk-singer Pete Seeger and folk-entertainer John Henry Faulk. The audience got to hear Sid Lens call Schlesinger "a fascist."

The Government's brief, filed August 7, advanced a new claim—that "technical information" was not "an essential part of any exposition of ideas" and hence was, like obscenity, beyond the protections of the First Amendment. It was a breathtakingly broad argument, and it further weakened the Government's position.

Hansen, meanwhile, announced that he was sponsoring a "Design the H-Bomb Contest," with a promised $200 prize for the first H-bomb schematic to be classified by the DOE. His aim: to "annoy and harass humorless DOE classification officers." He received entries from a physics graduate student at Berkeley and a high-school student in San Jose. He passed these on to the DOE, which tried and failed to get the FBI to investigate Hansen for conspiracy to violate the Atomic Energy Act of 1954.

On August 27, Hansen set forth his objections to the Government's "purely political" case against *The Progressive* in an 18-page, single-spaced letter to Senator Charles Percy of Illinois. Hansen attacked the DOE's double standard in suppressing the Glenn letter while doing nothing to prevent truly monumental breaches committed by three of its favored consultants: Teller, whose published diagram gave away much of the H-bomb secret; Ted Taylor, a physicist who in 1974 assented to a series of uncleared interviews that resulted in John McPhee's book, *The Curve of Binding Energy* (Taylor reportedly received a reprimand); and MIT Professor George Rathjens, for his recorded contacts and alleged help to Morland. Hansen also speculated as to the nature of the Teller-Ulam Idea and the concepts underlying H-bomb design. He provided a bomb schematic with two fission (A-bomb) triggers, one on each end, which would somehow be timed to go off at the same instant, compressing the fusion fuel between them.

When the DOE on September 7 received a copy of the technical portions of this letter, submitted by Hansen for "classification review," it didn't bother to respond. But five days later, when the DOE learned that the same information had, along with Hansen's critical comments about the DOE's behavior, been sent in a letter to a U.S. Senator, they classified the letter. "In a sense," quipped Hansen at the time, "I won my own contest." Government agents showed up at Percy's office and Hansen's home, demanding surrender of all copies. There was a familiar problem: By this time the letter had been sent to seven newspapers, including the *Wall Street Journal,* the *Chicago Tribune* and *The Daily Californian*. The Government dispatched a flurry of warnings to these recipients, asserting that the letter contained Restricted Data. But, as its desperation showed, the Government's case was blowing up.

On September 13, the Seventh Circuit Court of Appeals in Chicago heard oral arguments on *The Progressive* case. The Government's request that the arguments be heard in secret had been denied, and the courtroom was packed. The panel of three appellate court judges took a skeptical view of the Government's claims. Judge Wilbur Pell Jr. at one point told Justice Department attorney Tom Martin, who had just delivered a paean to the Atomic Energy Act, "In candor, I'd be more impressed if you were just trying to keep secret our secret. But you're keeping the whole world's secrets, aren't you, under this act." Martin was forced to concede the point. Judge Walter Cummins, meanwhile, proved how hard it was to keep track of what was and what wasn't secret when he accidently mentioned the articles by Joe Manning, which had been declared off-limits. His slip occasioned a media feeding frenzy for copies of Manning's hitherto overlooked series.

Knoll was certain the appellate panel would come down strongly against Warren's decision, vindicating *The Progressive* and giving future courts yet another clear precedent for rejecting prior restraint. At a press conference afterwards, Knoll summed up the Government's case: "The Atomic Secrets Act says the Department of Energy should decide what is secret and we'll decide what is secret and we decided this is secret, so trust us." His hope and expectation was that "the court will sneer at this." But a funny thing—actually, a few of them—happened instead.

CHAPTER THIRTEEN

Victory

Of all the known recipients of Chuck Hansen's letter to Senator Percy, the one the Government was most worried about was *The Daily Californian*. The Berkeley student paper had defiantly printed the Argonne scientists' "classified" letter to Senator John Glenn. Now it was refusing to give the Department of Energy's leak-moppers the absolute assurances they sought that Hansen's letter would not be published. On Saturday, September 15, the Government of the United States went into a federal district court and obtained a judicial restraint against publication under the Atomic Energy Act of 1954, something that had happened only once before, to Erwin Knoll and *The Progressive*. Just as Judge Warren had six months earlier bollixed *The Progressive*'s plans to publish Howard Morland's H-bomb article, California Judge Robert H. Schancke barred *The Daily Californian* from publishing or otherwise communicating Hansen's letter.

News of this latest spasm of censorship rocked the *Madison Press Connection*. That Saturday morning, the strike paper had come out with a story under the banner headline, "H-bomb papers obtained by PC." The article by John Junkerman did not say how these papers were obtained. The *Madison Press Connection* was not among seven papers known by the Government to have received the letter, and all day long the paper's staff half-expected that the door would burst open to reveal the grim visages of federal marshals in search of the forbidden document.

At noon, the *Press Connection* staff met to discuss what to do with Hansen's letter. By this time, the national media were scornful of the DOE's censorship campaign. Several other recipients pointedly refused to give the letter up. "We are deeply troubled," declared Stanton R. Cook, publisher of the *Chicago Tribune*. "We will use all necessary resources to prevent the Government from harassing private citizens and members of the media." The *Press Connection* staff decided to publish Hansen's letter on Monday, its next scheduled issue.

That afternoon, word came that the Government was moving against *The Daily Californian*. The paranoia level at the *Press Connection* reached critical mass, and the idea was hatched to run the article sooner, in a special Sunday edition. Ron McCrea, the paper's editor, was out of the office when these discussions began. By the time he returned late that afternoon, printers and editorial staffers were being called in for the task. McCrea headed to the bar in the building's basement. He had a martini (or two), and pondered his options: "Either go upstairs right now and resign or else accept the possibility of being tied up in a court case and conceivably going to prison. It was one of those real moments of truth: 'Are you willing to go to prison for the First Amendment?' I decided I was."

So were a lot of other people. The tiny office was jammed with activity. Between the hours of 6 p.m. and 2 a.m., the staff, racing against the still-anticipated arrival of the federal marshals, put together a special eight-page edition. McCrea came up with the letter's headline, "A citizen writes to a senator." "This had to be as understated and unsensational as possible," he says. "We knew it was explosive. We wanted to make sure our sense of responsibility showed through in every stick of type." The *Press Connection* also ran a front-page editorial about its decision to print the letter, and an article about the Government's crackdown on *The Daily Californian*. The page boards were sped to the paper's printer in Stoughton, which published 8,000 copies, two-thirds the usual press run. Volunteers made early morning drops at the usual outlets. Then everyone went home, and waited for the sky to crack open.

It did, but not right away. The *Press Connection*'s publication of the Hansen letter was noted in articles the next day, along with the *Chicago Tribune*'s declaration of its intention to publish excerpts later that week unless taken to court. (*The Capital Times* of Madison also planned to publish Hansen's letter in its Monday edition.)

Knoll applauded the strike paper: "I thought it was a splendid thing for the *Press Connection* to do." Indeed, the paper did precisely what Knoll, in retrospect, wished he'd done: assert the right to publish through an act of publication.

But the consequences were horrific. On the afternoon of Monday, September 17, the Justice Department held a press conference to declare that it was dropping its lawsuits against *The Progressive* and *The Daily Californian* because "the publication of an article containing Restricted Data . . . by a newspaper in Madison" had rendered the issue moot. That's when the sky cracked open.

The tiny *Madison Press Connection* was deluged with media attention, much of it negative and sensational. "It was a zoo," says McCrea. "The national television networks came in. We were inundated. It was an incredible media onslaught. We received many really hateful calls and death threats." Junkerman, for his part, hid from the media: "I was afraid if I talked to them they'd find out I was the one" who had obtained the Hansen letter—and start asking how. Junkerman had good reason to be afraid. Whoever passed the letter on to the *Press Connection* had committed a clear violation of the Atomic Energy Act.

The Progressive claimed victory. "We are obviously delighted that this attempt to deprive Americans of information to which they are fully entitled has been beaten back," said Knoll, before popping open the champagne for photographs that would appear around the world. "We hope the Government will think a long, hard time before it mounts this kind of censorship again." Knoll said the magazine was "looking to see if we can prevent" the Government from getting off without a court decision.

Privately, Knoll and the other defendants were bitterly disappointed. Even Judge Warren, semi-retired but still on the bench past the age of 70, feels the Government's attorneys had decided to "cut their loses." In fact, he says, "I was a little disgusted with the Government. If they started this thing, they should have had faith in their cause. And apparently, they didn't."

Brady Williamson of LaFollette & Sinykin complained bitterly that the Government had folded its cards because it expected to lose: "Still up in the air are the validity of the Atomic Energy Act and the ability of the Government to impose prior restraint." But, without a

Toasting the Government's decision to back down (left to right): Teri Terry, Kate Juderjahn, John Buell, Knoll, Margot Olmstead, Ron Carbon, Laura McClure, Sam Day.

plaintiff, the defense was powerless to compel a decision from the court. The Atomic Energy Act of 1954 would remain over the heads of U.S. journalists like the Sword of Damocles—its power being not that it swings, but that it hangs there. And while the Government dropped its civil cases against the two publications, it explicitly reserved the right to pursue criminal charges against whomever it pleased.

McCrea and Junkerman both soon regretted having published the Hansen letter, not only because of the barrage of negative reaction but because of the jarring note on which it ended the case. It would have been a much more noteworthy act of defiance had the letter been first published, as threatened, by the *Chicago Tribune*, one of the nation's most editorially conservative newspapers, rather than by a small, rag-tag strike paper in radical-hotbed Madison. And maybe the Government's threats would have kept the letter from being published long enough for the Seventh Circuit to issue its decision, expected within days.

John Mitchell's dream newspaper, *The Washington Post*, clamored for prosecution of the *Press Connection*. The DOE, in secret letters to the FBI, did too. Shortly after the article appeared, the local FBI office phoned McCrea, imparted an odd message about a criminal at large and asked him to read it back. A half-hour later, the office called again, telling McCrea to disregard the message. "It took me a while to figure out," he says, "that I probably had just been voice-printed."

The *Press Connection* was not long for this world. It folded in January 1980, after a twenty-three-month run. Its last days were not happy. Soon after the H-bomb imbroglio, more hell broke loose over the newspaper's acceptance of an ad from an anti-abortion group. The ad argued that if the Left supported *The Progressive*'s right to publish nuclear secrets it ought also decry the defacing of the group's billboards. Some staff members threatened a walk-out; a planned editorial explanation was pulled from the page. On WORT, the local community-access radio station, future national radio funnyman Michael Feldman bizarrely compared the *Press Connection*'s editors to Nazis. The paper was also picketed by feminists after it ran a health-club ad picturing a shapely woman in a bathing suit. Says McCrea of the newspaper whose very name is PC, "Here we were, having committed one of the last radical acts of the 1970s, being hit with the sharp winds of political correctness in the 1980s and 1990s. If I got paid for irony, I'd be rich."

Not as rich as *The Progressive*. The resolution of the H-bomb case is the irony that dared not speak its name. For fifteen years, the story of how Junkerman obtained his copy of the Hansen letter remained a secret. The most Junkerman revealed was that the article was "borrowed" from "a source in the case." Knoll told Doris he suspected someone in particular, but never said who. "I'm not sure," he'd say. She thought it was the Argonne scientists. David Knoll thought it was Sam Day. "Erwin," says Day, "did not want to know." Day knew.

On the evening of September 13, after oral arguments had been heard by the Seventh Circuit, Day had called Junkerman from Chicago. He mentioned that the Government was moving to block publication of the Hansen letter, and also that Morland had a copy. The next day, Junkerman called Morland at *The Progressive*. Morland, whose copy camc from *The Daily Californian*, told Junkerman "I don't know where you can get a copy and I can't talk right now because I'm going out to lunch. I'll be back in an hour, and when I come back, I have some work to do so I assume that my desk will not be disturbed." The two men never again discussed the matter until November 1994, when they met at Knoll's memorial service in Madison. Junkerman, says Morland, "confirmed he had violated the sanctity of my desk."

"That's great!" exclaims former associate editor John Buell, hearing this story for the first time sixteen years after the fact. "That's the Howard I know and love." Publisher Ron Carbon, who also didn't know, is less forgiving. "We really felt we had a winner in Chicago. We talked with people and publicly hoped nobody would publish something like this. When the Government dropped the case, we were heartbroken. Howard shot himself in the foot."

But, like much of the H-bomb case, it was an accident.

Judge Warren's preliminary injunction against publication was formally voided on September 28, 1979. *The Progressive* printed up advance copies in early October, and Morland—wearing his H-bomb T-shirt in public for the first time—helped hand them out. The story appeared in the magazine's November issue, along with articles about various aspects of the case. "It was an uneven match," Knoll chided in print. "We had the Government licked from the beginning, and we knew it."

Morland's piece ran exactly as it had been prepared for publication six months earlier—including, as much as it pained Knoll, a couple of typos that had been noticed too late. Knoll also refused to let Morland correct a fundamental flaw in his design. The error had been noted by the Government in secret filings to the court, but the security-cleared defense attorneys could do no more than give Morland broad hints. That summer, ACLU attorney Bruce Ennis reassured Morland that he need not worry about protecting "Vernon Kendrick," the former Los Alamos worker. Kendrick could be named and would not get in trouble, Ennis said, because the information he imparted was not correct. Indeed, Morland's understanding of the role of "radiation pressure" was faulty to the core.

In other words, the Carter Administration pulled out all the stops to prevent publication of speculations about H-bomb design it knew to be incorrect, and in the process publicly disclosed and authenticated much more accurate information. Afterwards, DOE officials demanded greater secrecy and more authority to enforce it.

In hearings before Glenn's subcommittee that October, Assistant Secretary Duane Sewell said the DOE's still-ongoing review of 19,000 declassified documents had led to security upgrades of 127 documents, including eight deemed to contain "highly sensitive" information. Sewell blamed hog-wild declassification mandates imposed earlier that decade by that leak-loving chief executive, Richard Nixon. And an official question-and-answer packet prepared by the DOE in March 1980—and released to Hansen in 1992 under the Freedom of Information Act—calls for independent DOE authority "to conduct investigations and to enforce security policies [regarding] classified information." The DOE also wanted it made "mandatory that FBI responsibility for investigations in this important area . . . be carried out in all cases." This is the same agency that for years purposely subjected unsuspecting Americans to dangerous levels of radiation, to see what would happen.

Knoll never found a publisher for *The Progressive*'s proposed book on the case, but he did let the four Argonne scientists—Ted Postol, Alexander DeVolpi, Gerald Marsh, and George Stanford—use its title for their own book, published in 1981. *Born Secret* presents a wealth of documentation and a substantial technical discussion; it concludes that the Government should have stuck to its never-deny-or-confirm rule and ignored Morland's article. The scientists also argue that efforts to classify concepts that can be discovered independently—as opposed to precise experimental data produced in the laboratory—are futile and damaging. In 1994 and again in 1996, DeWitt and DeVolpi had their security clearances revoked after criticizing the DOE for classifying information in the public domain.

Morland's book, *The Secret That Exploded*, centered on his own role and dwelled on his disagreements with Knoll, an "opposite and incompatible" character. It was poorly received, especially at *The Progressive*. Knoll, on reviewing the draft manuscript, wrote Morland: "I regret, of course, your petty and neurotic references to me. What troubles me more, however, is the unfortunate image you project of yourself. You've managed to trivialize and discredit your own role in an immensely important undertaking. But it's your book. . . ." Day was even angrier, lashing out at Morland's "effort to distort, belittle, and malign the efforts of others. . . . The book is garbage."

Morland's book, actually an enjoyable read, sold only about half its 15,000-copy initial printing. The film rights were optioned by Glenn Silber, who in 1979 produced *The War At Home*, an acclaimed documentary about the Madison anti-war movement. About $50,000 was invested to work a script through several rewrites, but the poor commercial performance of the 1983 anti-nuclear films *The Day After* and *Testament* put the project on ice. Morland went on to work as a Capitol Hill lobbyist and organizer for a now-defunct arms-control group, as a legislative analyst for Democratic members of the House of Representatives, as a high-school teacher, and as a computer programmer. He gave lectures on the H-bomb and its secrets in forty-one states, using a scale model of a bomb he built using such materials as a garbage can and soccer ball.

Taking a break from building an addition to his home in Arlington, Virginia, Morland credits *The Progressive* saga with helping change "the cultural attitude" toward secrecy claims. Today, he says, "the cult of military secrecy is a thing to be ridiculed. And I'd like to think part of that has to do with what we were doing in the 1970s and 1980s to create a new national consensus."

Contrary to the Government's alarms, publication of Morland's article never did spur a run on global proliferation. Indeed, some observers say *The Progressive* article may have undercut other nations' incentive to join the H-bomb club. Proliferation, this theory goes, is driven largely by the desire of nuclear scientists within given countries to prove they are as capable as the scientists of H-bomb-equipped countries; the glut of information that poured forth during *The Progressive* case proved that achieving the technical know-how was really no big deal.

Because *The Progressive* punctured this secrecy myth, DeWitt would later say, "American peace groups and scientific groups interested in curbing the ongoing nuclear arms race were able to bring forth much better informed arguments in the debates in favor of the Comprehensive Nuclear Test Ban and other arms control agreements." For what it's worth, the height of the anti-nuclear movement occurred on June 12, 1982, when a million people converged for a rally in Central Park.

The DOE could not let go. In August 1982, technical advisor William Grayson prepared a voluminous report alleging violations that might still be prosecutable under the Atomic Energy Act. The document identifies more than a dozen targets, including Morland, Knoll, Day, Carbon, Buell, Hansen, Franklin-Ramirez, Rotow, the *Madison Press Connection*, Caldicott, Forsberg, and even the anonymous student at the University of Alabama who in January 1978 answered Morland's question about the secret of the hydrogen bomb. Grayson admitted the list was "highly speculative" since it was based "on limited sources of limited credibility." He speculated—highly—that Knoll "probably revealed RD [Restricted Data] at least by broad hints in his many media events." And he wrote, "Conceivably, the whole case involved conspiracy of some sort between Morland, Day, CDI [Center for Defense Information], Mobilization for Survival, or others."

Grayson's report includes Appendixes, listing recipients of DOE-classified letters, the names of defense attorneys, twenty-five in all, who received security clearances, and an itinerary of Morland's visits to H-bomb factories. There's even a DOE-generated index for Morland's book, something his editors at Random House hadn't thought necessary. Hansen, who in 1992 pried the Grayson report into public view, is grateful: "I never saw a book that needed an index more badly than Morland's does."

Hansen, at the time of *The Progressive* case, had been working for eight years to learn all he could about thermonuclear weapons; he put in eight more years of research before publishing, in 1988, a remarkable book entitled *U.S. Nuclear Weapons: The Secret History.* Hansen's book was a shot across the bow of nuclear secrecy, but the Government did not seek to block publication. In fact, although the Atomic Energy Act is dusted off now and then to threaten impudent reporters, the Government has never again sought to impose prior restraint on national-security grounds.

Dozens of articles have explored the constitutional impact of *The Progressive* case. The clear consensus is that the evidence presented to Judge Warren did not justify the imposition of prior restraint and that the Supreme Court, had things gone that far, would have ruled to this effect. But it didn't, and instead the case stands as an example of how the Government, aided by a federal judge, successfully used the Atomic Energy Act to block publication. Many of the early legal assessments were downright dour: "Judge Warren's issuance of the preliminary injunction substantially broadened the availability of prior restraints"; ". . . courts using *The Progressive* test will invariably err on the side of restraining publication"; "Judge Warren saw the State's asserted interest as preeminent and simply refused to enforce the plain language of the First Amendment and First Amendment case law that has existed since *Near v. Minnesota*"; the case shows that the Pentagon Papers decision "can be interpreted so broadly by the courts that it provides no sure protection for freedom of the press."

Williamson, of LaFollette & Sinykin, looks on the bright side: "Nobody went to jail and the article got published." What about the precedent of granting prior restraint? "This case," says Williamson, "will be remembered as the time a federal judge appointed by Richard Nixon accepted at face value a series of Government affidavits that on their face were incredible, and were proved so." Thomas Martin, the Justice Department's lead attorney, conceded in a 1982 article in the *American Bar Association Journal* that the Government screwed up: "Most Government officials associated with *The Progressive* case would conclude, I think, that more was lost than gained."

Judge Warren still doesn't get it. "I won't take second seat to anybody in terms of my belief in the freedom of speech," he says. But, now as then, the judge feels that whatever point Knoll was trying to make could have been made without "insisting on wanting to publish the recipe for a hydrogen bomb. You don't have to stand up and shout something dangerous to exercise your freedom of speech." The judge says that while "the liberals" want to "canonize" the man he calls Edwin Knoll, "I didn't have any admiration for what he was trying to do." Neither did former Attorney General Bell, in his own petulant dismissal of the case: "The rag-tags of the press took it upon themselves to judge what was in the public interest, a dangerous precedent and one that in the future could well lead to censorship."

Warren makes no apology for siding with the Government, even though he believes it misrepresented matters of fact. "I was raised in a time when country was important," he says. "And the protection of country and its security had a very high priority among our panoply of values. Now, these days, if the U.S. and its Government decide they have to engage in some action around the world, I'm appalled by the way everybody feels free to question it, beyond what I think is reasonable. Look at the way our great President [Clinton], who I don't think much of, stayed out of the Vietnam War. That's a development of recent times. And I think I'm of a generation that felt that, if it was necessary to protect the integrity of the United States, you didn't challenge it. On the other hand, nowadays it seems that you grab a placard and away you go. Or sit down and pour blood on books or something."

Finally, Warren defends suppressing Morland's article because, he thinks, there really was an H-bomb secret: It had to do with "the way in which the fusion explosion was triggered." Warren believed this secret had to be contained "because a country like China, or a country like Russia, could save literally years by being pointed which direction it should go." But hadn't Russia and China already—by 1979—figured out this "secret" enough to build their own H-bombs? "I can't answer that. I don't remember. Atomic bombs, maybe, but this is thermonuclear, and of course there's a vast difference, and the way they're triggered is different." But he says it's hard to remember. All this happened "over twenty years ago." (Warren said this after a morning in court in April 1995, sixteen years after *The Progressive* case had, in an act of random selection, come to him.)

Sam Day was not long for *The Progressive*. Some of the cracks that had opened in his tight bond with Knoll would soon become fissures. In years to come, Day would dramatically escalate his commitment to the anti-nuclear cause. He was arrested dozens of times, even after losing most of his eyesight in prison in 1991—the same year he published a detailed inside account of the H-bomb story in his autobiography, *Crossing the Line*. In an interview conducted from prison in Omaha, Nebraska, where he was serving a maximum six-month sentence for handing out antinuclear leaflets (i.e., "trespassing") at a U.S. Air Force base, Day explained why he never talked about his role in disseminating the Hansen letter: "I felt a bit queasy about it afterwards, because of what it did to the case."

Erwin Knoll spoke and wrote often about the H-bomb story, always encountering the same problem: There were so many *misunderstandings* to clear up. One of the last things he wrote—it came out only after his death—was for the Winter 1994 issue of the *William & Mary Bill of Rights Journal*. Knoll stated, more absolutely than ever before, his "sincere regret" over one thing: his decision to obey Warren's injunction. "If such circumstances were to arise again," he promised, "I would publish and be damned."

Former U.S. Attorney Frank Tuerkheimer, now (by chance) a member of the Madison law firm of LaFollette & Sinykin, in May 1995 testified before the U.S. Senate Subcommittee on Terrorism, Technology and Government Information regarding the proposed banning of certain information—such as instructions on how to build bombs—from the Internet. "Efforts to curtail the flow of information are doomed to fail," he said. "The lesson of the H-bomb case is that it's the wrong way to go." Senator Dianne Feinstein, Democrat of California, was offended by this argument, coming just days after 168 people died in the savage bombing of the federal building in Oklahoma City: "I have a problem with people using their First Amendment rights to teach people how to kill."

But perhaps Tuerkheimer figured he had to speak out anyway, because it was the truth. That, too, was a lesson of *The Progressive* case. Tuerkheimer, as one of the Government's attorneys, watched in amazement as Knoll was "fucked over by the liberal establishment press" and still stood his ground. "Erwin withstood that kind of pressure. He had a peculiar form of courage—the greatest form of courage. In *An Enemy of the People*, Ibsen says that the strongest man in the world is the man who stands alone. That was Erwin. He stood alone."

CHAPTER FOURTEEN

At *The Progressive*

Three months after the Government abandoned its prosecution of *The Progressive*, a small cadre of the magazine's employees dropped a bomb of their own. Teri Terry, the magazine's bookkeeper, had with Sam Day's clandestine assistance drafted a statement to present to the board of directors: Gordon Sinykin, Morris Rubin, Mary Sheridan, and Erwin Knoll.

"I had to write the board to ask to be heard," says Terry, still irked. "They had to vote on whether or not to hear me." Terry was permitted to appear at the board's regular meeting of December 14, 1979. She held the four-page manifesto in her trembling hands, and began to read.

"Sit down," demanded Sinykin, asserting his dominion. Terry was furious. "Gordon," she remembers saying, "I have prepared this talk and I plan to give it, and I plan on you listening to me." What followed was a strongly worded appeal from Terry and three other poorly paid women who comprised the magazine's clerical staff. That December, after a round of raises, the four clerical workers averaged $9,078 a year, compared to Knoll's salary of $35,400. These women, who came to be known as the Gang of Four, also wanted greater input into workplace decisions.

"*The Progressive* magazine has reported on, and apparently supports, worker democracy, worker control and participation," read Terry. "It condemns secrecy and ignorance and supports the right of the people to know and be heard. Yet the very structure of the office belies those beliefs."

When Terry finished, the board moved on to its next item of business. "There was no discussion, nothing," she says. Afterwards, Knoll reproached her, putting the issue in personal terms, as she recalls: "He gave me the 'How could you? Aren't we friends?' crap." Terry would have none of it. Throughout its history, *The Progressive* had run on a shoestring, dependent on the sacrifices of the people who worked for it. For some, this meant doing without cars, vacations, even a place of their own to live. Until 1976, when Knoll importuned the board on his employees' behalf, the magazine did not have a policy regarding vacations and sick days. The quarters were cramped, the hours were long, the pay was low.

"It was a sweatshop," says managing editor Day, still ashamed about the amount of carcinogenic fumes to which he, Knoll, and other heavy puffers subjected nonsmokers in the office. "Most of *The Progressive*'s workforce," Day once wrote, "had little say about anything at the magazine, let alone the air they breathed." For all its "high-sounding rhetoric about workers' rights," the magazine "operated essentially like a cotton plantation. The editor was its 'massah' and the rest of the editorial and business staff its house niggers, some with privileges but few with any real power."

As a result of the Gang of Four's rebellion, Knoll and other board members agreed to let a staff representative attend their monthly meetings, so long as salaries and personnel issues remained "off limits." The workers' modest call for a built-in, cost-of-living adjustment tied to the Consumer Price Index was rebuffed. "The board agreed that such a provision is beyond our financial capabilities at this time," wrote Sheridan in a memo.

Day and others in the office backed the clerical workers' demands. "We had an understanding that if the women were to go out on strike, we would honor the picket line," he says. "We told that to Erwin. Erwin told us, in so many words, that he would put out the magazine single-handed if need be." Knoll made no bones about the fact that his commitment to the magazine exceeded his empathy for the dissident workers.

He had even less sympathy for the dissident worker who sent the *Madison Press Connection* a copy of the clerical workers' manifesto. Reporter John Junkerman showed up at *The Progressive* to ask about it. Knoll refused to comment. No story ever ran. But Knoll was steamed. While he tolerated—at times welcomed—the expression of dissent in the workplace, he felt betrayed by this attempt to invite the critical attention of other media. Apparently, his commitment to free speech was not all-encompassing. "Now we really have a problem—a problem with disloyalty," he said after Junkerman left. "That is beyond the pale." The next day Knoll met with staffers—including Day, Carbon, Terry, and editorial secretary Kate Juderjahn—to issue a reprimand: "I'm terribly distraught that one of you should go outside the family."

Juderjahn, feeling the heat of Knoll's accusation, was near tears. "I didn't do it," she protested. Day, suffused with guilt, couldn't stand it any longer. "I was the one," he confessed. Day had sent the statement to the *Madison Press Connection*, just as he had helped the paper obtain Chuck Hansen's letter. "Erwin was stunned," says Day. But his response was subdued. He stared at Day for a long time and said, "I think you used very, very poor judgment." Day, on reflection, agreed. And although Knoll never again mentioned the incident, Day understood that his days at the magazine were numbered. "The editorship of *The Progressive*," he realized, "could not be shared. Neither I nor anyone else would ever be more than an associate." Soon Day left, to start an anti-nuclear group.

Within a year, three of the four Gang members were also gone. One was edged out after she skipped a whole day of work. "I think it would be best if you were to find employment elsewhere," Knoll wrote. She did. It was the only time Knoll fired anyone. Juderjahn announced plans to leave the magazine to have a baby, and Terry was seen as her ideal replacement—if only she knew shorthand. Terry went to the local vocational college and "did a two-year course in one semester." In mid-1980, she took Juderjahn's place.

It was emblematic of Knoll's relationship with his employees that he could on occasion clash with them ferociously, as adversaries, and later embrace them warmly, as respected colleagues. Some workers felt bruised by the intensity with which Knoll pressed his points. Or else they decided it was useless to argue with him, because he was so determined to win, and so intractable. But Terry and Knoll respected each other, and his example emboldened her. She'd tell him he was full of it right to his face. Sometimes she would make her points and he'd say, "You're right." But, she concedes, "He wasn't often wrong. I hated it, too."

Every morning, before Knoll began dictating his first batch of letters, he and Terry talked about their families, things in the news, whatever. Knoll was, she says, "an excellent dictator." He would never forget to say "comma" or "period" or "new paragraph" or "upper case." It was as though he were reading from a text in his brain.

Throughout his more than two decades at the magazine, it was Knoll's policy and practice to respond personally to *every* letter addressed to him or the magazine: every unsolicited manuscript, even ones so awful they were not passed around for comment; every subscriber who took issue with an editorial or article; every request for information; every prisoner seeking a free subscription, which the magazine always granted, asking only that copies be shared with other inmates.

Terry estimates that throughout her fifteen years as Knoll's secretary, Knoll dictated an average of twenty-five to thirty letters a day. Even routine rejection letters were often personalized, containing specific references to the manuscript being rejected or the correspondent's concern. Each and every letter was signed by Erwin Knoll. "He just felt it was a personal touch," says Terry. "When someone took the time to write the magazine, he would respond."

Knoll himself had been drawn to *The Progressive* because it provided good editing and broad editorial freedom. He preserved these advantages for other writers, including his old friends Jules Witcover, Morton Mintz, and Judy Randal. All say Knoll was among the best editors they've ever known, not only because of his mastery but also his courtesy—a quality in terribly short supply among editors. In a business where some writers have never seen a rejection letter that bore the name of an actual human being, where articles are butchered without apology and compliments are as rare as people who think they make too much money, Knoll set out to do things differently.

"He was straightforward, a man of his word," says John Egerton, a frequent contributor to *The Progressive* who had been one of Knoll's editors at the Nashville-based Southern School News Reporting Service. "He'd edit your copy as your copy needed to be edited. I loved to write pieces for *The Progressive*. I never felt that I didn't have humane and personal and professional treatment by him. It was how he thought an editor should be."

Knoll would take time to instruct even novice writers on how to turn their badly flawed submissions into salvageable ones. "As a rule," he wrote one prisoner who submitted a hopelessly shrill screed, "it's better to make strong points by speaking softly than by engaging in rhetorical overkill."

Once he had an acceptable manuscript, Knoll would reach for his red felt-tip pen and go to work—expunging extraneous words, smashing passive verbs, substituting more vivid adjectives. But he took pains to preserve a writer's meaning and as many of the writer's words as possible. Contributors always got to see the edited version, and were invited to make "fixes." Knoll always had time for writers who wanted to make last-minute improvements or quibble with his decision to cut a certain point.

The Progressive, more and more, was becoming Erwin Knoll's magazine. Morris Rubin died on August 8, 1980, one day after his 69th birthday. A few months later, associate editor John McGrath was eased into retirement, ending his more than three decades of service to the magazine. These vacancies presented opportunities for Knoll. He hired a series of strong, opinionated associate editors, beginning with Lawrence Walsh, Carol Polsgrove, and Mary Williams. And magazine stalwarts Sid Lens and Milton Mayer, who held the titles of senior editor and roving editor, respectively, continued to make substantial contributions, keeping the issues of labor and pacifism on the front burner. Both served as mentors to Knoll, pushing his politics in radical directions.

In mid-1981 the magazine moved for the first time in thirty-five years, to a slightly larger office on the ground floor of an old brick building at 409 East Main Street, four blocks from the state Capitol. "I think it's appropriate that we landed on Main Street," Knoll wrote at the time. "From its beginnings earlier in this century, *The Progressive* has always represented a peculiarly American kind of radicalism—based on the best traditions of this country and on the assumption that we could build, right here in the United States, a society devoted to peace, freedom, and economic justice. We've always believed that a majority of our fellow citizens shared that vision—or could be persuaded to share it. In a sense, then, *The Progressive* has been on Main Street all along."

Knoll's greatest complaint about the magazine was its appearance. Madison Mayor Paul Soglin once told Knoll that *The Progressive* was the only magazine he could think of whose look had not changed in twenty-five years. In 1980, Knoll and publisher Ron Carbon succeeded in wooing Patrick J.B. Flynn from *The New York Times* to become the magazine's art director. Flynn, who grew up in Sioux Falls, South Dakota, didn't want his two young children to have to grow up in New York City. Flynn demanded complete control over the magazine's artwork and appearance. Knoll, who insisted so firmly on controlling the magazine's editorial content, agreed. Although he loved art—and for a year served as president of the Madison Print Club, a group that commissions artworks—Knoll didn't feel competent in this area. And he had high regard for Flynn.

"Thirty years from now," Knoll said with uncharacteristic humility, "most of the words we print in *The Progressive* will be tired old gibberish. But the graphics will still be interesting and sometimes profound."

Under Flynn, the magazine has featured some of the nation's best political artists, including Stephen Kroninger, Brad Holland, Sue Coe, Henrik Drescher, and Frances Jetter. A persistent complaint among readers of *The Progressive* is that the artwork is too heavy and harsh. Knoll always defended Flynn against such criticism. "I'm not out to make the reader's life more comfortable," he said. "I'm not out to ease anybody's way through *The Progressive*."

But over time Knoll did find occasion to suspend Flynn's complete control. "If it's something I really find objectionable, which happens maybe two times a year," he said, "then I have my way." Only twice, says Flynn, did Knoll flat-out reject a piece of artwork. Once was in the summer of 1984, when Knoll refused to print a cartoon by regular contributor Arnold Roth ("The Gripes of Roth") that depicted the caricature of an Arab. "I wouldn't be able to defend it," he said.

Knoll's most arduous task at *The Progressive* was raising the money to keep it going. Several times a year, he wrote letters used in direct mail fund-raising appeals. In 1980 and 1981, these letters invariably referred to the H-bomb case, which Knoll called "the most severe crisis" facing the magazine since it nearly went under in 1947. "We cannot sustain our crushing publication costs under the present circumstances," Knoll wrote in one letter. "At this moment, when *The Progressive*'s independent voice is needed as never before, the magazine faces such rapidly escalating costs that we may be forced to suspend publication," he said in another.

While Knoll, in the spirit of fund-raising appeals, may have overstated the case, *The Progressive*'s H-bomb legal debt was in fact a huge drain on the magazine's already meager finances. In the spring of 1980, Carbon wrote a memo to the magazine's board suggesting that *The Progressive* ask LaFollette & Sinykin to reduce or forgive the balance due, then just short of $55,000. The board never even discussed the matter. A copy of Carbon's memo was given to Sinykin's law partner Earl Munson, who fired off an indignant letter to Knoll.

"We have concluded that any further reduction in the fees is utterly unjustified," Munson wrote, asking Knoll to remember that "the editors forced this litigation on the magazine without warning and contrary to the judgment of some directors"—a reference to objections raised by Sinykin, Rubin, and Sheridan, all of whom disliked Howard Morland's piece. Knoll responded with a letter that, while conciliatory in the main, reverberated with rage. He professed, for instance, to be "puzzled" by Munson's comments about the article's merits: "These matters are quite irrelevant to the lawsuit and the legal fees, and of no concern to our attorneys."

The struggle to retire *The Progressive*'s legal debt led to the creation of The Progressive Foundation, a nonprofit arm that allowed supporters to make tax-free donations to the magazine. The magazine also capitalized on its cache of sudden celebrities by setting up The Progressive Foundation Speakers Bureau, which arranged talks by Knoll, Day, Morland, Sid Lens, Michael Klare, and other luminaries on the Left.

Knoll's foray into the public eye during the H-bomb case also got him a gig as commentator on National Public Radio's "All Things Considered." For a little more than a year, beginning in July 1980, Knoll considered all manner of things during his weekly three-minute segment. He declared his distaste not just for GOP challenger Ronald Reagan but also incumbent Democrat Jimmy Carter, who that year tried to firm up his Cold War credentials by resuming draft registration, boycotting the Moscow Olympics, and giving thumbs up to "probably the most extravagant boondoogle of all time, the MX missile." Knoll in one commentary told the "probably apocryphal" story of the woman who, when asked by a pollster how she would vote, replied, "Oh, I never vote. It only encourages them." He also quoted Socialist Eugene Debs, a five-time presidential candidate: "I'd rather vote for what I want and not get it than vote for what I don't want and get it." In another commentary, Knoll ripped the League of Women Voters for excluding third-party contenders from presidential debates. The League, he said, serves "to perpetuate the monopoly of the two major parties—and helps ensure that minor parties will never become major."

Knoll liked to rub it in when politicians he loathed had an inadvertently good idea. He praised President-Elect Reagan's call to abolish the Department of Energy, which "has actually been an obstacle to the production of safe and economically sound alternative energy sources" and spent nearly half its budget on nuclear weapons. President Reagan, of course, soon broke his pledge.

Another of Knoll's NPR commentaries was on the issue of draft registration. He noted that, under a federal law that "not only contradicts the First Amendment but insults it," he would risk five years' imprisonment and a $10,000 fine were he to advise his nineteen-year-old son not to register for the draft. He said his son had not asked for advice; a few days later, he gave him some anyway.

Jonathan was at the time in Israel, pursuing an interest in Biblical archaeology. (It was there he had his bar mitzvah—something his parents, disgusted by the materialism of many of these affairs, had avoided.) He had received letters informing him of his obligation to register, and more threatening letters when he didn't. Doris Knoll was worried; she didn't want Jonathan to get in trouble avoiding a draft that might never happen. But Erwin urged his son to do nothing until he returned to the States: "It should be clear, by then, how many people are resisting." Jonathan knew his father was opposed to registration, but never felt pressured: "He was 100 percent supportive, whether I did or I didn't. He said, 'You should do what you think is right.'"

Perhaps Knoll's best NPR commentary was about Bobby Sands, the imprisoned IRA activist who in the spring of 1981 starved himself to death to protest the English occupation of Northern Ireland. "There should be no doubt that Bobby Sands gave his life in a great cause," Knoll told his coast-to-coast audience. "It takes a great cause, after all, to make a young man, only twenty-seven years old, deliberately sacrifice himself." But, he went on, "I am weary of all these great causes that must be served by bloodshed and martyrdom. On one side or the other, hundreds and thousands have died in Northern Ireland in a struggle that is no closer to solution than it was decades ago, and I am certain many of the dead had only the vaguest notion, if any, of the great cause that claimed their lives."

Whereas the tremendous attention generated by the H-bomb article had a negligible effect on *The Progressive*'s readership, Knoll's exposure on NPR pushed the magazine's circulation to an all-time high of 51,475 in 1982. It remained strong throughout the mid-1980s, as the nation lurched radically to the right. Indeed, the election of Ronald Reagan, though properly regarded as a disaster for the political Left, was in many ways a good thing for *The Progressive*. "The Reagan Administration," Knoll wrote, "has thrown into sharp relief the most acute contradictions of our country's official policies and programs: preaching peace while making insane preparations for war; providing new subsidies and tax advantages for the rich while withdrawing vital services and benefits from the poor; meddling in our lives while claiming to get government off our backs." Or, as Carbon put it in a fund-raising appeal: "The Reagan Administration, the Moral Majority zealots, and the rest of the Neanderthals currently running amok have inadvertently caused hundreds of thousands of people across the country—people who care about the issues *The Progressive* has always addressed—to become more energized and more open to a magazine like *The Progressive*."

But this newfound success stoked the embers of staff discontent. If *The Progressive*'s fortunes were rising, why weren't their salaries rising too? If its paeans to workplace democracy and workers' rights made sense, why weren't they practiced at the magazine?

In October 1980, staff members pressured the board of directors to include an elected worker representative. The next year, several employees agitated for raises; this was nothing new, except that they did it collectively. In 1982, the board failed to approve a salary increase for Jonathan Burack, the magazine's development coordinator. The staff, in response, urged that meetings of the board be open to all employees. Board Chairman Sinykin flatly refused, and urged employees to be "realistic about your personal expectations from *The Progressive*. Unless we all work together, the only alternative will be to close our shop."

That summer, Carbon announced plans to take a job at *The American Lawyer*, and Burack declared his interest in the publisher's job. His candidacy was supported by several other workers. But it was not to be. Knoll did not like Burack, and he detested the notion of making decisions collectively. "One person has to be in charge," he'd say. The job went instead to Pat Vander Meer, previously with the Chicago-based weekly, *In These Times*. Further conflict was now unavoidable.

Meanwhile, Knoll was beginning to pay the piper for a lifetime of health neglect. Knoll never had much interest in exercise, as his waistline testified. In August 1983, Vander Meer arranged the first of what became an annual softball game between the staffs of *The Progressive* and *In These Times*. Knoll never played. Worse, he had smoked heavily for decades, up to four packs a day. David Knoll says, not entirely in jest, that his father needed to strike only one match each morning. After that, he lit each successive cigarette with the smoldering remains of the last.

"He lived in his head," offers David. "He thought of his body as a vehicle that carried around his head." But Erwin Knoll's body would not stand for it. In 1982, Knoll got the bad news that he was diabetic, just like his sister. This meant restrictions in diet, at least some of which he obeyed.

But Knoll did, during this time, manage to give up smoking. One impetus was Knoll's friend Ralph Nader, who was constantly on his case about it. In June 1980, when Knoll was visiting Washington, D.C., he appeared on a 2 a.m. radio call-in show hosted by his friend and former neighbor, Shelly Tromberg. The producer in the next room gave Knoll a message: "Ralph Nader just called. He says he can hear you breathing into the microphone. You *MUST* stop smoking." Knoll's doctor in Madison gave him the same advice.

Knoll stopped smoking, cold turkey and for good, in December 1980. Seven years later, he went on a 1,200-calorie-a-day diet, also on advice of his doctor, and lost more than forty pounds. These changes impressed his wife Doris and son David: Erwin *did* care enough about his health to do what his doctor told him. Later, this became a larger issue in their minds, as they contemplated the quality of health-care advice that Erwin, in his final years, received.

Photo by Joseph Blough

The editorial staff: Matthew Rothschild, Erwin Knoll, Mary Sheridan, John Buell and Keenan Peck, May 1984.

CHAPTER FIFTEEN

No Competitors

When Matthew Rothschild arrived at the airport on the edge of Madison in October 1982, Erwin Knoll was there to greet him. Knoll was easy to spot; he was, as promised, "the person holding a copy of *The Progressive* magazine." They walked out to Knoll's car, and Rothschild's chin dropped. The Knollmobile was not, as he expected, some sensible, high-mileage import but a Chevy Blazer, "a big, macho outdoorsman's car with fat wheels." This vehicle, the kind of car Knoll always drove once he moved to the hinterlands of Wisconsin, was emblematic of other contradictions that Rothschild soon perceived.

Rothschild, a native of Highland Park, Illinois, was in town to interview at *The Progressive* for the position of associate editor. For the past two-and-a-half years, Rothschild had worked at *Multinational Monitor*, a monthly magazine founded by Ralph Nader to investigate the role played by giant corporations and lending institutions in the Third World. He got the job right after graduating from Harvard University in 1980, and worked his way up to editor. But Nader, as any former employee will attest, is an unrelenting workaholic who expects the same from those around him. Rothschild sent letters announcing his availability to *The Progressive, The Nation,* and *Mother Jones*, the top three Left publications. His letter arrived at *The Progressive* just as the magazine's associate editors, Lawrence Walsh and Mary Williams, were leaving for law school and a journalism fellowship, respectively. In their place, Knoll hired Rothschild and Keenen Peck, like Williams a former editorial intern. Rothschild, at twenty-four, was a year older than Peck.

Matt Rothschild was smart and well-connected among the political Left. He was a capable writer and editor. And, like others Knoll brought on as associate editors, he had plenty of ideas for improving the magazine. But soon after he started in January 1983, Rothschild encountered Knoll's most troubling contradiction—the way he could go from familial to ferocious. "He could be quite belligerent," says Rothschild. "He would think nothing of resorting to ad hominem attacks if it was to his advantage."

One of Rothschild's earliest and most persistent quarrels with Knoll was about the magazine's "Comment" section, the unsigned editorials that are written in-house. The editors deliberate about what topics to comment on, and then an individual editor is assigned to write the piece. Rothschild felt the editorials should be signed: "I thought the writing might sparkle more. Maybe it wouldn't have the homogenous, run-through-the-mill tone and the Olympian stance that some of these unsigned editorials have." Knoll hated this idea, as Rothschild recalls. "He would say, as emphatically as possible, his chin jutting out and his shoulders scrunched up, rocking forward as he did, that the 'Comment' section is the institutional voice of the magazine and that readers have a right to know our collective position on the issues of the day." This was a fine and valid argument. But when Rothschild persisted in pressing his point, Knoll would shift effortlessly into low gear. "Well," he'd say, "you just want to get your name in the magazine more often."

There were times when Rothschild felt that arguing with Knoll was like banging his head against a wall: It was pointless, and he felt lousy afterwards. Still, Rothschild had a vision of the magazine that was different from Knoll's, and after years of headbanging much of it came about. Rothschild sought to broaden *The Progressive*'s coverage of cultural issues, which for a long time consisted mainly of film reviews and Nat Hentoff's column on jazz. He grasped, more clearly than Knoll, the need to share a common cultural vocabulary with younger readers. He pushed for more columnists, and regular interviews. And he wanted the magazine to do more investigative reporting.

Rothschild thought *The Progressive* needed to be more proactive, to reach out for writers and stories. Knoll was looser and more egalitarian: He simply trusted that timely articles worth publishing would arrive in the mail. "I would criticize this approach, saying we had made the Postmaster General our assignment editor, but that didn't seem to bother Erwin," says Rothschild. "While he was editor, at least 50 percent of the magazine was material that just floated in out of the blue, or over the transom, as he put it. I would neurotically ask at editorial meetings, 'What's going to be in the next issue?' because there would be absolutely no copy on hand and we weren't assigning any either. And he'd say, 'The Lord will provide.' This from an atheist."

Knoll was proud that *The Progressive* published pieces by free-lancers and first-time writers. He never held it against a writer that his or her work was previously unpublished; sometimes, if Knoll could see ways to make major improvements, it didn't even matter if the writing wasn't very good. He'd contrast this open approach with that of Left publications like *The Nation*, which tend to rely on a small stable of contributors. Rothschild, for his part, questioned whether the articles the magazine accepted "just because Erwin thought they were making an important point" were worth the bother—some, after many hours of work, were still only so-so. But Knoll thought the magazine was doing what it ought to do. "He was always content with the product," says Rothschild, adding that Knoll "would just recoil" to hear the word "product" applied to the magazine.

During his job interview, Rothschild put a question to Knoll: "Who are *The Progressive*'s competitors?" Knoll answered, "We have no competitors." *The Progressive* was, of course, in competition with other Left publications for subscribers and advertising; Knoll's point was that he didn't care what these other publications did in their pages. Nor was Knoll concerned about pleasing his own magazine's subscribers; the only criticisms he welcomed were those from staff members and journalists he trusted. "We're editing the magazine for ourselves," he often said, "not for anybody else."

In early 1984, a class at the University of Wisconsin helped the magazine conduct a detailed readership survey. It concluded that most readers were "well-educated, professional, middle-class white males" and recommended that the magazine seek new readers among "the burgeoning class of young urban professionals." Says Rothschild, "I don't think Erwin even looked at it. He was against the whole idea of a readership survey. He'd say, 'If we wanted to be popular, we could be *Time* magazine or *Reader's Digest* or *Parade*. But we're not in the business of being popular.'"

In the mid-1980s, Knoll seemed more inclined than ever to pick fights with his readers, and others on the Left. "One of the joys of editing *The Progressive*," he told writer George Vukelich in 1985, "is we feel it's part of our job to offend our readers. We're not here to stroke them but to provoke them. It's a poor issue of *The Progressive* that doesn't make a chunk of its readership angry." Knoll acted as though nothing gave him a greater sense of righteous satisfaction than when a reader cancelled his or her subscription over this or that article or editorial. "He would talk about it with glee," says Ralph Nader, who occasionally advised his friend Knoll on how to increase circulation. "But privately, he'd be upset."

One blowout occurred over the magazine's acceptance, in late 1984, of an advertisement from a group representing tobacco industry unionists. The ad was headed, "We're the tobacco industry, too." It pictured three tobacco workers with dour expressions. "By astonishing coincidence," observed Knoll, "one is black, one is a woman, and one is middle-aged." The text went on to lament that their good, union jobs in the tobacco industry were threatened by "well-meaning people who haven't stopped to consider how their actions might affect others." The reaction was intense. "You have prostituted your magazine, compromised your integrity, and shaken the faith of your readers," wrote one subscriber. "We won't renew," wrote another. Several writers wondered whether the magazine would run an ad from weapons workers in defense of military spending. Knoll used his "Memo" column for January 1985 to give his answer: Yes, it would. So long as an advertisement—any advertisement—"did not violate the law or minimal standards of good taste," the magazine would accept it for publication at its usual rates.

The tobacco workers' ad, Knoll continued, struck him as "cheap-shot propaganda." He gathered that others who saw it thought so, too. But unlike the people who complained, Knoll didn't think his readers "had to be shielded" from the ad. "Our position is that people who subscribe to *The Progressive* are mature, responsible, intelligent human beings who can be exposed to points of view we find wrong or downright obnoxious without being led down the primrose path to perdition. Anybody want to take issue with that?"

A few months later, a similar controversy arose when *The Progressive* ran an ad from Feminists for Life, a group that opposes abortion. June Makela, the executive director of the Funding Exchange, wrote a terse letter saying her New York-based advocacy group "had decided not to renew its subscription" and would find it difficult to help the magazine financially, as it had in the past. This baton-brandishing by the Politically Correct Thought Police infuriated Knoll, who responded by bashing—publicly, since he published his letter in his "Memo" column—the Funding Exchange's "intellectual intolerance" and its zeal for "censorship." He said the ad had already cost the magazine more in lost subscriptions than it produced in advertising revenue, and concluded by telling Makela, "We will do our best to get along without your subscription and without your financial help, because as much as we prize both of them, they don't mean nearly as much to us as our integrity and our commitment to freedom of speech."

Knoll's somewhat sanctimonious response earned him plaudits from *Village Voice* columnist Nat Hentoff. But Alexander Cockburn, the acerbic and brilliant writer for *The Nation*, wrote a scathing indictment of Knoll's "pious self-deception." The advertisements that appear in *The Progressive*, Cockburn felt, are clearly "a reflection of its editorial policy" and Knoll's acceptance of this particular ad "has everything to do with opportunism and petty greed and nothing to do with free speech and the First Amendment."

Shortly thereafter, Knoll attempted to set forth some policies regarding advertising in a memo to publisher Pat Vander Meer. "Obviously, we're obliged to reject advertising that is patently illegal, or that poses a direct and immediate threat to health and safety," he wrote, recalling an ad offering instructions on how to turn a rifle into a semi-automatic weapon. The magazine could also refuse ads that were "clearly fraudulent," such as one that promised respondents several thousand dollars a week in easy income. Finally, it could bump ads that are "grossly offensive—displaying gratuitous obscenity, or using repellent racial, sexual, or ethnic epithets." But in these cases, Knoll said, efforts should be made to "persuade advertisers to modify their language without changing the essential thrust of their message." In sum, he said, "I am convinced that we should *never* reject an ad because we disagree with or disapprove of the individual or organization sponsoring the ad, or because we have political objections to its content."

Knoll wrote this memo at about the same time *The Nation* published his letter in response to Cockburn's column. Knoll's letter began by calling Cockburn "one of those strange birds that take special pleasure in fouling their own nests," a reference to his penchant for picking fights with other leftists—one of the many ways Knoll and Cockburn could properly be described as birds of a feather. Knoll said true opportunism and greed would have dictated that he reject the ad "and thereby refrain from offending those readers and contributors who can't bear to see an opposing view in print." He accused Cockburn of having this "totalitarian mindset." In his inevitable reply, Cockburn called Knoll's reasoning "preposterous," citing a letter he received from Eric Parker, a worker at the magazine, as evidence of Knoll's duplicity. Parker wrote that Knoll "refuses to publish letters by staff members wishing to express perspectives dissenting from those of the editorial staff." Cockburn got the better of Knoll, thanks to one of *The Progressive*'s own employees.

It was becoming a real problem—the contradiction between *The Progressive*'s egalitarian ideals and its top-down management style. In May 1983, after pay increases approved by Knoll and Vander Meer were rejected by the board, the magazine's employees decided to unionize. They filed for representation with District 65 of the United Auto Workers, one of the nation's most militant unions. The elected union president, Beth Burack, issued a statement saying the union was needed to counter a board that was "extremely undemocratic in structure and spirit" and, worse, headed by Gordon Sinykin, who "has treated the employees with paternalistic disdain."

Knoll never quarreled with the right of his employees to form a union, although he did join Sinykin and other board members in trying to exclude four workers—all union activists—by claiming they were "management." Among them was the magazine's telemarketing coordinator, who after three years on the job had just been denied vacation time and health benefits on grounds that he was still "part-time," despite his forty-hour work week. *In Business*, a local publication not known for defending anybody's right to unionize, ran an account of the magazine's labor conflict under the headline,

"How Progressive is *The Progressive*?" Sinykin is quoted as saying the magazine's workers have long understood "they're not going to earn what they're entitled to."

From this mindset, Sinykin viewed the union's formation as though it were an advancing dustcloud containing the four horsemen of the apocalypse. "The real issue," he wrote in a letter to contributing writer Hentoff, who had inquired about the labor situation, "is whether there is any possibility that we can keep going." The union, in reply to such histrionics, pointed out that its salary demands would add just $12,000 to a $1.2 million annual budget.

The membership issue was resolved, mostly in the union's favor, and negotiations on *The Progressive*'s first union contract began in the summer of 1984. For at least two afternoons a week, the union's negotiating team of Rothschild, Peck, and circulation assistant Bonnie Urfer met in the magazine's small conference room with Knoll and Vander Meer. Knoll had ample opportunity to engage in his favorite pastime—arguing—but for the most part he played good cop to Vander Meer's bad lieutenant. It was her voice that could be heard blaring from the conference room, drowning out the bells of St. Patrick's church across the street. Early that summer, union members made up protest signs ("How about, '75 Years of Unfair Labor Practices'?" suggested Peck, in jest) and picketed a meeting of the board of directors at the magazine. The board, recalls Terry, "drew the blinds and had a fit."

The issue the union pressed most ardently—and the one management fought hardest—was for worker involvement in decisions. "We wanted equal decision-making with department heads," says Urfer. "The editorial workers wanted equal editorial say and the business workers wanted equal say in business decisions." Knoll, she remembers, would sit there, rocking back and forth, leaning back in his chair so far she thought he might fall. Then he'd rock forward and say, "I'm not going to let *The Progressive* be a guinea pig for cooperative management." The union team, in response, brought in articles on cooperatively run businesses throughout the country that were doing just fine. Vander Meer would pound on the table and shout, "We're not going to do this!"

Ironically, while repelling the dread prospect of workplace democracy, management caved in on almost everything else. Union members received substantial pay hikes, a huge increase in vacation time, complete health-care coverage, a clause giving workers who go to jail for civil disobedience the same rights as those who are drafted into military service, and one of the best baby-making incentives this side of Sweden: six weeks fully paid leave, followed by two-and-a-half months of partially paid leave, for any new mother—or father. The union also forced the magazine to part with stock holdings it had acquired in corporations with ties to South Africa.

Contract negotiations concluded on the last day of 1984, just in time for the Knolls' annual New Year's Day Party. Once the ordeal of negotiating was done, the anger on both sides dissipated. Says Urfer, "There were no grudges, no long-lasting hard feelings."

In time, says Rothschild, Knoll grew to like having the structure that the union provided: "He stated openly and regularly that it clarified office issues, so that people weren't always running back to him with every little problem." It also gave him a swatter with which to slap things down. When the union in January 1985 presented Knoll and Vander Meer with the tabulated results of a performance evaluation conducted by employees, Knoll replied that the survey was "appreciated" even though "such exercises are of very little usefulness." Then Knoll—whom the workers rated high on technical skills and low on managerial ones—refused a union request to discuss the findings at a full-staff meeting, on grounds that "business between the union and *The Progressive*'s management is to be transacted by the union's designated stewards."

Nineteen-eighty-four was an election year, and Knoll, not surprisingly, was disgusted by the choices. The Democrats' answer to Ronald Reagan was a sacrificial liberal named Walter Mondale. "The Democratic Party," Knoll said at the time, "is an institution that no longer serves any purpose except to elect candidates. It has no real body of principle, no ideological context of any substance. I think it's morally and intellectually bankrupt." He couldn't wait for the presidential election to be over, "so we can start talking rationally about politics again."

By this time, Knoll's rejection of liberalism was so complete that he corrected anyone who applied the term to him. "You can call me a progressive or a radical or a socialist or even an anarchist," he'd say. "Just don't call me a liberal." Rothschild never quite understood Knoll's need to draw this line in the sand: "I think it's largely a semantic exercise; most people identify liberal as left-wing." But from Knoll's point of view, if Walter Mondale was a liberal, he was not.

Unlike liberals, Knoll did not believe that the state—the Government, the capitalist system, the two-party system, the network of people and institutions making up official power—could be redeemed or reformed. He relished rather his role as a person who would have no truck with official power. In 1983, Knoll got a letter from someone who wanted to submit an article to *The Progressive* but wondered whether this would "automatically" result in his inclusion on "the FBI subversive list." Knoll, as always, took time to reply:

"I wish I could assure you that writing an article for *The Progressive* would guarantee you a place on 'the FBI subversive list,' " he began. "Unfortunately, I have no reason to believe that such honors are accorded 'automatically' to *The Progressive*'s writers. To be on the safe side, your article for this magazine ought to be complemented by other, equally 'subversive' activities." After suggesting various acts of protest and civil disobedience, Knoll concluded: "Then you can go ahead and write your piece for *The Progressive* secure in the knowledge that your Government counts you among its enemies. It's a grand feeling."

In terms of editorial content, *The Progressive* was better than ever. Rothschild and Peck hit their stride as writers. Rothschild's topics included CIA recruitment on campus, the Reagan-era heyday of corporate crime, and an investigative report on the murder of Mexican journalist Manuel Buendia. Peck focused on the threats to civil liberties posed by Government wiretappers (given new license by the Reagan Administration), the Federal Emergency Management Agency (which, he reported, was monitoring political dissent and seeking powers to censor communications and imprison dissidents in the event of a national emergency), and the American Civil Liberties Union (which agreed to a CIA exemption from the Freedom of Information Act). For the magazine's January 1985 issue, Rothschild and Peck teamed up on a major article debunking Star Wars, Ronald Reagan's mad scheme to build a shield that would—with luck and many billions of dollars—help the United States "win" an all-out nuclear war.

Beyond a doubt, though, the magazine's crowning journalistic achievement during this period was free-lance writer Allan Nairn's May 1984 expose, "Behind the Death Squads: An exclusive report on the U.S. role in El Salvador's official terror." The article fingered the CIA as the prime mover behind the murderous activities of the Salvadoran Death Squads. It was great reporting, based in large part on interviews with named sources who should have known better than to say what they did to Nairn. *The Progressive* used its cover to shout the first 112 words:

> Early in the 1960s, during the Kennedy Administration, agents of the U.S. Government in El Salvador set up two official security organizations that killed thousands of peasants and suspected leftists over the next fifteen years. These organizations, guided by American operatives, developed into the paramilitary apparatus that came to be known as the Salvadoran Death Squads. Today, even as the Reagan Administration publicly condemns the Death Squads, the CIA—in violation of U.S. law—continues to provide training, support, and intelligence to security forces directly involved in Death Squad activity. Interviews with dozens of current and former Salvadoran officers, civilians, and official American sources disclose a pattern of sustained U.S. participation in

And then it continued on Page 20.

Knoll, who had clashed with Nairn over the editing of the piece ("That was as close as I've ever come to a physical confrontation with a writer," he later said), used that month's "Memo from the Editor" to defend the magazine's rare use of the word "exclusive": "We break our share—and more than our share, I think—of exclusive stories, but as a rule we feel no need to crow about it. We're in business, after all, to do what the mass media don't do: to report the news they neglect and provide the analysis they withhold. In that sense, *The Progressive* is chock full of exclusives every month. Only once in a rare while do we have an article of such transcendent importance that we feel justified in calling attention to it by labeling it *exclusive*."

Throughout that summer, *The Progressive* sought to draw attention to Nairn's story. Press releases were sent. Phone calls were made.

But to Knoll's great disappointment, most media ignored the story entirely. It seemed to Knoll that if every newspaper in the country could report on *The Progressive*'s H-bomb article they ought to at least notice a piece on how the U.S. Government was actively aiding and abetting mass murderers. In frustration, *The Progressive* raised money to publish a version of the article as a full-page ad in *The Washington Post*, Knoll's alma mater. Still, the story was overlooked. In 1993, Nairn's allegations were substantially confirmed by a United Nations Truth Commission report. This, of course, was long after media attention to this ongoing slaughter might have helped stop it.

Another article of note appeared in the July 1988 issue. "The Poverty Palace" by Knoll's old friend John Egerton accused the Southern Poverty Law Center—a respected liberal organization—of getting rich by soliciting money to fight the Ku Klux Klan. The story took a hard-edged look at a group that enjoyed broad support among people on the Left; Knoll was delighted with it. "That sort of thing really tickled him." says Egerton. "When you could take conventional wisdom and put it on its ear."

Knoll usually wrote the magazine's lead editorial and one or two shorter editorials for the magazine's "Comment" section. He also compiled the popular "No Comment" feature, consisting of quirky, true items discovered by the editors or sent in by readers. Example: "Received at Disneyland—a letter from the Selective Service System addressed to Mickey M. Mouse and opening with these words: 'Dear Registrant: Our records indicate you have not responded to our initial request for necessary date-of-birth information." It ran under the headline "Draft Dodger." In 1984, a collection of Knoll's "No Comment" items was published as a book.

It was a time of change at *The Progressive*. John Buell, the magazine's in-house political scholar, moved back to his home in Maine, while remaining on the masthead as associate editor. He stepped down from the unpaid position in 1993 because his pieces, and his editorial suggestions, were not being used. In 1985, Peck left the magazine to attend law school. The following spring, Rothschild leveraged a promotion to managing editor. Vander Meer left to become publisher of *Harvard Magazine* and was replaced by Ruth Greenspan, another alumnus of *In These Times*.

At the end of 1985, Gordon Sinykin retired as chairman of the board. The staff, which had recently held an "emergency meeting" to press for Sinykin's resignation, was ecstatic; Knoll, who boycotted that meeting, was not. Although Knoll didn't like Sinykin's imperial style, he feared the loss of his financial stewardship, and especially his ability to hold creditors at bay. There was nothing forced about Knoll's declaration to readers that, were it not for Sinykin, "*The Progressive* would have passed into history long ago." Knoll took over as chairman of the board. Sinykin stayed on as the magazine's attorney, keeping a watchful eye on its ledgers and legal affairs until his death in January 1991. Mary Sheridan remained book editor until her retirement in June 1991; she died four years later at age 83.

In 1986, Knoll made a series of Freedom of Information Act requests for files kept on *The Progressive* by the FBI, CIA, and U.S. Army. The FBI eventually released 400 pages of documents, while withholding another 400 pages as being too secret to see the light of day. The released documents were, from Knoll's point of view, mostly a disappointment. "There are, unfortunately, no scandalous disclosures," Knoll wrote in *The Progressive*, "except for the scandalous disclosure that . . . the national police force preoccupied itself for almost four decades with the most detailed scrutiny of this political magazine."

The released portion of the file contained new material about the FBI's involvement in the H-bomb case, including the list of questions its agents put to citizens to whom Howard Morland had given a copy of his article before it was banned. ("Did you make copies of the material?" "How many?" "Have you distributed the original or any other copies to any other person?" "If so, to whom?" "When?" "What are their addresses?") They also revealed that FBI snoops had poured over Jeremy Rifkin's 1971 article for the magazine, "The Red, White and Blue Left." FBI director J. Edgar Hoover, in one of his last days before his death, received a detailed memo containing such incendiary excerpts as, "The new awareness that this country is in the midst of a grave crisis . . . [ellipses in original] can lead to a mass-based revolutionary struggle if the movement will discard its self-imposed ideological isolation and begin to re-identify with the revolutionary principles and symbols of the American heritage."

But the FBI's interest was short-lived. Less than two years later, in October 1973, the bureau decided to not renew its subscription to the magazine, as it had each year done "discreetly" through an FBI contact in New York. "By not renewing subscription," a released memo said, "bureau saves $8 a year." Ouch.

Knoll's FOI request to the U.S. Army produced an equally disappointing document. It was a detailed analysis of *The Progressive*'s content produced in October 1954 in response to concerns that the magazine may be unfit for soldiers to see. Knoll, who had at this time been an enlisted man at Fort Sheridan, Illinois, must have winced to see the Army analyst's conclusion: "From all available indications it appears that 'The Progressive' is a liberal publication which is entirely legitimate and gives no grounds for suspicion." The CIA, last and least, coughed up documents revealing its involvement in the H-bomb case, as well as copies it had made of Knoll's articles in *The Progressive* about CIA abuses.

Erwin's father Carl, his health deteriorating, moved to Madison in 1983, at the invitation of Erwin and Doris. Jonathan Knoll, then twenty-two, was on his way back from Israel and drove his grandfather from New York. Carl Knoll lived for a spell with the Knolls at their McFarland home. This was not ideal, and Carl soon entered Elder House, a Madison retirement home. He lived out the remainder of his days fighting senility. "I may forget something that happened to me a short time before. It may or may not come to my memory a short time later," he wrote in an aborted attempt, in the late 1980s, to record his personal history in a spiral notebook. "Life means hope. I don't give up the hope that someday my memory will start to work like in the past." It never did. The same notebook contains a half-dozen failed efforts to compose a letter to his daughter Alice; the words flow forth haphazardly, their meanings too obscure to decipher. Carl Knoll died of heart failure on June 8, 1986. He was buried in New York City. A year later, in accordance with Jewish tradition, a memorial service was held to unveil a tombstone. Erwin, in a letter to Jonathan, hoped "you and David will steadfastly refuse to succumb to any such foolishness in my behalf."

Jonathan, by this time, had moved to Boulder, Colorado, to pursue his interest in bicycle racing. He had, throughout his life, enjoyed his father's support to chart his own course. When Jonathan developed a fanatical interest in tae kwon do, beginning at age 14 and continuing for more than a decade, his father went to tournaments, and developed a liking for the sport. "There's nothing like seeing Erwin Knoll at a tae kwon do tournament, cheering his son, the blackbelt," says Jonathan, who won several major titles.

In early 1987, Erwin and Jonathan had their only falling out. Erwin, in a note, cast gentle aspersion on his son's casual lifestyle. Jonathan responded with an angry letter. His father backed down right away. "Let me be clear," he wrote. "I have no criticism of the life that you are leading in Boulder. I am concerned about your future—that's only natural, I think—but not concerned enough to question your judgment or challenge your decisions. On the contrary, I'm proud of you for being an autonomous human being who lives by his own standards instead of conforming to anyone else's (including mine)."

David, meanwhile, was still wandering. His first marriage ended in divorce. He hung with a crowd that was, if not dangerous, at least interested in playing the part. Like the majority of his associates, David "affected a swaggering hood attitude, including the appropriate accouterments of being a swaggering hood"—i.e., he packed a pistol. In the mid-1980s, David made the modest transition from hood to businessman, running a stereo and video repair store in downtown Madison. His custom during this time was to show up at the Knolls' Fourth of July get-togethers wearing the briefest of bikini briefs, a gesture everyone understood was designed to torture his dad. When his father would object, David would say, "You've got a problem: You're either an anarchist, or a Victorian, but you can't be both." By 1987, having learned through bitter experience the wisdom of his father's advice about finding enjoyable work, David put on some clothes, got his G.E.D., and applied for admission to the University of Wisconsin.

David graduated from college, and went on to the UW-Madison Law School. Erwin always had an interest in the law, and got a vicarious thrill out of David's law-student days. In the spring of 1994, Erwin sat in on a whole semester of classes—a UW law seminar about the death penalty, a topic on which he planned to write a book. (Knoll was gathering articles and studies and planning to witness an execution, probably in Florida, as part of his research.) David was struck by the sharp contrast between the attitudes of his father and those of his classmates, who "were far enough in their law-school careers that most of their intrinsic sense of moral outrage had been weaned from their system." His father, he realized, was fundamentally different: "He was an idealist." He had faith in people and the power of persuasion; he believed it was possible to talk one's way into a fairer, more humane society.

At least he was determined to try.

Photo by Zane Williams

CHAPTER SIXTEEN

On Building a Movement

The most famous member of the Knoll family, before Erwin, was Israel Knoll, a rabbi in Galicia in the 1800s. This was a position of keen importance—not only for religious reasons, but because Galician Jews, having no expectation of justice from the courts, turned to rabbis to settle disputes. Rabbi "Reb" Knoll's wisdom was legendary. In 1934, his great grandson, Samson Knoll, then a twenty-one-year-old refugee from Nazi Germany, met an elderly Jew in a cafe in Strasbourg, France. The older man, on discovering Samson's connection to Israel Knoll, exclaimed, "When I was a child, my grandfather used to hold me on his knees and tell me what a holy man your great grandfather was."

Erwin, too, was someone people turned to for guidance. He was never at a loss for words—or convictions. "In times of crisis, he was a rock," says Matt Rothschild. "People who were confused, concerned, or distraught could take great solace in Erwin's courage and steadfastness and clarity."

Over the years, Knoll developed opinions about a great many things, and shared them at every opportunity. He almost never turned down an invitation to speak. And he was just as willing to lead a discussion for the Junior Great Books reading students in Madison as he was to address the Coalition for Nuclear Disarmament in New Jersey.

Knoll understood that, to build a movement, progressives had to cultivate an audience. In 1987 he premiered a weekly half-hour radio program, "Second Opinion," in which he interviewed guests—some local people, some nationally known figures who happened to pass through town. The show was taped at WORT, Madison's listener-sponsored community radio station, and sent by tape and satellite to stations throughout the country. In time, "Second Opinion" was carried by more than sixty stations, from big cities like Chicago, Little Rock, and Honolulu to tiny towns like Alamosa, Colorado, and Magdalena, New Mexico.

By the end of each episode of "Second Opinion," listeners had indeed heard two opinions—Knoll's guest's, and Knoll's. In 1987, guest Midge Miller, chair of a local liberal think-tank, casually asserted the conventional wisdom that low voter turnout for national elections constituted a "failure of citizenship." Knoll dissented: "I think people decline to participate because they don't think it's going to make a difference. And that's not a lack of citizenship on the part of the people who choose not to vote, it's a failure of the candidates to meet their responsibilities." Sometimes Knoll's questions were so loaded it's a wonder they didn't blow up in his face. Once, during the waning years of the Reagan presidency, he began an interview with a university economist by asking, "Am I wrong in believing that this economy is rotten to the core and the so-called Reagan prosperity is a sham?"

Knoll's goal was to jar the members of his audience out of their usual ways of thinking. To this end he often took what others regarded as extreme positions. None was more extreme—or more controversial—than his decision not to vote for president.

In the summer of 1988, having sized up the two major party candidates, George Bush and Michael Dukakis, and the array of obscure third-party contenders, Knoll decided that, for the first time since he was old enough, he wasn't going to vote for President. Instead, as he wrote in an article for *Isthmus*, a Madison weekly, he was choosing "to reject our pathetically inadequate electoral system by the only means available to me: my refusal to join in the pretense that I've been given a choice." The essay, which ran under the headline "Wake Me When It's Over" (subtitled "A Nonvoter's Manifesto)," drew a deluge of outraged reaction. One reader wrote, "I am shocked! Twice! First, that Erwin Knoll wrote such an article, and secondly, that you would print it." "I think Erwin Knoll has done a terrible thing by exposing himself as a nonvoter," wrote another. Knoll, in his published reply, was unapologetic: "I'm impressed with the vehemence, if not the logic, of many of the responses to my modest manifesto. I must have touched an exposed nerve. . . . I'm ready to admit that I underestimated the value of the electoral process—not as an instrument of political change, but as a balm to soothe the tender consciences of well-intentioned liberals."

Knoll's "Manifesto" won an award from the Milwaukee Press Club as the best piece of analytical reporting in Wisconsin that year. Knoll said that "in forty years of writing for publication, I have never had a more vehement response"—until he set forth the same position in *The Progressive* in 1992. Then, the choice was between Bush and Bill Clinton, which Knoll felt was in itself ample evidence that a lot of work still needed to be done: "We can speak and write, meet and march, agitate and demonstrate, educate and organize. And eventually, when we've built a constituency for change in this country, we can start thinking again about electing somebody who will address our needs and carry out our wishes."

It wasn't just weak-kneed liberals who had a problem with Knoll's refusal to vote for president. His wife Doris, a counselor at a Madison abortion clinic, had little trouble preferring Clinton over Bush because of their respective positions on reproductive freedom. (In retrospect, she says, "Erwin was absolutely, 100 percent right. Clinton is a total loss.") Others preferred the Democratic contender to the GOP incumbent because they were concerned about Supreme Court appointments, or with the idea that he would do a better job protecting people in need. "That's enough for them, and I don't fault them," said Knoll. "But it's not enough for me." Rather, he sought to preserve through his conduct "the commitment to aspire to something better." And that meant telling the Democratic Party to shove off.

The two-party system, said Knoll, had become "the enemy of Democracy in America." He vowed to never vote for a Democrat again, "because my first obligation is to assist in the dissolution of that party." That July, before Bill Clinton had finished making campaign promises, let alone got around to breaking them, Knoll declared: "These folks who earnestly and sincerely and with the best of intentions believe Bill Clinton is by far the better road are going to be betrayed. I've had people say to me, 'First we get Clinton elected and then we push him to the left.' With what? What's the lever that's going to push him to the left when he's in office if he can't be pushed to the left now, when he needs our votes?"

For some, such as Knoll's old friend Morton Mintz, suggesting that people not vote for president was just plain irresponsible. "It's all very well for someone in your position—or mine—to say it doesn't matter, that both parties are corrupt and that you don't have a choice," Mintz recalls writing Knoll. "But I take into account the consequences of a Republican victory for helpless and downtrodden people."

James Weinstein, editor and publisher of *In These Times,* also distances himself from Knoll's position: "Erwin was much more of an anarchist than me. He believed the political system was a fraud. My belief is that you have to participate in that system. We live in an institutional two-party state."

Knoll's friend Ralph Nader takes a more positive view. "Of course, if everybody did what Erwin did, where would we be? But if you look at it as an attempt to communicate a message in a bold way, there's a lot of value to that."

Knoll liked and admired Nader, but thought he was naive to respond to injustices in the capitalist system by calling for greater regulation. The federal regulatory apparatus, Knoll said, had become "all but useless because it is so thoroughly run by the interests it is supposed to regulate." Besides, the idea that regulation could fix the problems of the system—a belief also held by his predecessor, Bob La Follette—struck Knoll as akin to believing an improved deck-chair arrangement might save the Titanic. (Nader, in response, says regulation is only a first step, and must be followed with more creative strategies.)

"There is really a fundamental difference in the way Ralph and I view how this economic system works," Knoll said. "Something comes along like the [explosion-prone] Ford Pinto, and Ralph says, 'Look at this terrible abuse. We've got to make them do the right thing.' I look at the Ford Pinto and I say, 'Look at the way this system works: This goddam corporation would rather kill people and make more money than stop killing people and make less money.' Not because it's an aberration. Not because they're evil guys. Not because they have a twisted set of values. It's because every manager knows what his board, what his owners, what the people he's accountable to demand of him: a balance sheet and a bottom line that says, 'Okay, these cars explode on impact, so we may have to pay out $10 million in injury claims. But if we fix it it might cost us $11.5 million, so if we don't fix it we're a million-and-a-half bucks ahead.' And that, I think, is inherent in the nature of capitalism, and anyone who doesn't do that bottom-line calculation is not faithfully serving in his job."

At times, Knoll was not out to enlighten people so much as to provoke them. What bothered him most about what he saw happening in the world around him was that other people were not as mad about it as he was. He noted the damage done to the prestige of the Presidency, beginning with Eisenhower's prevarications over the U-2 incident and continuing with Kennedy's Bay of Pigs, Johnson's Vietnam, Nixon's Watergate, and Reagan's Iran-contra arms scandal. "Few Americans still cling to the cherry-tree myth that their President cannot tell a lie," he said in one speech. "But I'm afraid we've succumbed to something far more pernicious—a cynical acceptance of falsehood as a way of government and a way of life. . . . We all know the emperor has no clothes, but we seem to have become comfortable with the sight of his bare behind."

At the heart of the problem, Knoll was convinced, was liberalism itself. He thought liberals were too willing to compromise: "Liberals in my judgment are people who will try to promote just enough change to allow themselves to sleep comfortably at night, and no more than that, and I don't think that's enough." Conservatives, he felt, at least stood for something, however offensive to his sensibilities it might be.

When Knoll was asked by the Wisconsin-based Johnson Foundation to deliver a paper in response to the question, "On what common ground do liberals and conservatives agree?" he wrote back, "I would answer, on altogether too much common ground. That's why I am not a liberal." He did, of course, deliver the paper. He said he had come up with a few "tattered remnants" of common ground between the Left and Right: "We may not be able to stitch these together into a flag we can all march behind, but we can, at least, improvise a blanket under which we can huddle together."

Knoll told the group he admired such staunch conservatives as Senator Robert Taft, Republican from Ohio. True to his party's anti-interventionist roots, Taft in 1945 opposed the post-war commitment of U.S. troops to Europe, warning that they'd still be there in twenty years. "All the Democrats, all the good liberals, all the internationalist moderates in the Republican Party laughed at Taft's silly prediction," Knoll said. "But here we are, not twenty years later but forty-seven, and the troops are still over there." He also praised a conservative Republican congressman from Kansas who in 1951 introduced a resolution condemning the United States' deepening involvement in Korea. The resolution said the President's commitment of troops without prior approval of Congress violated "the fundamental precepts of the Constitution"; it called on Congress to memorialize "those who have already fallen on the bleak wastes of the battlefields of foreign theaters, by taking immediate appropriate action" to preclude this from happening again.

"Boy, how we who opposed the Vietnam War could have used the eloquence of that Kansas conservative who wanted to summon Congress back to its constitutional responsibilities," Knoll said. "And we could have used him when Ronald Reagan dispatched troops into Grenada, and when George Bush invaded Panama, and when the United States went to war in the Persian Gulf. But by then that principled young conservative was gone. His name was Bob Dole, he had become the Republican leader in the U.S. Senate, and he had long forsaken conservative principle for partisan expediency."

Knoll outlined his idea of exemplary conservatism: "I'm talking about the kind of conservatism that says, 'The free market is a great and glorious device, but when it doesn't work it doesn't work. It doesn't work to provide decent housing for poor people, so we must do something different. After all, we can't have people sleeping in the streets. And it doesn't work to provide medical care for millions upon millions of Americans, so we must do something different. After all, we can't have people ailing, suffering, or dying for want of medical care.'" He identified areas of concern: respect for individual liberties and human rights, for resources and the environment. "It seems to me that all of these are obvious conservative issues, and I can't imagine why the Right has abandoned them to be looked after by the Left."

As caretakers of this legacy, the Left needs all the help it can get. In March 1992, Knoll did his part by delivering a speech at the annual dinner of the Women's International League for Peace and Freedom in Madison. He began by seeking to disabuse his audience of the then-popular notion that the nation's political woes all traced to the election of Ronald Reagan. "We have terribly short memories," he said, recalling President Truman's decision to use atomic bombs and sign the National Security Act—"the basic document legitimatizing the Cold War and the pursuit of American empire." The act created the CIA and "converted our War Department, which at least had the virtue of being honestly named, into the Department of Defense."

After that, Knoll stated, the United States became the "preeminent international aggressors" on earth. "Everywhere in the world, we have undermined and subverted indigenous attempts to redress monstrous inequities, to redistribute land, to combat the repressive legacy of colonialism. Everywhere in the world, we have sided with the rich ruling elites and the despots who did their dirty work."

Back at home, the gap between rich and poor widened and the quality of life declined. Knoll set forth a nightmare vision, not of the future but of the present: "We are curtailing civil liberties and rolling back due process. Our jails and prisons are packed, and construction of correctional facilities appears to be one of the few growth industries in America. The rate of homelessness in our cities is rising. Our schools are neglected, our culture is in decline, our environment is being destroyed by polluters hell-bent on maximizing profits, and our health-care system, or lack of a system, is a worldwide disgrace."

What's a progressive to do? First, advised Knoll, let go of the notion that the Democratic Party offers any kind of real alternative. "Today," he quipped, "the United States is second only to China as the world's largest one-party state." And while the emergence of third parties was a good sign, Knoll said the most important work to be done had nothing to do with the ballot box. "It has to do with rekindling a political culture in this country in which fundamental issues are addressed squarely and openly—in a way that can't be done in ten-second sound bites or even the dog-and-pony shows that pass for presidential 'debates.'"

Concluded Knoll, "We need to talk about these issues to our neighbors on the block where we live, to our fellow workers, to people we see in church or at the bowling alley or in the tavern. This is the stuff that matters. And, having said all that, I'm not at all suggesting that we will necessarily prevail. There *are* tough times ahead.

But as the great Italian socialist, Gramsci, wrote, we must sustain pessimism of the intellect but optimism of the will. He was in a fascist prison when he wrote these words. Can we say less? Whether we win or lose, we should try to revive the kind of politics that will give us the patriotic satisfaction of knowing that we did our best to make a country we can be proud of again."

CHAPTER SEVENTEEN

First Things First

Erwin Knoll believed any position worth holding had to withstand scrutiny. "It was the Nazis who proscribed speech," he said. "It was their conduct that could not tolerate the challenge of speech." Knoll's boyhood experience as a Jew fleeing Nazism formed his core political values; it was the reason he found censorship, like killing, so reprehensible: "When you kill somebody, and when you gag somebody, you're committing irreversible acts. You kill somebody and you can't bring them back to life; you cut off speech and you foreclose the debate. So those are *terminal* actions. That's why I despise them, because I know how capable of error human beings are."

In the late 1980s, Knoll first typed out his standard speech on free speech, which he revised and delivered many times. The First Amendment's guarantee that "Congress shall make no law abridging freedom of speech or of the press," he told his audiences, is "the most clear, the most categorical, the most absolute statement to be found in the Constitution of the United States." Why, then, "do we spend so much time arguing about it, legislating about it, and suing each other about it? Why do some of our most corrosive and divisive controversies arise over what kind of speech, or print, or art, or music, or movies, or any other form of expression is or is not covered by the First Amendment?"

The reason, he'd say, is that most people—audience members included—occasionally came across something that prompts them to say, like the Nuclear Regulatory Commission chairman who in 1979 wanted to suppress news about the accident at Three Mile Island, "Which amendment is it that guarantees freedom of the press?

Well, I'm against it." The First Amendment is "in deep trouble," Knoll said, because of this popular yearning. Then, like a rabbi addressing his congregation, he asked members of his audience to look within:

"What aspects of the First Amendment do *you* find troublesome? That it allows Nazis and members of the Ku Klux Klan to publish hate literature? That it permits sleazy supermarket tabloids to engage in sordid speculation (true or false) about the extramarital activities of presidential candidates? That it is invoked by your newspaper as a rationale for reporting on local troubles that might be better kept out of public view? . . . Can you honestly say that you've never encountered a news story or an editorial or an opinion column that you wouldn't gladly have suppressed if you'd had the power to do so?"

He'd pause to gaze at his audience of would-be censors, then say, "I'm glad that you don't have that power. I'm even more glad that I don't have that power. Why? Because I don't trust either of us—not you, not me—to decide what our fellow citizens should read or hear or write or say."

Knoll conceded that nearly all assaults on the First Amendment are made with the best of intentions—for instance, to spare others from "racist fulminations." This in no way lessened Knoll's contempt for what he called "the censorship mentality."

"You know," he'd tell his audiences, "the censorship mentality has always baffled me, because it must be based either on profound ignorance or on incredible arrogance. The ignorant censor says, 'I haven't read this, or listened to it, or seen it, but I just know it's terrible, so I can't allow you to see it or say it or read it or write it or listen to it.' And the arrogant censor says, 'I have read or seen or heard this, and it hasn't hurt me because I'm a very good person, but you're not nearly as good as I am, so I must make sure that you can't have access to this dangerous or filthy stuff.'"

Knoll would update his speech with current examples, such as the case of a twenty-four-year-old Florida man who in 1994 was fined $3,000, placed on three years' probation, ordered not to have contact with children, to perform 1,248 hours of community service, and attend a college class in journalism ethics—all because a judge didn't like his "crude and ugly" (Knoll's words) comic book. He would retool it for addresses to librarians, or for teachers—telling, for instance, about the teacher in Irvine, California, who assigned her class to read *Fahrenheit 451,* Ray Bradbury's horrific tale about book-burning, after blacking out such words as "hell" and "damn" from every classroom copy of the book. Or the high-school principal in Oregon who wouldn't allow the student paper to report on sports losses.

Invariably, Knoll would conclude his remarks on the First Amendment by talking about *The Progressive*'s H-bomb case, in which the "extremely narrow exception" to the rule against prior restraint carved out by the U.S. Supreme Court's decision in *Near v. Minnesota* became, in the hands of Judge Robert W. Warren, a wedge to give the Government sweeping powers to censor and suppress. The lesson: "Even the narrowest of exceptions is too broad." And that, he concluded, is why the First Amendment was written "so simply, so clearly, and so absolutely."

Protecting the First Amendment became a driving passion. In 1985, Knoll testified before a Wisconsin Senate committee in opposition to a proposed new state obscenity law, called Senate Bill 31. "The history of such statutes, in this state and elsewhere, is uniformly dismal," he said. "At best, obscenity laws are overly broad, vague, and confusing—defects that ultimately result in court decisions that hold such statutes to be unconstitutional. At worst, obscenity laws are repressive, resulting in assaults on freedoms we cherish."

Finally, Knoll quoted from the Wisconsin Constitution, which guarantees: "Every person may freely speak, write and publish his sentiments on all subjects, being responsible for the abuse of that right, and no laws will be passed to restrain or abridge the liberty of speech or of the press." This language, Knoll told the committee, "not only bars the kind of effort you are undertaking here today, but it also offers recourse to anyone who sustains genuine injury. Any person who can prove that he or she has been harmed by spoken or written words, by performances or by works of art, can recover damages. That is the constitutional remedy in Wisconsin. Senate Bill 31 is not." The bill died in committee that year but substantial parts of it were passed two years later and signed into law by Republican Governor Tommy Thompson.

Knoll's most pitched battle in behalf of freedom of speech was over the issue of free expression, or the lack thereof, in shopping malls. It began in 1984, when a local mall named East Towne barred a local dance troupe called Nu Parable from performing an antinuclear routine. In response, Knoll and a small group of accomplices, mostly employees at *The Progressive*, went to the mall to hand out leaflets containing the full text of the Bill of Rights. Knoll often told the story of a young girl, perhaps twelve years old, who accepted a leaflet from him and, after looking it over, asked, "Is this really the Bills of Rights?" "You bet it is," Knoll answered. "Wow!" said the girl, getting more copies to give to her friends. Moments later, a security guard tried, without success, to rip the leaflets from Knoll's hands to prevent further exposure of the citizenry to this radical tract.

In a letter to mall manager Dave Van Dusen, Knoll said he was "appalled to learn that the free-speech rights guaranteed to all Americans by the First Amendment to the U.S. Constitution are held in contempt by the management of East Towne." He said he was sending a copy of his letter to the managers of the three stores at which he and Doris had charge accounts. "I hope, as a customer, that they will take steps to dissociate themselves from your dangerous and offensive position."

Days later, the mall's attorneys filed a lawsuit against Knoll, three other leafletters, "and all persons acting in concert with them or under their direction." Its goal: to bar them from the premises, except for the express purpose of shopping. Defendant Keenen Peck, the magazine's associate editor, wrote a brief arguing that the shopping mall was the modern equivalent of public markets and town squares. Knoll, in an affidavit, warned that "If these areas are to be closed to public discourse on matters of most vital concern to citizens of a democracy, our free society will have been dealt a serious blow, and my own civil liberties will be substantially diminished." A local judge refused to grant a preliminary injunction, but that didn't stop the mall management from continuing to harass leafletters. In March 1985, six leafletters, including Sam Day, *The Progressive*'s former managing editor, were dragged from the premises by mall security while Madison police officers looked on. Day wrote a letter of protest to then-Madison Police Chief David Couper, whose wall was adorned with pictures of Mahatma Gandhi and Dr. Martin Luther King Jr. The next time out, the police protected the protesters.

In June 1987, the Wisconsin Supreme Court issued a ruling in the Nu Parable case. "Malls, shopping centers, department stores, and specialty stores," it said, "exist for primarily one function: profit for their owners." Thus the mall owners, the court concluded, could prohibit any speech they saw as threatening to that end. Knoll, in a column, recalled again the twelve-year-old girl who had been so excited to encounter a copy of the Bill of Rights. "I think the Wisconsin Supreme Court let her down."

It certainly let Knoll down: The Nu Parable decision was quickly followed by a lower court ruling against Knoll and his co-defendants. All were henceforth barred from East Towne and its crosstown counterpart, West Towne, "except strictly in the capacity of a customer or shopper."

At times, Knoll had to fight for *The Progressive*'s own First Amendment rights. Most commonly, this meant defending the right of prison inmates to receive their free subscriptions to the magazine, which was occasionally deemed too subversive. Knoll would lodge bitter protests with wardens, state prison officials, and lawmakers—and keep at it until he won.

In 1990, a sophomore of conservative bent nearly succeeded in getting *The Progressive* barred from the library of his high school in Colonie, New York. The student, Michael Elmendorf, wrote at the time that "a few nationwide conservative groups have been extremely helpful in terms of providing me with support, materials and direction." Elmendorf also claimed that his 400 fellow schoolmates who signed a petition against censorship had been duped, because the people circulating these petitions "never mentioned *The Progressive*, nor showed anyone the magazine." In contrast, all 124 students who signed his petition to ban *The Progressive*, he boasted, had seen it. They just didn't think their peers could be trusted to see it also.

An even more outlandish threat emerged in 1986, when the UW-Madison prohibited the campus sale of monthly magazines. This was eyed as a possibly constitutional way to banish three soft-porn magazines—*Playboy, Playgirl* and *Penthouse*—that enjoyed brisk sales on campus. This restriction applied also to *Harper's, The Atlantic Monthly, Reader's Digest,* and *The Progressive*. Knoll, in a letter to *The Capital Times*, unloaded: "They would have been better advised to proscribe all publications whose names begin with the letter P; that would have made just as much sense, and they could have snared *Playboy, Playgirl,* and *Penthouse*—and *The Progressive*, too—without putting *Scientific American* on their Index of Banned Periodicals.

"Have you ever noticed that censors—the folks who arrogate to themselves the power what others should see, or hear, or read—have an uncanny knack for making fools of themselves?" The ban was rescinded after two months.

In 1992, Knoll again testified before a state legislative committee, this time regarding the University of Wisconsin's proposed "hate-speech" rule creating penalties for campus expression deemed to create a hostile environment for others. Such a rule, Knoll said, "could all too quickly become a full-scale assault on many other kinds of speech." And the victims of this next assault, he predicted, "are likely to be some of the very same groups that are supporting this insidious regulation—racial minorities, women, lesbians and gays, and political dissidents."

Besides, Knoll continued, "the proper response to bad speech is not censorship, is not a gag rule, is not punishment. The proper response to bad speech is good speech. If we cannot prevail in full and open debate with the forces of bigotry, we might as well shut down this university, because we've already lost the struggle for a rational and humane society."

Knoll's opposition to the hate-speech rule pitted him against the UW's liberal elite. James Sulton, the UW System's special assistant on minority affairs, squared off against Knoll in a live radio debate. He said the rule (later struck down as unconstitutional) was needed to keep minorities from being driven away by epithet-spewing fellow students. Knoll responded by noting that the university, which has never done a good job recruiting minority students, had just approved another tuition hike: "I think that's just monstrous hypocrisy, to give lip service to the idea of getting more minorities, and then freeze them out with money."

If Knoll was appalled by the censorial impulses of liberals, he was even more affronted when the same proclivities were displayed by the Left. That summer of 1992, he sent a scathing letter to the editor of a local left-wing tabloid, *The Madison Insurgent*, regarding an article it ran attacking the ACLU as "racist" for opposing the UW's hate-speech rule. "What astonishes me about [writer Mario] Compean's peevish little diatribe is this statement: 'Any first-year law student can tell these folks that the purpose of all laws is to regulate conduct that has a harmful effect on society or violates the rights of others.' For this we need *The Madison Insurgent*?

"I'm sure there are first-year law students who subscribe to Compean's naive notion of 'the purpose of all laws,' but I know bright junior-high students who understand that the purpose of all laws is to protect the interest of society's ruling elites. Folks who can't pursue their politics without invoking and defending the power of the state have no business calling themselves 'insurgents.' "

More and more, Knoll liked to mix it up, to engage in debate. "I'd rather test my ideas against someone who disagrees with me than simply present them," he said. "But I do believe strongly in the things I believe in, and I'm going to articulate them as forcefully as I can, without reservation, without hesitation, and certainly without embarrassment. I think people ought to arrive at their judgments the same way I've arrived at mine—by hearing every kind of point of view expressed as forcefully as it could be."

A common judgment among people who heard Knoll express himself was that he was a bit too forceful. "He could be a real bear, pompous, hard to deal with," says Ruth Conniff, who interned at *The Progressive* in the summer of 1988 and came back as associate editor in January 1991. "He was like a lawyer: He could put together a very coherent and forceful argument for any position." On one occasion, a concern arose over the adequacy of the fact-checking done by the magazine. Knoll began arguing that the huge fact-checking operations at larger publications were simply beyond *The Progressive*'s means. Before long, says Conniff, "He basically backed himself into a corner, against any form of fact-checking. It was absurd."

Another tussle came when Conniff questioned the magazine's use of the word "mistress" in a 1991 interview with writer Graham Greene, who died shortly thereafter. The original version had referred to this person in Greene's life as a "lady friend." "Mistress," Knoll insisted, "is a perfectly appropriate word." Conniff suggested that "lover" might be better. Knoll: "Now you want to censor the truth!" He told Conniff to write a letter to the editor. She's still ticked off: "He was so self-righteous about it." But the next week, when the two of them went out to lunch, Knoll told Conniff, "You should never think I don't want to hear your opinion."

Imparting knowledge to interns was one of Knoll's fundamental commitments at the magazine. He started offering internships—unpaid, except for writing accepted for publication—soon after he came on board. Over the years he worked with dozens of young writers. Knoll was always patient and encouraging—a good teacher. And, says Conniff, "he did not forget to tell you when you did a good job."

When Conniff first came to *The Progressive*, "I thought Erwin was wonderful. He was very affectionate, very grandfatherly. Other people just couldn't bear Erwin. But I was blind to his foibles."

Conniff recalls how Knoll would prowl the office, his fists clenched ("There was a lot of anger in there"), looking for a fight. One day the editors were discussing an article about homeless children that made mention of a child prostitute. Knoll was disgusted with this aspect of the story, and wanted to put it lower in the piece. "Did you see that movie?" Conniff asked, about to mention its name. "Erwin flew into a rage," she says. "What a piece of shit!" he fumed. "That movie was incredibly dishonest!" He went on and on until Conniff asked, "What movie are you talking about?" "*My Own Private Idaho*," he answered. Oh. The movie on her mind was *Paris is Burning*.

As frustrating as it was to argue with Knoll, he was a great debate coach. He would prep Conniff before she made public appearances. Once, before going on a radio call-in show to discuss an article she had written in defense of AFDC, she asked Knoll what to say to callers who claim all welfare recipients are lazy bums. Knoll knew: "Just say, 'I know people on welfare, and they aren't lazy. Maybe the people *you* know are lazy. . . .' " Laughs Conniff, "He loved ad hominem attacks."

Knoll reveled in tales of his own rebellions—how he quit jobs on principle with no new job in sight. He always mentioned how nice it was that Doris supported him in these decisions. And he was pleased to find a rebellious spirit in others. One internship candidate, being put through an interview process that invariably included a sparring match with Knoll, hit the ball out of the park when the conversation turned to the subject of his disability. "I'm colorblind," the applicant said, looking at Knoll. "I see by your tie that you are, too." Says Conniff, "Erwin hired him for that alone."

Even though Knoll didn't mind being talked back to, he exerted an authoritarian presence in the office. A case in point: the magazine's ill-fated sexual-harassment policy. Knoll once said that the only First Amendment issue on which he hesitated to embrace an absolutist position was that of sexist pinups in the workplace. "If it's my workplace, I'm going to tear them down," he recalled telling an audience, "because I don't want my people working in that environment. I don't want them to feel embarrassed, or intimidated, or exploited." This issue, apparently, never came up. But in October 1991, as the Clarence Thomas scandal unfolded, then-publisher Matt Rothschild thought the waters were safe to propose a policy to "ensure that sexual harassment does not occur at *The Progressive*."

Rothschild's proposed policy called for no workplace propositions, no physical contact with employees, no telling of dirty jokes, no discussions about anybody's sex life, no discussions about sex, no "general comments" about sex, and no comments on employees' appearance or dress. Managers were instructed to have only minimal contact with employees outside the office. Rothschild says he wasn't sure how Knoll would react.

Knoll, as Rothschild recalls, "put his hands behind his neck, rocked back and forth four times, jutting out his chin, and said something like, 'This is the most bizarre and objectionable memo I have ever seen.'" Knoll was enraged. He said the proposed rules would severely curtail freedom of speech and association: "Who am I to tell managers with whom they can go to lunch?" Perhaps Knoll was most piqued by the item about physical contact. Rothschild had written, "Even seemingly innocuous hugs, arms around shoulders, pats on the back, or kisses goodbye could be interpreted by employees as unwanted and untoward. What might look innocent to you could be gross to an employee and look gruesome in the media or in a courtroom." Knoll was big on arms around the shoulders, a gesture Rothschild never really liked.

"I felt humiliated after that meeting," says Rothschild. "Erwin treated me as though I were a fool, and made no bones about it."

Conniff, for her part, felt the proposed harassment code was "stupid," but also that Knoll was wrong not to see his duty to act affirmatively to prevent sexual harassment. "What if I were sexually harassed," she asked him. "You can't go crying to some big daddy," he answered. Then what should she do? "Picket the office," he said. She thought this was ridiculous: "He wasn't ready to acknowledge his own power to intervene."

Knoll's saddest moment as editor of *The Progressive* was the untimely death of Keenen Peck. A bright and funny fellow with a shock of red hair, Peck had gone from *The Progressive* to law school to the Washington office of U.S. Senator Herb Kohl, Democrat from Wisconsin. "Keenen was one of Erwin's favorite people," says Doris. "Erwin thought he was very gifted." And although he would not discourage anyone from studying the law—or whatever else they wanted to study—Knoll privately opined that Peck's career move was journalism's loss. A far greater loss, sadly, was yet to come: In the early morning hours of June 6, 1990, after working late preparing for a hearing on a bill he had drafted, Peck died in his sleep of an aneurism, at the age of twenty-nine. Erwin, says Doris, was "devastated." Peck, he wrote in eulogy, "was a gifted journalist, a brilliant lawyer, an indefatigable champion of human rights and civil liberties, an affectionate friend, and a joyous presence in the lives of all who knew him."

Teri Terry, Knoll's secretary, remained his friend and confidant. When she left the magazine for another job in 1986, Knoll proclaimed, for perhaps the first time since he won big at the track nearly two decades before, a desire to get drunk. Knoll and Terry still got together for lunch at least once a week. Two years later, Terry came back to the magazine. It was uncanny, she says, how often both of them were on the same wavelength: She would say something he was just about to say, or retrieve a long-buried folder he was just about to ask for. Knoll gave her the benefit of his opinion on the issues of the day, and she, in turn, "taught him everyday things he was not aware of."

Like what? "Garage sales," Terry answers without hesitation. On Friday afternoons during the summer, Knoll would ask Terry, "Are we on today?" The two of them would get in his car and drive around to some of the weekend garage sales listed in the local papers. Terry also went shopping with Knoll for clothes, things he knew little about, as his ties attested.

After the Knolls' two sons were out of the nest, the nest looked large and empty. In May 1989, Erwin and Doris moved again, to a house on the northeast side of Madison. They had lived in McFarland for more than a decade, a family record. Their new home, a tastefully outfitted ranch-house at 528 Woodward Drive, was just across the road from homes on the shoreline of Lake Mendota. Knoll often said he wanted a lakefront home; this was the closest he got. Erwin fell in love with the house at first sight. Doris's reaction: "It's a ranch-house. It looks like the Midwest. I hate it."

Erwin Knoll was not the kind of home-owner you'd see trimming the shrubs on Saturdays or watering the lawn as the sun went down. He cut the grass, under duress, and would occasionally attempt a home repair. He kept a well-stocked workbench in the basement, but he wasn't handy. Says Doris, "He was the only man I ever knew who would hammer a nail with a pliers." Erwin loved his library and his array of prints on the walls. He told Doris early on, "I don't care if they wheel me out of that house." After that, she liked it even less.

Every other Wednesday, Erwin played poker with his club, whose members included Sam Day and Matt Rothschild. Occasionally, David Knoll would sit in. It was a medium-stakes game, where players might win or lose as much as $100. Erwin was a smart player and a good bluffer, but over the years he lost more than he won because of his great poker shortcoming—an inability to fold. He liked to stay in the game, even if it was not in his best interest.

While Knoll was greatly fond of poker, it was not just a game. He saw it as stimulating, a test of his abilities. Just as David never once saw his father under the influence of alcohol, he cannot recall him ever engaging in "a purely trivial, self-indulgent exercise" of any sort. "He really felt leisure time should be carefully invested in improving yourself," says David, "although Erwin could give watching *The Maltese Falcon* for the 200th time the patina of self-improvement." When David took up boat-racing, his father "never understood why I would go out there and race around a lake and actually care about doing it better." Similarly, David says Erwin "wanted to like baseball, but he couldn't bear to sit there and watch it."

Knoll's closest friend during his years in Madison was Joseph Kepecs, a local psychoanalyst who had treated Morris Rubin.

Though Kepecs was nineteen years older than Knoll and not as politically inclined, the two men shared many of the same interests in art, literature, and music. Joan Kepecs and Doris Knoll also got along well, and the two couples would go out together to dinner, movies, and concerts. Knoll especially liked Mozart, and, says Kepecs, "would tolerate Beethoven and Schubert, but after that . . ." Kepecs used to tease Knoll that he worked for a magazine called *The Progressive* yet only liked music from long ago. The two men traded books; Knoll had a special interest in Sigmund Freud ("one of his cultural heroes," says Kepecs) and Franz Kafka, whom Knoll felt "really expressed what the 20th Century was all about."

But even the dark visions of Kafka and Freud did not quell Knoll's essential optimism—the same quality that kept him holding on to bad poker hands and placing long-shot bets at the track. Indeed, Kepecs felt his friend was too much of a "utopian." He'd ask Knoll what he was working toward. "A socialist society," Knoll would say. "But where on earth has socialism succeeded?" pressed Kepecs. Knoll: "It hasn't been tried yet."

Knoll, for all his alacrity of expression, had a hard time talking about his personal life, says Kepecs: "He was not the sort to bare his soul to others." When asked how he was doing, Knoll always answered "Just fine"—even though there were times Kepecs knew his friend was feeling ill or depressed. Kepecs traces Knoll's stiff upper lip to his traumatic childhood: "I think he developed his toughness and energy as a kind of reaction to what was a frightening, helpless situation. The certainty he conveyed to himself and others was to some extent an attempt to cope with his own fears and uncertainty."

"Erwin worked very hard to keep himself above his vulnerabilities," says Kepecs. "It was one of his strengths, and also one of his weaknesses."

CHAPTER EIGHTEEN

Never a Just War

There was nothing Erwin Knoll liked better than telling stories, usually about himself. Someone would say to him, "Nice day, isn't it?" and it would trigger a story. "That reminds me," he'd say. "Once when I was covering the Johnson White House in Washington—it was a day like this, a beautiful day. . . ." Knoll's stories always flowed forth fully formed, sometimes word-for-word the same as the last time he told them. It was like someone pressed a button that activated a tape in his brain. He'd conclude with a chuckle, or just open his mouth in silent mirth. Even if people didn't like the story, it was hard not to laugh. His enthusiasm was contagious.

At times, though, Matt Rothschild found Knoll's tendency to tell stories "stultifying," even "asphyxiating." It bothered him especially that most of Knoll's stories were about his past as a reporter in Washington or about the H-bomb case. "It was as though he saw his glory days behind him and not in front of him," says Rothschild. "I always thought that was sad." The first time Rothschild came to *The Progressive*'s office in 1983, Knoll threw an arm around his shoulder and launched into a story whose significance was hard to fathom. "I had the sense," says Rothschild, "that this was a man who was acting older than he was."

In fact, Knoll's greatest glory days were still in front of him. From 1991 until his death in 1994, Erwin Knoll was beyond a doubt the nation's most visible, vocal, and articulate proponent of radical ideas. He was the exception to the rule that, in an age of almost total corporate media domination, truly leftist voices cannot get on the air, let alone on prime-time TV. His big break came toward the end of 1990.

Part of Rothschild's strategy for rescuing *The Progressive* from its perennially bleak financial situation was to translate Knoll's gift for public speaking into new subscribers. Rothschild pushed hard to expand the audience for "Second Opinion," Knoll's weekly radio interview show. The idea was that people who heard Knoll would be more inclined to pick up his magazine.

When Saddam Hussein of Iraq in August 1990 sent his troops to invade what Knoll called "the neighboring sheikdom" of Kuwait, the reaction from the Bush Administration was fast and furious. Bush declared the Iraqi ruler to be "worse than Hitler" and immediately began dispatching U.S. troops, mostly reservists, to the Persian Gulf. This build-up, which had all of the appearances of being a prelude to an invasion, was officially known as "Operation Desert Shield." Knoll was against it from the start.

"The hypocrisy of the rhetoric emanating from our Government and its cheerleaders in support of the dispatch of U.S. troops to the Middle East boggles the mind," Knoll wrote in a column for *Newsday.* Just look, he said, at the extent to which the U.S. Government had previously armed and encouraged this same Saddam Hussein. "Let's be clear about it: The only principle connected with the U.S. military intervention in the Middle East is the principle that might makes right. The United States believes its 'interests' are threatened, and so it sends in the troops. That, by curious coincidence, is exactly the same way Saddam Hussein behaved when he believed Iraq's 'interests' were threatened."

Rothschild sensed the potential of this issue to catapult Knoll back into the national limelight. At a time when others were clamoring for war, his was a firm, reasoned voice for peace. Surely some of the nation's major media would be interested. Rothschild, telling a disbelieving Knoll "I'm going to make you famous again," mailed off Knoll's *Newsday* column to "Nightline," "The CBS Evening News," "Good Morning, America," "The Today Show," "This Week with David Brinkley," "Face the Nation," "Meet the Press" and "The MacNeil/Lehrer NewsHour." Seven of the eight never responded; the folks at "MacNeil/Lehrer" did. And one was enough.

"MacNeil/Lehrer," public television's premier daily public-policy program, was at the time frustrated in its desire to present a variety of perspectives on the impending Gulf War. "We found, surprisingly, that many voices we considered to be liberal or left-of-center, while harboring some reservations, were generally rallying around the Administration's positions," says Peggy Robinson, a senior producer for the show. "We felt the need to counter a wholesale endorsement of those positions." Another impetus may have been the program's desire to counter a recently released report by the left-wing media watchdog group Fairness and Accuracy in Reporting (FAIR) that documented an overwhelming conservative bias in "MacNeil/ Lehrer's" choice of guests. For whatever reason, Knoll got on the program.

Knoll's first "MacNeil/Lehrer" appearance, on September 12, 1990, set the tone for those that followed. The topic was President Bush's nationally televised speech on the Persian Gulf the night before. Co-host Robin MacNeil asked the members of the show's editors' panel for their reactions. "I thought it was a very effective speech," said Lee Cullum of *The Times Herald* of Dallas. "It seemed to me the President made it clear why we're in the Persian Gulf and what we're there to defend. We're there to defend a principle, non-aggression, and we're there to protect our own national interest, access to the world's principal oil supplies. I think the people in Dallas support Bush and were pleased with the speech." Cynthia Tucker of *The Atlantic Constitution* called it "a very good speech" that "set an excellent tone." Gerald Warren of the *San Diego Union* praised it further as "a very unwarlike speech"—a difficult feat for someone threatening to go to war. Ed Baumeister of New Jersey's *Trenton Times* called the speech "the perfect response."

Knoll, in turn, called it "cleverly manipulative. I think the President pulled out all the stops, used all the applause lines, did everything he could to build a consensus and, in fact, to make it disreputable to oppose the U.S. course of conduct in the Persian Gulf. . . . The tenor of the speech was that anyone who opposes lowering the capital gains tax is, in effect, stabbing in the back our brave soldiers sweltering in the desert sands of Saudi Arabia. I think that's obnoxious. I think that's a thoroughly disgusting political tactic. I think the main problem with the speech was that while the President talked about a New World Order, this policy reflects the old world order of solving disputes by military means."

Photo by Joseph Blough

On "MacNeil/Lehrer"

The folks at "MacNeil/Lehrer" liked Knoll's perspective and made him a regular member of the editors' panel. Most of the time, the same pattern played out: The other editors would regurgitate conventional wisdom on the issues of the day, which usually meant they agreed, with varying degrees of enthusiasm, that the emperor's new outfit was dazzling. Knoll, disgusted by having to look at the emperor's bare behind, would take a dissident view, and at times change the course of the discussion.

"The quality he brought to the program was a really gritty independent liberalism," says co-host Robin MacNeil, applying a term Knoll would cringe to hear. "He was a fierce and unapologetic representative of the Old Left, extremely eloquent and uncompromising, and quite willing in the case of the Gulf War to take really unpopular stands and stick to them, which is a rare quality today. He reminded me of I.F. Stone, and there was a Mencken quality about him too, although he wasn't as angry a man as Mencken. He could also be quite funny."

MacNeil recalls that Knoll, in his initial appearances, came across as though he felt "he had to represent the entire vanished Left"—all the voices that were not being heard—and hence seemed more "ideologically rigid." But "as he became a 'regular' and had more interchange with other members of our regular panel, he then began to soften in a way and was more willing to enter a kind of discourse and say 'Yes, that's a good point' and 'I agree with this person but I disagree with that.' In other words, he became part of a colloquy rather than sort of the captain on the deck of the sinking ship, going down with all his wounds streaming blood into the sea. It was a rather interesting little transition."

But Knoll never softened in his opposition to the Persian Gulf War, even as other commentators went from voicing opposition early on to becoming resigned to war once it appeared imminent. "Is this war really necessary?" asked Knoll in an opinion piece that appeared in *The New York Times* on November 8. "What will we win in exchange for the sacrifice of thousands—perhaps scores of thousands—of American and Arab lives?"

From Knoll's point of view, the Bush Administration's professed desire to deter aggression was monstrously hypocritical. Not only had the United States made aggression a key component of its own foreign policy—in Chile, in Nicaragua, in Grenada, in Panama, to name a few—but it had a long history of coddling despots, including Saddam Hussein, who were loyal to the U.S. "China gobbled up Tibet exactly the way Iraq gobbled up Kuwait, and it continues to impose its will there," Knoll said in November on "MacNeil/Lehrer." "I don't see anyone excited about it. I don't see President Bush sending 400,000 troops into India as a counterforce to the Chinese threat."

As the President banged the drums for war, most of the nation's pundits fell in step. But Knoll believed, optimistically, that the public would not stand for it. On January 11, 1991, Knoll told his television audience about a rally at the state Capitol in Madison a few days before. Some 1,000 people turned out for a discussion on the Gulf situation, he said, and "the sentiment ran more than ten to one, perhaps as much as twenty to one, against the war. And that includes all kinds of people, rural people, church people, labor union people. Many groups that were in favor of the Vietnam War and supported it, at least at the outset, are absolutely opposed to this military exercise from the very beginning."

Unlike Vietnam, though, the high point of public resistance to the Persian Gulf War was before it began. On January 15, 1991, just hours after Congress authorized the use of U.S. military force, American forces unleashed a devastating air assault against Iraq that lasted for weeks, followed by an invasion of U.S. troops; officially, "Operation Desert Shield" had become "Operation Desert Storm." Throughout the country, millions of yellow ribbons appeared in support of the 450,000 U.S. servicepeople sent to do George Bush's bidding in the Persian Gulf. That night, about 200 protesters—one-tenth the number at an anti-war protest a few days before—marched through the streets of Madison. This time the demonstrators were countered by UW-Madison students shouting "U.S.A.! U.S.A.!" from dorm windows.

Knoll, in his appearances on "MacNeil/Lehrer," continued to take a sharply dissident position on the war. When his fellow panelists offered uniform praise of the high-tech devices being put to use by Nintendo-trained fighter pilots in the Persian Gulf War ("It's impossible not to feel enormous pride in their performance," gushed Cullum), Knoll had a different take: "I watched the video displays of [bombs hitting their targets]. It looks like a video game and it makes people forget what war is about. We get all these images of successful technology, and we forget because we don't see it on the screen, but those electronic flashes that look so pretty represent lives being taken, buildings being destroyed, civilization being wiped out in many instances. I think it's appalling that people are subjected to this kind of high-tech game instead of what it is—a really bloody exercise that shouldn't happen in the advanced stage of civilization that we supposedly have attained."

The Persian Gulf War was perhaps the most carefully orchestrated media event in the history of the United States. The military—drawing on its successful past experience in Grenada, where it banned the press altogether, and Panama, where it set up a "press pool" to keep out all but a few officially approved reporters—asserted broad, new authority to manipulate and censor the news coming out of the Persian Gulf. Again, there was a pre-approved press pool; reporters were not allowed to go anywhere without a military escort, and all video footage and written dispatches had to be cleared by military censors. Prior restraint had, in the hands of the U.S. military, become automatic.

On January 10, 1991, just two days after the Pentagon announced these restrictions, *The Progressive* and eight other news organizations—including *Harper's, The Nation, Mother Jones, In These Times*, and Pacifica News Service—filed a lawsuit against the U.S. Government. The suit, joined by writers Sydney Schanberg, E.L. Doctorow, William Styron, and Michael Klare, charged that the real purpose of these press restrictions was "to deter independent inquiry by the press, and to control and manipulate information available to the American public. . . ." Or, as Knoll told *The Capital Times*, "These regulations amount to a military assault on the First Amendment." That the suit was brought by a few smaller, left-leaning news outlets and not the major U.S. news organizations most directly and severely affected, squared perfectly with Knoll's belief that the mainstream media's relationship with official power was that of a lapdog to its master. Indeed, after the case was dismissed as moot when the war ended, representatives of major media including *The Washington Post* met with Pentagon officials—none of the plaintiffs were invited to participate—and agreed to similar restrictions in future conflicts. At war's end, General Norman Schwarzkopf praised the press for its "cooperation," saying "We couldn't have done it without you." "Most of the press," Knoll said in a speech, "didn't even have enough sensibility to be embarrassed."

Knoll spoke out against the Persian Gulf War as often—and as emphatically—as he could. "I don't want to temporize or equivocate or be polite about this war," he told an audience on February 9 at the College of the Atlantic in Bar Harbor, Maine. "I believe it is a crime and a horror and a disgrace. I am ashamed that it is being fought by my Government, which claims to be acting in my behalf, and which is certainly spending my money. I believe it is a war that will leave the world, and the Middle East, and this country in worse shape than they were before the war began—so it is not merely a crime and a horror and a disgrace, but also an act of mind-boggling stupidity."

In this speech and in his writings on the subject, Knoll recounted the various rationales for the Gulf War that the Bush Administration put forth. First, it was to protect Saudi Arabia from Iraqi invasion. Later the administration, in apparent response to opinion polls, began putting out what Knoll called "exaggerated rhetoric" regarding Iraq's nuclear threat. Later still, it was stated that the troops were needed to protect the territorial integrity of Kuwait. This last reason, surmised Knoll, probably hadn't occurred to the Bush Administration early on; after all, the U.S. ambassador to Baghdad, April Glaspie, had essentially given Iraq a green light to invade Kuwait.

Despite these shifting justifications, Knoll noted in one speech, "It turned out that given the dynamics of modern propaganda technique and the pliability of the media, merchandising a holy war based on Iraq's aggression against Kuwait really wasn't all that difficult. And it would provide the excuse for doing something the United States had wanted to do ever since the Shah of Iran was overthrown in the early 1970s—establish an American military presence in the Gulf."

After the Persian Gulf War, Knoll warned, there would surely be other occasions in which U.S. soldiers would be asked to fight and kill for reasons that had nothing to do with the national defense and everything to do with the maintenance of fundamental inequities:

> Maybe it will be the tin miners of Brazil next time, and some union leader you and I have never heard of will be the next Saddam Hussein, the new archvillain who must be eradicated at all costs.
>
> We must ask ourselves whether this is the kind of New World Order we want for ourselves and our children and our children's children–crisis after crisis, war after war, butchery after butchery, until at long last our economy is bankrupt, our political system is in shambles, supplanted by a garrison state, and whatever decency and dignity we still lay claim to as human beings has been completely destroyed.

To Knoll, the Persian Gulf War was a singularly dark period in the nation's history. "During that time, we went through this spasm of gory, patriotic fervor," he later said. "I was giving a lot of speeches at colleges and in high schools. In the high schools I encountered kids whose only regret was that they were not old enough to go and kill for their country. I spent a lot of time thinking about that as I drove down those streets decorated by yellow ribbons. And I thought parents are so concerned today about violence. Well, they ought to be concerned about the violence that is part of the American pysche—about the notion that if there is a problem anywhere in the world, the way to solve it is to start killing people."

It wasn't just this transparently fraudulent Persian Gulf War—which caused countless thousands of Iraqi deaths and horrendous environmental damage and ended with Saddam Hussein still in power and U.S. soldiers still in the Gulf—that Knoll objected to. He was against *all* war—including the war supposedly fought to stop Hitler. As Knoll wrote in the Madison weekly *Isthmus*, "I've heard a lot of foolishness lately about this being a just war. There is no such thing as a just war. Never has been. Never will be."

That was the real message Knoll sought to convey in his ruminations on the Persian Gulf War, and for many people it was going too far. Knoll's essay drew an angry letter to the editor from Jonathan Burack, formerly with *The Progressive*. He called Knoll's position "self-righteous, condescending, and imperious" and urged him to "tell it to the countless numbers of thoughtful people who, through the ages, have agonized over the question of a just war. Or maybe you should tell it to the fallen black soldiers of the 54th Massachusetts, or the guys dead on the beaches of Normandy, or the young people throwing stones at Brezhnev's tanks in the streets of Czechoslovakia."

Knoll proceeded to do just that. The June 1991 issue of *The Progressive* contained Knoll's blanket defense of pacifism, an essay entitled "Not a Just War—Just a War." After quoting from Burack's letter, Knoll said this was an issue he, too, had agonized over, so he could sympathize with the "outraged reactions" of others to an absolute pacifist position. "The idea that it is sometimes necessary and, indeed, proper to slaughter our fellow human beings to stamp out a great evil or advance a noble cause has, after all, been drummed into all of us by Church and State, School and Family. To reject that notion is to dismiss the ultimate sacrifice made by ancestors, friends, relatives, and compatriots who laid down their lives in wars they—or at least their governments—deemed worthy. Perhaps it *is* self-righteous, condescending, even imperious to suggest that their last measure of devotion—as Lincoln described it at Gettysburg—was neither just nor justifiable.

"I make no apology."

Knoll proceeded to recount *The Progressive*'s long legacy of pacifism, beginning with founder Bob La Follette's unyielding opposition to World War I, a position that led to his being burned in effigy at the University of Wisconsin. During World War II, the magazine's writers and editors were divided over whether or not to support the war, with columnist Milton Mayer leading the pacifist flank. The Cold War struggle for economic dominion presented new conundrums, Knoll noted:

> How can I say to a long-suffering victim of South Africa's apartheid regime that he or she should not take up arms against such brutal oppression? How can I tell the Salvadoran teenager cited by one of my correspondents that he or she must resort only to nonviolent resistance against the savagely greedy oligarchs who exploit the people of that land?
>
> I respond that the casualties of war are hardly ever the patriarchs and oligarchs and despots who are supposedly its targets. Just wars claim the just—not the unjust—as their victims.

Besides, Knoll said, "Every revolution, every national-liberation movement that achieves its ends by dealing in death continues dealing in death once its ends have been achieved."

Such basic tenets of pacifism, Knoll continued, had made sense to him all his life. "Why, then, did I spend so much time agonizing over the question of just and unjust wars?" It was because of another question that is invariably put to anyone who professes pacifist ideals: "What about Nazi Germany?"

This was an especially difficult question for Knoll, because of his own boyhood experience of fleeing the Nazis and losing relatives to the Holocaust. He recounted how, as a teenager and even as a young adult, "I loved to go to old World War II films so that I could watch Germans die." But in time, he realized that not all Germans—not even all those who died in World War II–were like those depicted in these movies—"officers of the Waffen SS who invariably wore monocles, black uniforms, and permanent sneers."

Ultimately, Knoll concluded that "of all the ways to stop Hitler or to keep him from getting started, war was the worst—the way that inflicted the most pain, the most suffering, the most damage on everyone—especially on Hitler's victims." Far better, he said, had Hitler been resisted through "ingenious, nonviolent struggle."

Some people who heard this argument found it unconvincing. "Erwin didn't know what he was talking about," says his uncle, Dr. Eric Nash, who lost his wife and two-year-old son to the gas chambers at Auschwitz. "He obviously had no comprehension what Hitler was up to. Resistance was absolutely impossible." But the example of futile resistance Nash offers is a Jewish youth's assassination of a German diplomat in Paris, which was used as a pretext for the killing of dozens of Jews during *Kristallnacht*. This is not the kind of resistance Knoll was advocating.

Daniel Ellsberg, who got his start in peace activism by leaking the Pentagon Papers to *The Washington Post* and *The New York Times*, also has a hard time accepting Knoll's absolute pacifism. Although such World War II events as the bombing of Dresden by Allied forces were, says Ellsberg, "definitely war crimes by all previous standards," it doesn't follow that all aspects of the war were unjustified. Nor does he agree that nonviolent resistance is always a better strategy. For one thing, he questions whether "it is reasonable to think you're going to get that degree of concerted heroism."

Knoll's pacifism was indeed the position of an idealist, although one could argue that—in saying war leads to war crimes but is not inherently unjust—Ellsberg is also basing his comments on an idealized version of war. In fact, people have tried and failed at waging just wars far more often than they've responded to injustice with nonviolent resistance. And in a few instances, such as Gandhi's liberation of India from British control, the latter strategy has worked.

Another question arises: If Knoll believed so strongly in nonviolent resistance, why didn't he engage in it himself? Former associates Sam Day and Bonnie Urfer were by this time routinely serving prison sentences of up to six months for their flagrant trespassing at nuclear weapons sites and Project ELF, a low-frequency nuclear submarine communications system in northern Wisconsin. In August 1990, when the Gulf War mobilization began, Day and Urfer chained themselves to the front of the federal office building in Madison, just as Urfer and former associate editor Keenen Peck had done seven years earlier in response to the U.S. invasion of Grenada. Knoll praised all of these actions, and respected those who engaged in them. Still, he had his doubts about the usefulness of getting oneself put in jail.

"As a political tactic, I don't think it's particularly effective, and it has some negative connotations," remarked Knoll in a 1990 interview. "By submitting to imprisonment, they underscore their weakness and the state's might."

Day demurs: "I think exactly the opposite is true. Going to prison demonstrates that you as an individual can withstand the worst that the state can do to you for a political crime." Ordinarily, he says, "the fear of going to prison immobilizes us and forces us to curtail the extent of our resistance to evil—in my case, nuclear weapons. But by undergoing these things—arrest, prosecution, and imprisonment—we can have a profound effect, at least on other people. It is what moves other people to greater feats of resistance. Sure, you're preaching to the choir, but you're making the choir sing better."

Knoll also felt that most people who engage in "prison witness" languish in obscurity, ignored by the media and thought merely peculiar by those who happen to hear of them. Day says some acts of resistance do get noticed—surely Erwin Knoll would have gotten media coverage had he chained himself to a building in protest of the Persian Gulf War. But Day also says such acts ought to be done for their own sake. He likens it to being editor of *The Progressive*: "Why put out a magazine that only reaches 35,000 people? You do it because there are things that need to be said and things that people need to hear. Hopefully, it will have some effect."

Late in 1992, Americans were overwhelmed with media images of starving Somalians, as pressure grew to send in the Marines to open food lines in that East African nation. Knoll was against it from the start. "I don't believe this is a purely humanitarian intervention," he told his "MacNeil/Lehrer" audience. "Who are we to impose our will on the world, to refashion it in our image, to tell all the nations on this planet, here's what we want you to do and you'd better do it, or you'd better be prepared for the arrival of the U.S. Marines?"

When the editors of *The Progressive* met to hammer out the magazine's "collective position" on the Somalia situation, Knoll and Rothschild had a major blowout. "I found his argument exasperating," says Rothschild. "It was as though, for him, there was no other side, no possibility there was a valid moral reason to try to stop starvation. I was just outraged after that meeting." The two men went back to their respective office areas and wrote editorials for *The Progressive*'s January 1993 issue. The one by Knoll ran unsigned, as the institutional voice of the magazine. The one by Rothschild was published alongside it, as a signed dissent, the first in the magazine's history.

The editorial by Knoll posed a series of questions about sending U.S. troops to Somalia. How long would they be there? How, exactly, could their presence benefit Somalia in the long run? Was this the sort of intervention Americans could expect to see more of? Why shouldn't the U.S. be listening to the relief workers who were saying it would be better to have nonmilitary intervention? As always, Knoll's questions evinced a profound distrust of the Government. As his editorial went on to say: "This time, we're told, America is pursuing humane objectives without ulterior motives. Whence this sudden spasm of altruism? Who can recall another such case in the last few decades?"

Rothschild, in turn, wrote what he now considers an "intemperate" response: "Some on the Left oppose the U.S. role because it is yet another exercise in American hegemony. Maybe, but so what? Is that reason enough to let people starve?" If there were ever a legitimate role for the military, Rothschild wrote, the Somalia situation was it. Not to intervene amounted to "pacifism run amok. I'm sorry, but holding hands and singing 'Give peace a chance' will not stop the warlords from stealing food from starving babies."

The Marines did intervene in Somalia, a military exploit perhaps best characterized by the photograph of a U.S. Marine kicking a young Somalian boy in the butt with a steel-toed boot. Rothschild, later, was chagrined: "Most of what Erwin predicted came to pass in Somalia, so his position looks better than mine does with time."

photo ©1991 by Joseph Blough

Taping "Second Opinion" on WORT Radio.

CHAPTER NINETEEN

No Shortage of Issues

Throughout the early 1990s, the circulation of *The Progressive* rose steadily. By 1993, the number of paid subscribers was back up to 39,000, after dipping below the 30,000 mark three years before. Much of this increase was due to Knoll's exposure on "The MacNeil/Lehrer NewsHour"; the magazine used his televised image in print ads aimed at attracting new subscribers.

From Knoll's point of view, *The Progressive* was never better. It now had monthly interviews, and an array of columnists including Molly Ivins, June Jordan, Susan Douglas, and Elayne Rapping. Knoll used to boast that *The Progressive* had more women columnists than any other national political magazine. He used to crow, too, about being editor of *The Progressive*.

"I have the best job in American journalism, bar none," Knoll said in 1992. "I may have two or three or four years left in this job, more or less, depending on my capabilities. I feel very confident about the fact that if I were to drop dead this afternoon the magazine would be in good hands. I don't have to worry about that, so I'm glad."

Whom did Knoll have in mind to take his place? "Matt," he said, nodding toward an unseen corner of the office that housed publisher Rothschild.

Knoll, as it turned out, had only two years left, but they were among the most important. During these two years, Knoll found that he was able to get his opinions out all over—on "MacNeil/Lehrer," in op-ed columns printed in major newspapers, in interviews with the press, and on radio. And there was no shortage of issues on which he had opinions.

From his perch at "MacNeil/Lehrer," Knoll continued to be the lone radical voice in a chorus of conservative, neoconservative, and moderate views. Knoll commented on the charges of sexual harassment lodged against Supreme Court nominee Clarence Thomas ("Our own feeling here at *The Progressive* has always been that Judge Thomas was a terrible choice for the Supreme Court and we've heard nothing in the last few days to make us change that view"), the Democratic National convention ("I kind of envied the people who were able to watch *The Revenge of the Nerds Part III* on Fox Television. I think they may have gotten a more interesting show"), and the quixotic candidacy of Ross Perot ("I think Perot has two tremendous strengths right now. One is that he's not a Democrat. And the other is that he's not a Republican. I think his candidacy reflects nothing so much as the bankruptcy, the moral, the political bankruptcy of the two-party system that we've been ruled by for such a long time"). But perhaps Knoll's finest moment on "MacNeil/Lehrer" came toward the end of a long discussion on May 1, 1992, regarding the riots that erupted in Los Angeles after a jury acquitted four police officers in the videotaped beating of Rodney King:

> We've had three dozen people die in the last couple of days. We've had people dispossessed from their homes, their businesses. And that's terrible. But we have to remember too that the people who did those terrible things are the dispossessed, the alienated of our society, the people who have no stake whatsoever in it. I've been sitting here, listening to my colleagues and watching them on the monitor in this studio, and thinking how remote we all are from those people in the inner cities, how little we represent them, and how I, sitting here as a white, middle-aged male on the MacNeil/Lehrer show, convey the image to the rest of the country that we, the white, middle-aged males, are the people who own America and run it. And I can't help it that people feel enraged, furious, destructive, even murderous ultimately when that frustration and rage builds up in them."

Knoll constantly sought new outlets for his opinions. In February 1993, *The Progressive* launched the Progressive Media Project, a grant-funded program to get leftist points of view onto the op-ed pages of daily newspapers. Within a year, the project was soliciting, editing, and distributing an average of three op-ed columns a week through the Knight-Ridder and Scripps-Howard news services, to which hundreds of newspapers subscribe. Knoll wrote several offerings that went out over this wire. In April 1993, Knoll was one of the few voices on the Left who criticized the Government's siege of the Branch Davidian compound in Waco, Texas, a decision that led to more than eighty deaths. "Should we speculate that the Branch Davidians' real crime," wrote Knoll in *The Christian Science Monitor*, "was their stubborn refusal to bow to conventional orthodoxy and official authority? Are we so determined to be a nation of tractable subjects that all dissidents must be rooted out?"

In June 1993, Knoll wrote a column about Clinton's bombing of Baghdad in response to allegations that Saddam Hussein plotted the murder of George Bush. The real purpose of the attack, Knoll asserted, was to establish "that this President has guts; that his vacillating, hesitating, inept, and bungling first five months in office are not to be construed as weakness; that when the chips are down he's not a weakling—he's a killer with the best of them."

Knoll also wrote columns and editorials in opposition to U.S. military involvement in Bosnia. He said on "MacNeil/Lehrer" that "The only force that I might consider putting in there, although I'd want to think about it some more, is handing an M-16 to each of the columnists, pundits, and commentators in Washington and New York who are urging the President to send Americans in there to kill and die. I think they're being irresponsible."

Beginning in May 1994, Knoll began producing two-minute daily radio commentaries that within months were airing on thirty-eight radio stations, including many of the stations already carrying Knoll's weekly "Second Opinion" show. The daily commentary, called "Insight," gave Knoll a chance to remark on just about everything, from the caning of an American teenager in Singapore, to the news that the FBI spied on composer Leonard Bernstein, to the decision of prosecutors not to seek the death penalty against so popular a fellow as O.J. Simpson.

Knoll increasingly found himself being quizzed by reporters for his opinions on the issues of the day. He could always provide a clever quote and fresh perspective. Asked whether gays should be allowed in the military, Knoll responded, "My own preference, rather than admitting gays and lesbians, would be to exclude them along with everybody else."

The First Amendment remained Knoll's preeminent concern. He parted company with other progressives in opposing penalty enhancers for hate crimes—that is, crimes that are apparently motivated by bigotry. At issue was a 1988 Wisconsin law that allowed judges to add up to five years to the sentence of a person deemed to have committed a hate crime. The law, heralded as a breakthrough in the protection of gays and racial minorities, was in Wisconsin soon used *against* a racial minority. Todd Mitchell, a nineteen-year-old black man, was standing on a street corner with a group of friends discussing a scene from the film *Mississippi Burning*, which dealt with racism against blacks. Mitchell pointed out a fourteen-year-old caucasian youth on the other side of the street: "There goes a white boy. Go get him." The group of blacks proceeded to beat the white youth unconscious, causing permanent injury. Mitchell, who did not participate in the beating and summoned help to the scene, was sentenced to four years in prison—two for aggravated assault, and two more for the words he used beforehand. The Wisconsin Supreme Court struck down the law as unconstitutional, but the U.S. Supreme Court accepted *Wisconsin v. Mitchell* as a test case for hate-crimes statutes in place in more than two dozen states. The High Court, by unanimous decision, reversed Wisconsin and affirmed the law's constitutionality. Knoll warned that the decision could lead to wholesale speculation about and criminalization of "motives"—which are, after all, thoughts in a person's head.

"How does one establish a defendant's hateful intent?" Knoll wrote in his "Memo" for August 1993. "By scrutinizing the books he or she reads, the comments he or she makes, the company he or she keeps. When punishment can be based on a motive—or mere speculation about motive—rather than deed, abuses are sure to occur."

In 1994, Knoll again stood apart from most others on the Left in condemning the Supreme Court's decision upholding the use of federal racketeering (RICO) statutes against anti-abortion protesters. "This decision is going to be used against every demonstrator in America. It's going to be used against peace activists. It's going to be used against labor," Knoll was quoted as saying in *Isthmus*, the

Madison weekly. "I think the women's groups that brought this suit did a real disservice." Margaret McMurray, head of Wisconsin NOW, a strong supporter of the RICO decision, was quoted in response: "With all due respect to Erwin Knoll, I think he's misread the Supreme Court decision and doesn't understand the ramifications of RICO." But after reading Knoll's comments alongside hers in *Isthmus*, McMurray sent Knoll "just a note to let you know that I *do* think you understand the ramifications of RICO and the U.S. Supreme Court's recent decision. I spoke too hastily when [*Isthmus*] called me last week for comment. . . . I'll try not to insert my foot in my mouth as readily next time."

Curiously, Knoll's rising fortunes coincided with the decline of the political Left. During the years Knoll was on "MacNeil/Lehrer," the preeminent grassroots political movement in the United States was the Religious Right. While *The Progressive* continued to advocate for economic justice, socialism was dying, labor lost ground, and conservatives dominated domestic-policy debates. Knoll's response, as always, was to speak out.

On the issue of crime, Knoll noted on "MacNeil/Lehrer" that the public's fears were rising at a time when the actual incidence of violent crime was going down. "I think many people are almost obsessed with violence these days because there's a lot of guilt around. [They] understand that this society is becoming less and less fair, less and less just, that the gap is widening between rich and poor. And I think people feel that those who are disadvantaged in this society aren't going to take it lying down forever. They're going to become more and more violent. They're going to rise up against the injustices in their own lives. And I think that's why there's this great rush to build more prisons, put more people behind bars. . . . People sense that there is more lawlessness coming because the society has been less and less just."

Knoll saw the presidency of Bill Clinton—with his retreat on urban renewal, his crackdown on welfare, his abandonment of health-care reform, his preservation of massive military spending—as being every bit the disaster he predicted. He was, of course, unsparing in his criticism, and some readers of *The Progressive* took him to task for it. Knoll used his "Memo" column of March 1994 to respond.

"Why do we keep picking on Bill Clinton?" he asked. "Because he's the only President we've got. That's why we picked on George Bush and Ronald Reagan, on Jimmy Carter and Gerald Ford, on Richard Nixon and Lyndon Johnson, when each of them occupied the White House. In an era—it didn't start with Ronald Reagan—when the U.S. Government has engaged in bloody imperial adventures abroad while practicing malign neglect of its own people's needs at home, we see no reason to act as cheerleaders for whatever President happens to be in office. . . ." The column ran under the headline, "Unappreciative."

The last major piece Knoll wrote for *The Progressive* appeared in the October 1994 issue under the headline, "How the Left Was Lost." The review of several historical books on the American Left began by surveying "the barren, desolate landscape of the American Left" and asking,

> What happened? How did we arrive at this forsaken place? Where did we take a wrong turn—if we took a wrong turn?
>
> There were times in this century, after all, when the most solidly entrenched plutocrats thought a new American revolution was in the offing. There were times when labor unions were determined to transform—not merely meliorate—the lives of working people, times when movements of the Left mobilized millions of Americans, [and] times when radical newspapers rivaled the commercial press in circulation and influence.
>
> How did we come to lose all that? What brought us to the poor, shriveled prospect that is the Left today?

To answer these questions, Knoll wrote, the Left needs to ponder its past. In the reviews that followed, he mentioned some historic wrong turns, such as the Left's identification with Leninism, but his most useful clue was a quote from a book of short profiles called *The American Radical*. The quote is by Harvey Goldberg, the late, great radical professor of history at the University of Wisconsin: "For very compelling reasons, the study of American radicals should be essential homework for this generation because their record can give heart and stomach to Americans who are watching democracy weaken under the weight of conformism; and because their insights and errors, their accomplishments and failures can cast light, even many years later, on the problems of the present."

CHAPTER TWENTY

"We Have Lost a Lion"

On Tuesday, November 1, 1994, Erwin Knoll left the office of *The Progressive* for the last time. It was a week before the magazine's December issue was scheduled to go to press. The stories were all edited. The headlines were all written. The editorials for the "Comment" section were all assigned. "No Comment" was set in type. Knoll stopped by Rothschild's office on his way out.

"How's the cash flow?" he asked.

"Not very good," Rothschild replied.

"When's it going to get better?" Knoll asked.

"It's never going to get better," said Rothschild.

"All right," said Knoll. "See you tomorrow."

Knoll went to bed that night with a copy of his friend John Egerton's new book, *Speak Now Against the Day*, by his bedside. Egerton was scheduled to be taped November 3 as a guest on Knoll's "Second Opinion" radio show. Knoll's last radio interview, recorded in a Madison sound studio on October 24, was with Texas columnist Molly Ivins, then coming through Madison to hawk her own new book, *Nothin' But Good Times Ahead*. "Molly Ivins, welcome to 'Second Opinion,'" Knoll began. "That book title—*Nothin' But Good Times Ahead*—it's a lie, it's utterly preposterous. . . ." Ivins rose to the occasion. "There's a great thing that Texas liberals know, we're born knowing it, from our cradles: The reason you have to be cheerful right now is because things can always get worse."

Afterwards Ivins, Knoll, and other members of *The Progressive* staff went to a local pub. Someone asked Ivins to define her politics, and she could not. "I mean," she asked Knoll, "can you describe yourself in programmatic terms?" "Of course not," Knoll replied. ("Erwin," Ivins wrote of this encounter, was "the perfect anti-ideologue. What free mind would ever abandon its intelligence to someone else's creed?") He went on, "I have only two irreducible principles. One is nonviolence. I am a pacifist. I believe violence is never a solution. And the other is freedom of speech, the First Amendment."

Ivins's response? "Sign me up for Erwin's Party."

On the morning of November 2, Doris got up at 5:30 and began her day. About two hours later, she checked on Erwin, surprised he still was not up. She shook him, then took his pulse. She tried CPR. It was no use. She was a nurse. She knew.

Doris called 911 and her son David. David called Rothschild at home: "My mom says Erwin is dead and it's not the kind of thing she'd joke about." Rothschild went to Knoll's house, then to *The Progressive,* to break the news to staffers and make a few painful calls. By mid-day he sat down to write a press release.

"We have lost a lion," Rothschild wrote. "Free speech and nonviolence had no greater friend, and war-makers and opportunistic politicians no greater foe than Erwin Knoll." He called Knoll, "a pugnacious pacifist" who was "extremely skilled in arguing for left-wing views. . . . For all his outspokenness, he was a very lovable man. In the office, he was an avuncular figure, offering advice and reveling in anecdotes. The staff is terribly, terribly grieved."

Rothschild, in a column on Knoll's death in the magazine's December issue, concluded with a quote from W.H. Auden: "Every day they die among us, those who were doing some good, and knew it was never enough but hoped to improve a little by living. . . . To us he is no more a person now but a whole climate of opinion under which we conduct our differing lives."

Hundreds of letters poured into the Knoll residence and the magazine from all over the country. Teri Terry, Knoll's secretary, says that until he died, "I had no idea how many people admired Erwin. Not just liked him, but admired him and respected him for the work he did all his life." Terry, who knew Erwin well, echoes these sentiments: "Erwin was his own man, and nobody rocked that boat. It was a rock, and a lot of times he stood alone on that rock."

Howard Morland wrote to recall his glory days with Knoll, who had in March 1979 "faced the television cameras as the nation's newest villain and a radical editor gone berserk. . . ." Morland also recalled a conversation he had with Knoll about "the moment . . . I first glimpsed the possibility that the anti-war movement might actually stop the war in Vietnam." This cognition came to Morland when he saw pictured in the newspaper a young blond woman wearing a T-shirt that said, "Make Love, Not War." The woman had been among the protesters who greeted President Lyndon Johnson during his visit to Australia in late 1966. "I saw that woman!" Morland says Knoll exclaimed. "She was beautiful. She was mobbed by photographers. I warned her that her picture would be in every major newspaper in the world—and it was." Recalls Morland, "We shared a sheepish moment of male bonding, politically incorrect, no doubt, as we conceded the unequal distribution of female photogenicity and noted its political uses." *The Progressive*, in the sampling of letters that appeared in its January 1995 issue, ran Morland's letter but omitted this anecdote.

Word of Knoll's death received at least a small notice in hundreds of daily newspapers throughout the United States. Many ran substantial obituaries. "Erwin Knoll, the editor of *The Progressive*, an iconoclastic magazine that crusaded for civil liberties and against nuclear weapons and United States intervention abroad, died yesterday at his home in Madison, Wisconsin," wrote *The New York Times* in an obituary that recounted the H-bomb case and mentioned Knoll's appearances on the "MacNeil/Lehrer NewsHour."

The *Los Angeles Times* quoted Ralph Nader calling Knoll "the most versatile progressive journalist in America." *Time* called Knoll "amiably combative" and his magazine "proudly left-wing but non-doctrinaire." Columnist Colman McCarthy wrote in *The Washington Post*, "Many editors cater to their subscribers' beliefs. Mr. Knoll, the rare one, honored the faithful another way, by prodding and rebuking them."

Perhaps the best editorial eulogy appeared in the same paper that misidentified Knoll as a "liberal champion" in its headline announcing his death. *The Capital Times*, the Madison paper for which Knoll had been Washington correspondent, wrote, "Knoll's unyielding commitment to peace and social justice often put him at odds with the orthodoxy of his times. Yet he never surrendered to cynicism; to the end he believed that he had dedicated his life to worthy *and* obtainable goals. The struggle for a better world will go on without this great man. But for years to come, it will be said that each step forward was made possible at least in part by the wit, the intellect, the humanism, the passion, and the hope that are the legacy of Erwin Knoll."

Some honored Knoll by taking issue with the words said about him by others. John LaForge, a Wisconsin activist, wrote a letter ripping the *Milwaukee Sentinel*'s editorial claim to have "common ground" with Knoll "on the absolute commitment to freedom of speech." The paper, LaForge said, had not raised a fuss "when the U.S. Government imposed complete press censorship" during the 1991 Persian Gulf War. "Don't put on airs by equating yourselves with the principled likes of the late Erwin Knoll," LaForge scolded. "Some of your readers knew him."

There was more contention at the memorial service held for Knoll in Washington, D.C., on November 12. More than 100 people gathered as such notables as Ralph Nader, Daniel Schorr, and Daniel Ellsberg spoke. Nader made disparaging remarks about Knoll's role as the lone lefty on the "MacNeil/Lehrer NewsHour"; someone in the audience interjected that Knoll only got on the show due to pressure from FAIR, the media watchdog group. Mike Mosettig, a former colleague of Knoll's at the Newhouse News Service, now with "MacNeil/Lehrer," got up and assured the gathering that no such thing had happened, that MacNeil/Lehrer had been attracted to Knoll because of his stand against the Persian Gulf War.

On the evening of November 2, Jim Lehrer signed off for the evening with "the sad news, family news," of Knoll's death. "He was a delightful man, an outspoken curmudgeon, with strong opinions and strong humor." Lee Cullum, Knoll's foremost adversary on the program, cried when a "MacNeil/Lehrer" staffer told her the news.

After Knoll's death, according to co-host Robin MacNeil, the program set out to find another strong Left representative. But MacNeil, in an interview on the verge of his retirement, defended the dearth of such voices on the show: "We're trying to reflect what we see as the landscape of American opinion, and you can't pretend the weight is on the Left. The left wing in terms of political organization or representatives in Congress has eroded so that there's not much Left left in this country." There certainly isn't much Left left on MacNeil's old show, now "The NewsHour with Jim Lehrer." After a year of trying out various editors, the program settled on a line-up that runs the gamut from conservative to cautiously liberal. Says senior producer Peggy Robinson: "Erwin was irreplaceable. The voice he had was fairly unique."

Most people who knew Knoll were stunned by his death. He had not smoked in more than a decade and still hadn't gained back all of the weight he lost in the mid-1980s. He almost never missed a day of work due to illness and whenever anyone asked how he was feeling always said "fine."

But Knoll was not fine. He had high blood pressure, trouble with his eyes, and pain in his legs, all related to his diabetes, which was poorly controlled. He also began dozing off at work, and went through a lot of antacid tablets. Doris was concerned, but Erwin shrugged off her inquiries. The Sunday before he died, Erwin looked so bad that Doris wanted to take him to the emergency room, but he begged off, saying he had an appointment with his doctor that Wednesday. He later cancelled the appointment. He needn't have bothered. He died early that morning.

After Erwin's death, Doris obtained his medical records, and was shocked by what she saw. His blood pressure was dangerously high for a diabetic and, on two occasions during the last fourteen months of his life, his blood sugar tested in excess of 500. "At that level," says Doris, "every tissue in your body is deteriorating. Everybody knows that." The American Diabetes Association advises patients who test above 500 to "get to a hospital." Back in Spanish Harlem, where Doris trained as a nurse, a blood-sugar level of 500 would have resulted in immediate hospitalization. Instead, Erwin was called and his response recorded: "Patient feels 'fine.'"

Doris was never pleased with the quality of care Erwin had been getting at his HMO, Group Health Cooperative. She disliked the very concept of HMOs, which contain built-in incentives for medical professionals to treat less. And while Doris admits Erwin was in denial about his health, she says "lots of patients are in denial, and doctors have to cope with that." She points to Erwin's past success at stopping smoking and losing weight on the Nutra System plan as evidence of his discipline, and his will to live: "Had Group Health provided an organized, sensible program with supervision, he would have followed it." David Knoll agrees: "His primary-care physician did not make a significant effort to get him to do what he had to do. It's reasonable to suggest his death was probably avoidable." Dr. Benjamin Atkinson, Knoll's primary-care physician, instead blames his patient: "I felt he knew best how to be responsible for managing his care."

On November 13, 1994, a memorial service was held for Knoll on the University of Wisconsin campus. Some 500 people packed into the room and hallways. Among them were Knoll's old Washington friends Jules Witcover, Stuart Loory, Ted Schuchat, and Shelly Tromberg. Musicians performed Schubert's *Trout* Quintet, as a peregrine falcon swooped outside the windows overlooking Lake Mendota. Matthew Rothschild, Knoll's successor, spoke first.

"We gather here today to pay our respects to our dearest Erwin—to mourn, to remember, to salute, and to celebrate this man who meant so much to all of us," he began. "*The Progressive* magazine grieves, because we've lost a great editor. The progressive movement grieves; we've lost a great leader. We all grieve; we've lost a great friend."

Rothschild spoke of Knoll's courage, his conviction, his kindness to the people with whom he worked. He told of his skills as an editor, about how he would rewrite articles from top to bottom but do it so skillfully that in one case the author responded, "It's great. You barely touched a word." He credited him as mentor: "I came to *The Progressive* twelve years ago and Erwin taught me the trade. He taught me how to write. He taught me how to edit. He taught me how to speak in public, and he taught me how to think about politics. Radical politics. Visionary politics. Uncompromising. Undiluted. Unpragmatic. Radical politics. He taught me how to take the high ground and how to uphold the utopian banner."

Knoll's friend, the artist Warrington Colescott, spoke next. He told of how his 1993 cartoon depicting Rush Limbaugh being castrated by his own creation, the FemiNazis, drew a deluge of angry reaction from readers of *The Progressive*. "Erwin was in high glee," recalled Colescott. "We met and, sagaciously, he noted that the letters were all from men. And he said, 'I think you've touched a nerve.'"

Dr. Joe Kepecs, the third speaker, recalled how his friend loved "clarity and lucidity in music and writing." In Knoll's honor, he read from the work of Franz Kafka: "The laws were made to the advantages of the nobles from the very beginning. They themselves stand above the laws. . . ."

The last speaker was David Knoll, who recalled his father as a good family man "whose patience saw him through a determined effort on my part to exhaust his patience that went on for just about twenty years. He didn't have a vision for my brother and I. He didn't want to define us. He visited upon us a richness of existence. . . ." David lamented that he would never again go to the track with, or get advice from, his father. If only he could still call him up and ask him, "What's your take on this?"

David, who in May 1995 graduated from law school and soon set about "keeping ne'er-do-wells out of prison," as his father once proudly put it, with the Madison law firm of Elfers, Knoll & Hart, went on. "All of this has left a big hole in my life, in my mother's life, my brother's life, in all of our lives. And time will fill some bit of that in, and some bit of it I suppose just lasts. But when I'm at a loss for a quote, when I need to have an idea and have run dry, I'll reflect on the endless litany of wise things he said to me, and perhaps I'll come up with something that's appropriate."

Erwin Knoll, his son attested, taught his children well. "I never saw my father treat someone with disdain, until they had arrogated disdain for another. I never saw him dismiss a person or their ability. He despised unkindness, he disliked unconcern, and if he wanted anything from any of us it wasn't to be right, and it wasn't to be strategically appropriate, it was to be decent. And that's what I'm going to hang on to."

Of all the roles that Knoll played, the most important was as a teacher—a man who through word and example taught others to conduct their differing lives in a more humane and challenging way. He understood the need for conflict as an agent of change, and would zealously defend his patch of ideological turf. In so doing, he inspired others to assert themselves.

"Over the years I idolized him, fought with him and finally came to know and love him," wrote Ruth Conniff, now *The Progressive*'s managing editor. "I realize now how much I counted on Erwin to be there, solid as a rock. Clashing with him, testing myself against him, was something I came to take for granted. He never held a grudge, and his affection endured."

After one of their final arguments, Conniff had told Knoll, "You know, Erwin, I really like you. . . ." She's glad to have ended a spat on that note. Days before he died, Knoll complimented Conniff on her interview with writer Katha Pollitt for *The Progressive*'s December 1994 issue, Knoll's last as editor. He put his arm around her shoulder and said, "I read it with joy."

Knoll was cremated, and his ashes were buried in a small cemetery in McFarland. It was a place he always liked, a well-kept patch of earth with a metal gateway along a rural road, just a few blocks from the home he lived in longest. A small marker, unveiled a year after his death, bears the emblem from Trigonon, the NYU Evening Organization Honor Society, Knoll's name, birthdate, date of death, and the words "Reporter Editor 'Tell Them the Truth'."

Like "Fighting Bob" La Follette and Eugene Debs, Knoll stood at the forefront of the radical movements in his day. He got through to people, and changed the way they thought. Knoll was fond of Aristotle's definition of politics as being the contest between those who have been favored by fortune and those who have not. He was among the former, but stood with the latter. He believed that progressive values—taking care of the have-nots—made sense even in terms of society's self-interest. "You can't fashion a politics based on altruism," he said.

Out of the maelstrom of his own experience, Knoll fashioned a politics that was radical and compelling and consistent. The boy sent away in tears from a fruit-stand vendor who would no longer sell oranges to Jews became the man who defended the right of Nazis to freely preach hate. The Washington reporter who probed the machinations of official power became a self-proclaimed enemy of the state. The editor who stood up against the full might and authority of the U.S. Government became a national voice of reason in times of crisis.

Knoll's mission was to persuade people that a better world is attainable if only they would do a few simple things: Stop killing each other, stop shutting each other up, start looking beyond the coldblooded calculations of capitalism for a prevailing ethic, start working toward a more just and equitable society.

The American Left has perhaps never had more reason to despair than it does in these final years of the 20th Century. The promise of progressive political power, so alive in the 1920s (due in large part to the movement led by La Follette) and 1960s (spurred by a generation's rebellion against a stagnant social and political order), seems all but dead today. The Democratic Party appears every bit "as morally and intellectually bankrupt" as Knoll proclaimed it to be. Popular resentment is directed not against those who have confounded health-care reform and caused most Americans to work harder for less, but rather against immigrants, prisoners, and people on welfare. The Religious Right remains a more potent force for social change than any force on the Left.

People of progressive bent are understandably distraught by such trends. Bill Clinton has let them down. The Democratic Party has let them down. The prevalence of political opportunism and lack of progressive leadership fill them with dread. They don't know what to do.

Erwin Knoll would have known what to tell them: educate, agitate, organize, vocalize. True reform begins from the grassroots up, from the people to the politicians. Talk to your neighbors, to people at work, to the guy who comes to fix your furnace. The Left, Knoll believed, had one great advantage: It made sense, and thus was capable of winning people over. This was the optimistic message Knoll delivered every chance he got for decades—including many a time when, to his way of thinking, the political terrain was every bit as bleak as it is today. Like the Italian socialist Gramsci, he sustained pessimism of the intellect but optimism of the will. Erwin Knoll's greatest lesson was that he never abandoned hope. His legacy is our challenge.

Notes

The use of present tense denotes material from interviews conducted and correspondence received in 1995, while researching this book. Whenever "she says" or "he recalls," it is from this primary material. Quotations from Erwin Knoll, unless otherwise specified, are from a series of taped interviews with the author in 1992.

Chapter 1

Much information in this chapter is from George Berkeley's book, *Vienna and Its Jews: The Tragedy of Success, 1880-1980s* (Abt Books, 1988). Referenced material can be found as follows: Hitler's quote on Vienna, P. 101; "The Fuerher is deeply moved" quote, P. 302; Alfred Polgar's quote, P. 257; Berkeley's "mass conversion" observation, P. 303; the humiliations of Jews after the *Anschluss*, P. 259-260; the Gestapo report, P. 311; the quote from *Das Schwarze Korps*, P. 306; the quote from the Teachers Association journal, P. 230; the three spotlights and 17 papers tidbit, P. 217; the dissolution of Parliament, P. 14; the reference to the gift made on Sigmund Freud's behalf, P. 16; the Vienna "wrong profession" quote, P. 23; Berkeley's "first major city" quote, P. 99; the figures on Vienna's rising Jewish population, P. 35; the "naked self-preservation" quote, P. 156; the reference to declining Jewish birthrates, P. 232; the wording of "Horst Wessel," P. 242; the Nazi newspaper quote, P. 271; the reference to injured people outside the hospital, P. 278; the sex-with-prostitutes reference, P. 278-279.

The number of people killed and synagogues burned on *Kristallnacht* is from the U.S. Holocaust Memorial Museum in Washington, D.C. Referenced historian Marsha Rosenblitz's book is *The Jews of Vienna: 1867–1914: Assimilation and Identity* (State University of New York Press, 1984).

Knoll wrote about his childhood in "Homecoming to Vienna," published in *The Progressive* for April 1973. Quotes from Simon and Anny Knoll are from a tape recorded by daughter Renn Penn and her family circa 1990. Simon Knoll died in 1995.

Chapter 2

Primary sources are interviews and the Knoll family history written by Carl Knoll in 1964. The *New York Post* article on Felix Rohatyn is dated Sept. 27, 1975. Information about Carl's draft-dodging scheme is from the tape made by the family of Rita Penn, Simon and Anny Knoll's parents. (At this point in the tape, made more than seven decades after the fact, Anny interjects, to no avail, "I don't think you should tell this.") The story about the machine-gunning of Jews found in hiding in the Leopoldstadt is from Berkeley's *Vienna and Its Jews*, P. 334-335.

Chapter 3

Copies of *The Evening Star* were obtained from the NYU Library Archives in New York City. Knoll's letter opposing a consolidation of NYU campus papers appeared in the *Star* on Nov. 24, 1952. The editorial regarding the suspension of *The Vanguard* appeared Oct. 16, 1950. Knoll's appointment to the Student Committee on Educational Policy was reported Feb. 26, 1952. Chancellor Heald's remarks about academic freedom are quoted Feb. 26, 1952. Edwin Burgum's letter of defense appeared Oct. 27, 1952. The exchange between Hooks and Burgum appeared Nov. 10, 1952. Knoll's editorial responding to the reprimand of fellow student editor Harold Goodman appeared March 9, 1953. Quoted editorials by Sidney Hook appeared in *The Washington Post* on Sept. 10, 1949, June 10, 1950, and Nov. 12, 1949.

Chapter 4

The referenced correspondence between Knoll and Alan Lemberger, Doris Ricksteen, the U.S. Army, and Don Morris is from his personal files, provided by Doris Knoll. Anny Knoll's remark, "There's not much he doesn't have," is remembered by Renata Maas, a cousin. The U.S. military's National Personnel Records Center says its records on Pvt. Knoll's reassignment and his appeal of "flagging actions" have been destroyed.

Chapter 5

Primary sources, in addition to correspondence, include *The Washington Post: The First 100 Years* by Chalmers M. Roberts (Houghton Mifflin Company, 1977). Referenced material is as follows: Roberts's quoted description of Gilbert, P. 294; The story about Harry Truman's letter to Paul Hume, P. 267; Information on Phil Graham's decline and death, P. 361-364; the paper's labor woes in the mid-1970s, P. 247-252. Knoll's recollection about getting carbon paper by the sheet is from *Power, Privilege and The Post: The Katharine Graham Story* by Carol Felsenthal

(Putnam Publishing Group, 1993) at P. 168; the story of Phil Graham sending Knoll to his doctor is from P. 205.

Knoll's series on desegregation appeared Dec. 22 to Dec. 28, 1958. "Old Teaching in a New World" ran Dec. 25, 1960, through Jan. 1, 1961. His account about being embarrassed by the changes made to his stories on the racial composition of district schools is from a 1988 letter to Gilbert, who was writing a detailed history of race relations at the paper. Also from this correspondence is Knoll's conversation with Harry Gladstone and Knoll's efforts in behalf of William Raspberry (who doesn't remember anything about it). Facts about *The Washington Post* unit's 1960 bargaining sessions are from *The Guild Reporter*, Nov. 25 and Dec. 9, 1960.

Chapter 6

Knoll's correspondence with Ben Bradlee and the letter of recommendation from Philip Foisie are from his personal papers.

Lyndon Johnson's quote about Bobby Baker not having time to "take a piss" is remembered most vividly by Ted Schuchat, but confirmed to varying degrees as something the President either very plausibly would or did say by former press handlers Bill Moyers, George Reedy, and Joe Laitlin. Sources for background information on Bobby Baker include *U.S. News & World Report* on Feb. 3, Mar. 9, and Mar. 30, 1964, and Feb. 13, 1967, and *Time* magazine on Jan. 25, 1971. *The New York Times*' reference to the Baker townhouse was on Nov. 21, 1963. The *Times*, on May 10, 1965, also carried a story on Carole Tyler's plane crash.

"Influence" was written up in the *Charlotte Observer* for June 18, 1964, and the *Newark Star-Ledger* for on Sept. 6, 1964. The advertisement in *The New York Times* appeared on Aug. 8, 1964. The referenced "Scandal" article appeared in the April 1964 issue of *Esquire.*

Information on *The Progressive* is taken from a 1978 in-house history of the magazine and from "Morris H. Rubin: Memoirs of a Progressive Editor," a chapter in *The Old Northwest in the American Revolution: An Anthology* (State Historical Society of Wisconsin, 1977). Rubin's reflections on his depression are at P. 153-154. Johnson's quoted threat to the press is from *Decade of Disillusionment: The Kennedy-Johnson Years* by Jim Heath (Indiana University Press, 1975). on P. 177-178.

Knoll's account of Johnson's Camp Stanley speech and its significance is from his essay "A New World Order?" which appeared in *Isthmus* on March 1, 1991. The date of the Knolls' visit to the Johnson ranch is from the Presidential library in Austin. The story on Amidon school appeared in the *Saturday Evening Post* for Dec. 19, 1964. *The Long Island Press* hailed Knoll's prescience on April 1, 1968. Knoll's article on LBJ appeared in *The Progressive* for January 1969.

Chapter 7

The section on the 1968 Democratic National Convention draws from Knoll's articles in *The Capital Times* for August 30, 1968, and *The Progressive* for October 1968, as well as a taped and transcribed 1973 interview with Knoll on file (Tape No. 237) with the McCarthy Historical Project at Georgetown University Library. Loory's account comes in part from a letter he wrote to Knoll's family in November 1994.

Knoll's quoted analysis appeared in *The Capital Times* for Oct. 8, 1968. The referenced articles in *The Progressive* on Melvin Laird, Henry Durham, and Vienna appeared in the issues for April 1971, January 1972, and April 1973, respectively. The quoted reviews of *Anything But the Truth* are from *The Chicago Daily News* of June 29, 1968, and the Boston *Sunday Globe* of July 21, 1968. Knoll's article "The Oil Lobby is Not Depleted" appeared in *The New York Times Sunday Magazine* on March 8, 1970. Ikard's letter and Knoll's reply appeared on April 5. The anecdote about Ralph Nader and Knoll's car is remembered by Stuart Loory.

Chapter 8

Information on Bob La Follette is drawn from *The La Follettes of Wisconsin: Love and Politics in Progressive America* by Bernard A. Weisberger (University of Wisconsin Press, 1994). References as follows: The story of La Follette's 1922 speech, P. 242; the quote about "the Land of Never Return," P. 273; Weisberger's quoted account of La Follette's graveyard antics, P. 6; the exchange between Belle Case and Lincoln Steffens, P. 91. Other information on La Follette is taken from *Robert M. La Follette and the Insurgent Spirit* by David P. Thelen (Little, Brown, 1976; reprinted by University of Wisconsin Press, 1986) and *La Follette's Autobiography: A Personal Narrative of Political Experiences* (University of Wisconsin Press, 1986).

The *Chicago Sun-Times* article profiling the Knolls at home ran June 5, 1977. The Chomsky quote is from the documentary film, *Manufacturing Consent: Noam Chomsky and the Media* (Necessary Illusions Productions, Montreal, Canada). Carbon's comments about *The Progessive* are from an article by Sam Day in the Jan. 21, 1977, issue of *Isthmus*, a Madison paper.

Chapter 9

This chapter draws from *The Secret That Exploded* by Howard Morland and Peter Garrison (Random House, 1981). References as follows: Morland's account of the student at the University of Alabama, P. 41; his ruminations on "the Teller-Ulam trick," P. 40; his recollection of Gilbert's "bizarre simile," P. 64; his encounter with a former plant worker at a roadside fruit stand, P. 68; Morland's meeting with Rathjens, P. 89; his visit to Oak Ridge, P. 96-97; his visit to the Truman Library, P. 112; his interview with "Vernon Kendrick," P. 19-20; his meeting with Stanislav Ulam, P. 139; Morland's disputed account of his Feb. 12 conversation with Knoll and Day, P. 140-141.

General Groves's testimony on the Rosenbergs is quoted in *Born Secret: The H-Bomb, the Progressive Case and National Security* by A. DeVolpi, G.E. Marsh, T.A. Postol and G.S. Stanford (Pergamon Press, 1981), at P. 161. The information on the number of U.S. nuclear weapons built since 1945 is from *U.S. Nuclear Weapons: The Secret History* by Chuck Hansen (Orion Books, 1988). Correspondence between Morland and *The Progressive* and a copy of Forsberg's letter to Day were obtained from the magazine.

Other information comes from *Crossing the Line: From Editor to Activist to Inmate—A Writer's Journey* by Samuel H. Day Jr. (Fortkamp Publishing Co., 1991). The chapters of Day's autobiography that deal with the H-bomb case were initially written in 1979, in articles and as part of *The Progressive*'s planned book on the topic. The editors' initial reaction to Morland's article is on P. 102; Postol's comment regarding the damage this article posed to classification is P. 108. Knoll's remark to Rathjens is from Knoll's article in *The Progressive* for May 1979.

Chapter 10

Gordon Sinykin's assessment of Phil La Follette's 1940 defeat is from *The La Follettes of Wisconsin* at P. 305. Information on the pair's early partnership was provided by LaFollette & Sinykin. The memos to Sinykin detailing contacts between *The Progressive*'s editors and Government officials are from the magazine's files.

Day's Feb. 21 letter to Cannon is quoted in *Crossing the Line* at P. 108. Sinykin's reaction to reading the Atomic Energy Act and his statement about preferring restraint to sanctions is from P. 110. Conversations with Cannon are recounted on P. 110-113. Knoll's "I love it!" remark is quoted at P. 116. Day's assessment of Sinykin as "tense and uncommunicative" is from P. 122; Sinykin's "Let's have a lawsuit" remark is on P. 124.

Bell's *Taking Care of the Law*, written with Ronald J. Ostrow (William Morrow and Co., 1982) discusses the H-bomb case at P. 130-135. The D.O.E. document that reveals the Government's early response to Morland's article is entitled "A Brief History of the Progressive Case" by William C. Grayson. It was obtained in 1995 by Chuck Hansen at the Los Alamos National Laboratory's Oppenheimer Study Center.

Chapter 11

The federal court docket number for *The Progressive* case is 79-C-98. What follows is a list of referenced documents and, in parentheses, their court docket number and, where applicable, the pages on which they are quoted in the book *Born Secret*: The Government's complaint (1); the statement advancing the "born secret" doctrine (4, P. 59, 136); Sewell's public (8, P. 269-270) and *in camera* (8A3) affidavits; Van Doren's affidavit (6, P. 269); the transcript of Judge Warren's March 9 ruling (31, P. 61-62): the affidavits from Rosengren (23, P. 61), Postol (45, P. 65), DeWitt (56, P. 272), the three Argonne scientists (62, P. 278), and Kidder (74-75A), P. 67); Grayson and Rosengren's March 23 *in camera* filing (68, P. 108). The Government's statement regarding information "already available and in the public domain" appears in the court file as item 21 and is quoted in *The Secret That Exploded* at P. 159-160. The transcript of the March 26 hearing (item 83) is recounted by Morland at P. 184-192 and in *The Columbia Journalism Review* for July/August 1979.

Kendall's quote is mentioned by Morland at P. 167 and discussed by Day in *Crossing the Line* at P. 130. Knoll's incomplete press release and other primary documents are from *The Progressive*. His quotes at the March 9 press conference are from an original tape recording. *The Washington Post* ran Knoll's referenced column on March 13, 1979, and *The New York Times* quoted his "banana pie" remark on March 21, 1979. Other information comes from Knoll's article in *The Progressive* for May 1979.

The Washington Post's editorial, "John Mitchell's Dream Case," appeared March 11, 1979. Knoll's letter in response, his correspondence with James Kilpatrick, and his letter decrying Hans Bethe's "pusillanimous acquiescence" are from *The Progressive*'s files. Einstein's comments on secrecy were made in a Jan. 22, 1947, letter to the Emergency Committee of Atomic Scientists. The statement from the Federation of American Scientists appears in *The Progressive*'s files and is quoted in Day's article in *The Progressive* for May 1979. The same article recounts the drama regarding Kidder's affidavits.

Morland wrote about the Honolulu civil suit in an op-ed column in *The New York Times* for March 26, and about whiting out his earlier underlining in a "My Turn" column in Newsweek for April 9. An account of the Government's censorship of Hans Bethe's *Scientific American* article appears in *Science in the Cause of Man* by Gerard Piel (Alfred Knopf, 1962), P. 3-20. Knoll's remark that the Government was seeking "to intimidate and throttle all news media" was quoted in *The New York Times* for March 14. In his book, Morland tells of his unhappiness with such pronouncements at P. 171-72; of his hidden H-bomb T-shirt at P. 184, and of the press conference immediately following the March 26 hearing at P. 193.

Chapter 12

The New York Times' editorial ripping Warren's decision appeared March 29, 1979. Morland's account of the Alicia Patterson conference and its aftermath is told in his book at P. 204-205. Quotes from the conference are from an official transcript. Ennis's strategy letter, records of contacts between the DOE and the FBI, and the referenced New Solidarity press release were obtained from *The Progressive*.

Bell's June 3 reply to Justice Department lawyers urging abandonment of the case is from *Taking Care of the Law* at P. 133-134. Sid Lens's comments were quoted in the *Madison Press Connection* on July 14, 1979. DeWitt's difficulties at Livermore are discussed in *Born Secret* at P. 213. Rep. McCloskey's remark is quoted on P. 182. Judge Warren's quotes in this chapter and the next are from an interview with the author on April 18, 1995. The Government's brief about "technical information" appears in the court file as item 166 and is quoted in *Born Secret* at P. 209.

Hansen's stated goal "to harass and annoy" is from a May 11, 1988, letter to reporter Mary Madison. His line about winning his own contest is from the *National Journal* of May 7, 1988. Knoll's hope that the Seventh Circuit will "sneer at" the DOE's arguments is from the *Press Connection* of Sept. 14, 1979.

Chapter 13

Cook's comments are quoted in the *Madison Press Connection* on Sept. 15, 1979. Knoll's praise for the paper's publication of Hansen's letter is from its issue of Sept. 17. His remarks after the case was dropped are from *The Capital Times* of Sept. 18. Attorney Williamson's lament is from *The Capital Times* of Sept. 19. This last article, by Dan Allegretti, also reports that a "middle level" DOE bureaucrat decided there was no hurry to notify his superiors that the *Press Connection* on Sept. 14 reported having the Hansen letter since the paper did not (normally) publish on Sunday.

Knoll's boast about having the Government "licked from the beginning" is from his article in *The Progressive* for November 1979. Sewell's testimony before the Senate Subcommittee on Energy, Nuclear Proliferation and Federal Services was on Oct. 2, 1979. The information about the movie deal is from an interview with Glenn Silber.

DeWitt made his remarks on the H-bomb case in a paper delivered at the Pugwash Conference on Science and World Affairs, Sept. 15-20, 1990, in Egham, England. The four quoted legal assessments of *The Progressive* case are from papers by Janet Neese, Judge James L. Oakes, Arthur

S. Miller, and Michael Campbell Soper, respectively. Bell's put-down of the "rag-tags of the press" is from his book at P. 135. Tuerkheimer's testimony and Sen. Feinstein's rebuke were reported in *The Capital Times* on May 12, 1995.

Chapter 14

Salary figures, the statement from the Gang of Four, letters regarding union organizing and management response, and other quoted correspondence are from the files of *The Progressive*. Day compared the magazine to a "cotton plantation" in a column in *Isthmus* for Oct. 4, 1985. Knoll's "Main Street" reflections are from a fund-raising appeal in August 1981.

The letter from the authors of the FBI story and Knoll's defense of Flynn is in *The Progressive* for November 1987. Munson's letter to Knoll is dated April 11, 1980; Knoll responded the following day. Circulation figures, here and elsewhere, are as reported in the magazine, as required, each October. (These reports appear in the magazine's November or December issues.)

Knoll's NPR commentary on Carter aired Oct. 12, 1980; on the presidential elections, July 22, 1980; on the League of Women Voters, Sept. 9, 1980; on Reagan and the DOE, Dec. 30, 1980; on Bobby Sands, May 5, 1981; on draft registration, July 11, 1980. Knoll's advice to Jonathan is from a personal letter dated July 13, 1980.

Chapter 15

The 1984 readership survey, Knoll's memo on advertising policy, Beth Burack's statement, Sinykin's letter to Hentoff, and other union-management correspondence are from the magazine's files. Knoll's comments to Vukelich are from the March 1986 issue of *Milwaukee Magazine*. His "Memo" regarding the Feminists for Life ad appeared in *The Progressive* for June 1985. Hentoff's columns on Knoll ran in *The Village Voice* for June 25 and July 2, 1985. Cockburn's attack appeared in *The Nation* for July 20, 1985; Knoll's letter to the editor and Cockburn's rejoinder appeared in *The Nation* for Aug. 17.

In Business ran its piece on *The Progressive* in November 1983. The picket-sign party at the Buracks' was attended by the author; some details regarding contract negotiations are also from personal observation.

Knoll's comments on the 1984 presidential elections are from an interview with the author that appeared in the December 1984 issue of *The Crazy Shepherd*, a Milwaukee newspaper. Knoll's book, *No Comment*, is published by Vintage Books. Knoll's tribute to Sinykin appeared in *The Progressive* for February 1986.

The materials received from the FBI, Army, and CIA are from *The Progressive*'s files. Knoll's article on these appeared in the magazine for October 1986, but made no mention of the Army's 1954 finding or the FBI's decision to stop subscribing.

Chapter 16

Quoted exchanges from "Second Opinion" are from an article by the author for *Isthmus* on July 17, 1987. Knoll's "Nonvoters' Manifesto" appeared in *Isthmus* on Oct. 21, 1988; letters and Knoll's reply appeared the following week. Knoll said the article drew the most "vehement response" of anything in his career in a speech he gave Oct. 28, 1992, at the UW-Platteville and in an article he wrote for the Summer 1991 issue of *Peace & Democracy News*. His speech containing the "emperor has no clothes" comment was delivered in Monterey, Calif., on Jan. 30, 1988. His address to the Johnson Foundation was delivered Feb. 20, 1992.

All other quotes from Knoll, here as elsewhere, are from interviews with the author in June and July of 1992, and a followup interview in April 1993. These were done for profile articles that appeared in *The Milwaukee Journal* on Oct. 25, 1992, and in *Quill* magazine for July/August 1993.

Chapter 17

The mall-speech lawsuit was filed in Dane County Circuit Court, case number 84-CV-4427. The Nu Parable case is 84 CV 2216 at the circuit-court level and 85-0341 before the Wisconsin Supreme Court. Knoll's column on the Supreme Court's decision appeared in the *Wisconsin State Journal* for June 29, 1987.

Articles on the challenge by student Elmendorf ran in the *Albany Times-Union* for May 9, 1990, and the (Schenectady, NY) *Daily Gazette* for May 25.

Knoll's letter to *The Capital Times* regarding the UW's ban on monthly magazines ran May 14, 1986. He testified against the porn bill before the Wisconsin Legislature's Committee on Judiciary and Consumer Affairs on Oct. 29, 1985; his testimony against the hate-speech rule was on June 10, 1992.

The debate between Sulton and Knoll aired July 3, 1992, on WTSO in Madison. Knoll's letter to *The Madison Insurgent* was published on July 31, 1992. Rothschild's proposed sexual-harassment policy and other personnel-related correspondence is from Knoll's files. Knoll's eulogy to Peck appeared in *The Progressive* for August 1990.

Chapter 18

Knoll's *Newsday* column appeared on Aug. 15, 1990. His offering in *The New York Times* ran Nov. 8, 1990. Quotes from "The MacNeil/Lehrer

NewsHour" are from program transcripts. Knoll's first appearance was on Oct. 28, 1990; his remarks on Tibet were made Nov. 26, 1990; on the burgeoning war opposition Jan. 11, 1991; on "video displays" Jan. 18, 1991; and on Somalia Dec. 31, 1992. Robin MacNeil was interviewed in October 1995, the month he retired from the program.

The lawsuit over Gulf censorship was filed in the U.S. District Court in New York City by the Center for Constitutional Rights. *The Capital Times*' article about it appeared Jan. 11, 1991. Knoll's comment that the press did not have "enough sensibility" to be offended by Schwarzkopf's compliment is from a speech he delivered in Denver on April 15, 1991. His comments regarding "modern propaganda technique" and "New World Order" are from a Feb. 9, 1992, speech in Bar Harbor, Maine. His reminiscence of the "spasm of gory, patriotic fervor" is from a profile in the *Wisconsin State Journal* on Aug. 29, 1993.

Knoll's essay, "New World Order?," a version of his Bar Harbor speech, appeared in *Isthmus* for March 1, 1991. Burack's letter ran March 28, 1991. Knoll's remarks on the downside of prison witness are from an article by the author that appeared in *The Milwaukee Journal* on Sept. 2, 1990.

Chapter 19

The dates of Knoll's quoted "MacNeil/Lehrer" comments are: Clarence Thomas, Oct. 14, 1991; the Democratic National Convention, July 17, 1992; Ross Perot, June 5, 1992; the Los Angeles riots, May 1, 1992; Bosnia, May 7, 1993; and crime, Dec. 24, 1993. His column on Waco appeared in *The Christian Science Monitor* for May 12, 1993. His piece on Clinton's Baghdad attack appeared in the *Wisconsin State Journal* on June 30, 1991. The *State Journal*'s profile of Aug. 29, 1993, is the source for Knoll's quote regarding gays in the military. Knoll's comments on RICO are quoted in *Isthmus* for Feb. 11, 1994.

Chapter 20

Ivins's recollections of her last meeting with Knoll are from *The Progressive* for January 1995. *The Capital Times*'s eulogy ran Nov. 4, 1994. Conniff's written recollections appeared in *Isthmus* on Nov. 25, 1994. A fuller account of the circumstances of Knoll's death ran in *Isthmus* on Nov. 3, 1995.

Index

About the Author

Bill Lueders was born in 1959 in Milwaukee, where he attended Catholic elementary and high school and the University of Wisconsin–Milwaukee. He is the editor of *Gathering Place of the Waters: 30 Milwaukee Poets,* a 1983 anthology. He cofounded *The Crazy Shepherd,* a Milwaukee "free-expression magazine" that is now the city weekly, *Shepherd Express.* Lueders worked under Knoll as an editorial intern at *The Progressive* in the summer of 1984. Two years later, he returned to Madison to become news editor of *Isthmus,* a weekly paper. He has held that position since, winning the 1991 Golden Quill Award for editorial writing from the International Society of Weekly Newspaper Editors, as well as statewide awards for investigative reporting, civil liberties reporting, interpretative reporting, and column writing. He lives on Madison's east side.